OXFORD LEARNER'S GRAMMAR
Grammar Builder

Oxford
LEARNER'S
GRAMMAR

Grammar
Builder

John Eastwood

OXFORD
UNIVERSITY PRESS

OXFORD

UNIVERSITY PRESS

Great Clarendon Street, Oxford OX2 6DP

Oxford University Press is a department of the University of Oxford.
It furthers the University's objective of excellence in research, scholarship,
and education by publishing worldwide in

Oxford New York

Auckland Cape Town Dar es Salaam Hong Kong Karachi
Kuala Lumpur Madrid Melbourne Mexico City Nairobi
New Delhi Shanghai Taipei Toronto

With offices in

Argentina Austria Brazil Chile Czech Republic France Greece
Guatemala Hungary Italy Japan Poland Portugal Singapore
South Korea Switzerland Thailand Turkey Ukraine Vietnam

OXFORD and OXFORD ENGLISH are registered trade marks of
Oxford University Press in the UK and in certain other countries

ISBN-13: 978 0 19 437594 8
ISBN-10: 0 19 437594 3

Printed in China

ACKNOWLEDGEMENTS

*The authors and publisher are grateful to those who have given permission to
reproduce the following extracts and adaptations of copyright material*: p169:
The Story of Metals by L Aitchison, copyright © Ladybird Books Ltd 1971,
reproduced by permission of Ladybird Books Ltd. p169: 'Midtown
Manhattan', *Fodor's Budget Travel in America* © Random House Inc.

Although every effort has been made to trace and contact copyright
holders before publication, this has not been possible in some cases.
We apologise for any apparent infringement of copyright and if
notified, the publisher will be pleased to rectify any errors or
omissions at the earliest opportunity.

Illustrated by: Trevor Dunton and Joanna Kerr

Introduction

A   The *Grammar Builder* as part of Oxford Learner's Grammar

Oxford Learner's Grammar is a resource pack of reference and practice material designed for intermediate or advanced level students. The pack consists of the *Grammar Finder* reference book, with its *Grammar Checker* CD-ROM, and this *Grammar Builder* practice book. There is also an *Oxford Learner's Grammar* website at www.oup.com/elt/olg.

a   Teachers

The *Grammar Builder* contains exercises on the grammar points dealt with in the *Grammar Finder*. You can use it

- to give students grammar practice, whether in class or for homework
- to test your students' knowledge of a particular grammar topic
- to encourage students to improve their ability by using the *Grammar Builder* in combination with the *Grammar Finder* reference book.

b   Students

The *Grammar Builder* contains exercises on the grammar points dealt with in the *Grammar Finder*. You can use it

- to practise grammar topics in class or for homework, as directed by your teacher
- to practise grammar on your own independently of a teacher and to monitor your progress
- in combination with the *Grammar Finder*, which will explain points of difficulty.

B   How the *Grammar Builder* works

At the head of each exercise you will find a reference to the section in the *Grammar Finder* where the point is explained. There is also a key at the back of the *Grammar Builder*, where answers can be checked. Each answer has a reference to a specific part of the *Grammar Finder*, which you can then consult if any problems remain. The book is thus especially suitable for self-study, whether used independently or together with the *Grammar Finder*.

There is a wide variety of exercise types. These include activities such as sentence completion, sentence construction, transformation, gap-filling, multiple choice, correction, matching, ordering, and grammatical analysis. You will find a good number of key-word transformation exercises (e.g. Exercise 17), a significant part of the Use of English paper in the Cambridge First Certificate in English examination. As well as exercises on individual points, there are contrastive exercises and review exercises covering the content of a whole chapter. For example, alongside exercises on individual verb tenses, there are exercises contrasting different tenses, and others reviewing tenses as a whole.

Throughout the book the emphasis is on practice which involves the student not only in producing correct English but also in thinking about the meaning of sentences and in increasing their awareness of grammatical structure. Most exercises demand a choice of grammatical form rather than the mechanical production of a single form.

Good luck

The aim of the *Oxford Learner's Grammar* resource pack is to provide clear, accessible explanations and meaningful practice in order to facilitate learning. Author and publisher hope very much that teachers and students will benefit from the pack and enjoy working with it.

Contents

1 Word classes

▶ Finder 1

Look at the words in **bold** type and say what word class they belong to.

DETECTIVES

A police **inspector** was interviewing two people for **the** job of detective. The first **candidate** was a woman. The inspector showed **her** a photo of a man with green hair and asked her what was unusual **about** the man. She looked carefully at the photo and replied 'He's only got one **ear**.' This was not what the inspector had been **hoping** to hear. 'We can only see one ear **because** the picture is in profile,' he pointed out rather **crossly**.

The second candidate **was** a man. The inspector asked him the **same** question. The man said 'He's wearing contact **lenses**.' The inspector was **very** surprised. 'You're right,' he said. 'I happen to know **that** he really is wearing contact lenses. That's very clever **of** you.' 'It's quite **simple**,' said the man. 'He must have poor eyesight with only **one** eye. And he can't **wear** glasses because he's only got one ear.'

▶ 'Inspector' is a noun.
▶ 'The' is a determiner.

1	9 ....
2	10 ....
3	11 ....
4	12 ....
5	13 ....
6	14 ....
7	15 ....
8	16 ....

2 Words belonging to more than one class

▶ Finder 2

Say if the word is a verb, a noun, or an adjective.

▶ The officers will **police** the festival.
police = *verb*
▶ The golf ball rolled slowly onto the **green**.
green = *noun*

My sister wants to join the **police**.
police = *noun*
The man in the photo had **green** hair.
green = *adjective*

1 The police want to **interview** the man.
interview = ...

The **interview** took place at the police station.
interview = ...

2 I asked you a **question**.
question = ...

Detectives are going to **question** the man.
question = ...

3 We all have a **right** to freedom of speech.
right = ...

What do you think is the **right** thing to do?
right = ...

4 Mike told us a really funny **joke**.
joke = ...

It's serious. You shouldn't **joke**.
joke = ...

5 It's **criminal** to cause all this pollution.
criminal = ...

The man is a **criminal** known to the police.
criminal = ...

6 There was an **empty** bottle on the floor.
empty = ...

The security man made me **empty** my pockets.
empty = ...

3 Phrases

▶ Finder 3

Find the relevant phrase.

▶ The train leaves in fifteen minutes.
verb phrase: *leaves* . . . .

▶ I always feel so tired after working all day.
adjective phrase: *so tired* . . . .

1 I don't often buy a magazine.
adverb phrase: . . . .

2 Unfortunately I left my briefcase on the bus.
prepositional phrase: . . . .

3 That dress you wore yesterday looked really nice.
adjective phrase: . . . .

4 We must have lunch together some time.
verb phrase: . . . .

5 What about throwing all these old magazines away?
noun phrase: . . . .

6 My boss said that I had to finish this report by Thursday.
prepositional phrase: . . . .

7 Some strange things have been happening lately.
verb phrase: . . . .

8 Do you have to drive so slowly all the time?
adverb phrase: . . . .

9 Surely you must be joking.
noun phrase: . . . .

10 The forecast says it's going to be hot again today.
adjective phrase: . . . .

4 Basic clause structure

▶ Finder 4

Identify the clause element in **bold** type.

▶ We played **tennis**.   *object* . . . .

1 My boyfriend is **a student**.   . . . .

2 The meeting was **yesterday**.   . . . .

3 My back **is aching**.   . . . .

4 **The weather** is looking better.   . . . .

5 You know **the answer**.   . . . .

6 Everyone found the joke **terribly amusing**.   . . . .

7 I'm **on a diet**.   . . . .

8 I poured my drink **down the sink**.   . . . .

9 It was getting **dark**.   . . . .

10 Our exams are **next week**.   . . . .

11 **You** should go the doctor.   . . . .

12 Rick gave **us** a lift.   . . . .

13 The statue **stands** in front of the palace.   . . . .

14 The boss appointed his son **Marketing Manager**.   . . . .

5 Basic clause structure

▶ Finder 4

Look at the table and write sentences starting at column A. You must decide if the sentence ends at A, or if you need to continue with column B. If the sentence is still not complete, you should then use column C.

A	B	C
The train stopped	~~you~~	a tip
I'll send	some new flats	fit
We gave	the car	in the garage
These chocolates are	in Tokyo	~~an e-mail~~
Louise put	delicious	
The sun was shining	the driver	
My luggage is	the team	
They built		
Physical exercise keeps		

▶ The train *stopped.* . . . .
▶ I'll *send you an e-mail.* . . . .

1 We . . . .
2 These chocolates . . . .
3 Louise . . . .
4 The sun . . . .
5 My luggage . . . .
6 They . . . .
7 Physical exercise . . . .

6 Complements

▶ Finder 5D

Give the information in a structure with an object and a complement.

▶ The theory is wrong, you know. Someone has proved that.
   Someone has proved the theory wrong. . . . .
▶ The viewers voted. And in their opinion 'Coronation Street' is the best soap opera.
   The viewers voted 'Coronation Street' the best soap opera. . . . .

1 We've painted the walls. They're bright yellow now.
   . . . .
2 This coffee is very strong. But that's the way I like my coffee.
   . . . .
3 The members elected Alice. She's president now.
   . . . .
4 I was tired after the long journey. (Use the verb *make*.)
   . . . .
5 What's the name of their cat? Oh, I know. It's 'Biscuit'. (Use the verb *call*.)
   . . . .
6 The food will stay cool with the ice-packs. (Use the verb *keep*.)
   . . . .

7 Adverbials

Read this story and then write down the adverbials. There are two adverbials in each sentence.

STOP THIEF!

This incident actually happened a few years ago. One Saturday morning, in a small English town, a man entered a shoe shop. For a few minutes he carefully inspected some cowboy boots. Then he put his dirty old trainers on the floor and left the shop. He now had some smart new cowboy boots on his feet. Luckily the assistant saw immediately what was happening and rang the police. They soon caught the thief because he was moving too slowly. He couldn't run very fast in two right-foot boots.

▶ *actually* .... *a few years ago* ....

1 ....
2 ....
3 ....
4 ....
5 ....
6 ....
7 ....

8 *Give, send, buy, etc*

▶ Finder 6A–B

Write the words in the correct order to form a statement.

▶ the ball / the man / threw / to the woman
The man threw the ball to the woman.

▶ her friends / her holiday snaps / Karen / showed
Karen showed her friends her holiday snaps.

1 is going to cook / me / a meal / my boyfriend

....

2 his nephews and nieces / promised / a trip to the zoo / Uncle Robert

....

3 gave / the job / they / to a young man from Glasgow

....

4 some sandwiches / for his guests / made / Patrick

....

5 the guide / handed / a list of hotels / me

....

6 the company / the information / mailed / us

....

7 a car / are going to buy / her / Lucy's parents

....

8 have sent / a message / the protestors / to the Prime Minister

....

9 for our group / have saved / the organizers / seats

....

9 *To* or *for*?

▶ Finder 6C

Complete the dialogue. Put in *to* or *for*.

Gemma: I've got a message here for one of our visitors, but I don't know where he is at the moment. I can't fax it (▶) . . *to* . . him because he isn't in his office. And there's no point in posting it (1) . . . . . his home address.
Lisa: We've got his address somewhere. I can find it (2) . . . . . you if you like.
Gemma: But it's urgent. I ought to give it (3) . . . . . him today.
Lisa: Well, why don't you take it (4) . . . . . his hotel? He's staying at the International. You can leave it there (5) . . . . . him. They'll pass it on (6) . . . . . him when he gets back there this evening.
Gemma: OK. Where is the International?
Lisa: Near the station. There's a street plan in my office. I'll just get it (7) . . . . . you.
Gemma: Well, maybe I'll take a taxi.

10 Which structure with *give, send,* etc?

▶ Finder 6C–E

Complete the sentences using the words in brackets. The phrase in **bold** is new information, so put it at the end of the sentence. Sometimes you need to put in *to* or *for*.

▶ I'm depressed. I need cheering up. Why don't you tell . *me a joke* . . ? (**a joke** / me)
▶ I've given some clothes away. I gave . *two coats to Oxfam.* . . . (two coats / **Oxfam**)

1 You work really long hours. I think they should pay
. . . . (**more money** / you)

2 Have you heard about Mrs Newman's will? She left
. . . . (all her money /**an animal hospital**)

3 I hate choosing lottery numbers. You can choose mine. And pick
. . . . (six numbers /**my little sister**)

4 The chicken I cooked wasn't very nice, I'm afraid. I couldn't eat it, so I fed
. . . . (most of it /**the dog**)

5 Christopher is always very kind to me. Do you know, last week he lent
. . . . (**fifty pounds** / me)

6 The company treat their staff very well. They've offered
. . . . (**a free holiday** / all their employees)

11 *Describe, explain, etc* ► Finder 6F

Some of the sentences below are wrong. Find the wrong answers and correct them.

a) The postman delivered our neighbour the parcel by mistake.
b) Caroline described the doctor her symptoms.
c) I owe Martin some money.
d) The artist's family have donated the National Gallery the picture.
e) I was late, but my friends had saved me a seat.
f) Lucy explained us the rules of the game.
g) The government must communicate the public its message.
h) The judges awarded Emily the first prize.

► *a) The postman delivered the parcel to our neighbour by mistake.* ....

1 ....
2 ....
3 ....
4 ....

12 Introduction to sentence types ► Finder 7

Look at each sentence in **bold** type. What type of sentence is it, and how is it used?

	Type	Use
► **Would you mind carrying this bag for me?** ~ No problem.	*a question*	*a request*
1 **I want to know all about your holiday.** ~ Oh, I had a great time. Florida was wonderful.		
2 What shall I do with my coat? ~ **Oh, just leave it on that chair.**		
3 **Good Heavens!** ~ What's the matter? ~ Look at the time. We're going to be late.		
4 **Is it far to the restaurant?** ~ No, it's only five minutes from here.		
5 We're off to the disco now ~ **Well, enjoy yourselves.**		
6 Have you got enough money? ~ No. **Could you lend me a pound?** ~ Sure.		
7 How is the game going? ~ **We're winning easily.**		
8 **I need to see the printout now.** ~ OK, I'll just get it for you.		

13 The use of statements

▶ Finder 8

Look at these conversations and write down the use of each statement. Choose from these uses: asking for information, expressing sympathy, giving information, making a suggestion, not agreeing with a suggestion, offering, predicting, thanking.

1 Nicola: You must tell me about your job interview.   *asking for information*
    Paul: It didn't go very well, unfortunately. ....
          I'm definitely not going to get the job. ....
    Nicola: Well, I'm sorry to hear that, Paul. ....

2 Peter: We could go out for a meal tonight. ....
    Gemma: I'm too tired to go out. ....
    Peter: Well, I'll cook you a meal, then. ....
    Gemma: That's really kind of you, Peter. ....

14 Performative verbs

▶ Finder 9

Complete each conversation. Put in these performative verbs: *advise, agree, apologize, insist, promise, refuse, suggest*.

▶ What are we going to do this afternoon?
  ~ Well, I . . *suggest* . . we all go to the beach together.

1 This town is really ugly. These buildings look awful.
  ~ Yes, I . . . . with you.

2 You sold me a computer that doesn't work.
  ~ Well, we'll try to repair it for you. ~ No, I must . . . . you give me my money back.

3 Could you move to another seat, please?
  ~ Certainly not. I've paid for this seat, and I . . . . to move.

4 Do you think I can climb a mountain in these shoes?
  ~ No, I'd . . . . you to wear some proper climbing boots.

5 I'll meet you in the main square at seven.
  ~ Well, make sure you're on time. I don't want to be waiting around for you.
  ~ OK, I won't be late, I . . . .·

6 You're late. I've been waiting half an hour.
  ~ I'm sorry. I . . . .·

15 Negative statements

▶ Finder 10A–B

Mrs Probert is a government minister, and Mrs Conway is a member of the party in Opposition. They are having an argument on television. Put in Mr Conway's negative replies to Mrs Probert's statements.

▶ We are building a new nation.
  ~ What nonsense. *You aren't building a new nation.* . . . .

1 The economy is improving.
  ~ I disagree. It . . . .

2 We have put things right.
  ~ What do you mean? . . . .

3 Industry has been modernized.
  ~ Our industry is out of date. . . . .

4 This country leads the world in technology.
  ~ You must be joking. . . . .

5 People should be grateful to us.
  ~ You haven't helped them. . . . .

6 We saved the country from ruin.
  ~ You ruined the country. . . . .

7 Your ideas are ridiculous.
  ~ We have some good policies. . . . .

8 We will win the next election.
  ~ The people will reject you. . . . .

16 *Not* in other positions

▶ Finder 10C

Rewrite the parts in **bold** type. Use the word *not*.

▶ **Too little money** is spent on schools.
  Not enough money . . . . is spent on schools.

1 **Few companies** pay their workers so well.
  . . . . pay their workers so well.

2 **Very little** happens around here.
  . . . . happens around here.

3 The police should arrive in **five minutes at the most**.
  The police should arrive in . . . .

4 **A short distance away** we found an interesting museum.
  . . . . we found an interesting museum.

5 I saw that film **quite recently**.
  I saw that film . . . .

6 **There are people who don't have** a television.
  . . . . a television.

17 Negative words

► Finder 10D

Write a second sentence so that it has a similar meaning to the previous one. Use the words in brackets.

► I don't know anything about American football. (nothing)
I know nothing about American football.

1 There were few seats left. (many)

. . . .

2 All of these problems are minor ones. (major)

. . . .

3 There wasn't really much traffic on the road. (hardly)

. . . .

4 Everyone agrees with your suggestion. (disagrees)

. . . .

5 Louise doesn't like Mark, and I don't either. (neither)

. . . .

6 I don't suppose we will ever know the truth. (never)

. . . .

7 The new computer isn't any more expensive than the old one. (no)

. . . .

8 We don't go to that club any more. (no)

. . . .

18 The emphatic negative

► Finder 10E

Complete this letter to a newspaper. Put in these words: *absolutely*, *at*, *far*, *least*, *means*, *not*, *whatsoever*.

I would like to reply to what your reporter said last week in the article about the new tobacco-free 'healthy' cigarettes. He says that they are safe, but he does not by any (►) . . *means* . . persuade me that this is true. I am not in the (1) . . . . convinced by his ridiculous arguments. There is plenty of evidence that smoking this synthetic material is dangerous, but there is (2) . . . . no evidence to show that it is safe. There is no truth (3) . . . . in anything your reporter says. I simply do (4) . . . . believe his arguments. This product is (5) . . . . from safe. We should not have anything to do with it (6) . . . . all.

19 Inversion after a negative phrase

There are rumours that US President Ron Curtis has been dishonest in money matters. A White House spokesperson is denying everything. The sentences in brackets show what the spokesperson is thinking. What does she say? Put the negative phrase in the front position.

▶ (Mr Curtis would not be dishonest under any circumstances.)
    Under no circumstances would Mr Curtis be dishonest.

1 (The President is corrupt only in the fantasies of news reporters.)

. . . .

2 (He has not broken the law at any time.)

. . . .

3 (He didn't ever do anything wrong in his whole life.)

. . . .

4 (The President has not been late with his tax payments since 1997.)

. . . .

5 (These rumours are not in any way true.)

. . . .

6 (Mr Curtis seldom thinks about his own finances.)

. . . .

7 (The President does not cheat the people, and he doesn't tell lies either.)

. . . .

20 The imperative
▶ Finder 11A

Complete the teacher's sentences. Put in a positive or a negative imperative.

▶ *Sit down* . . . . . ., please. We're going to start the lesson now.
▶ *Don't shout* . . . ., please. There's no need to raise your voice.

1 . . . . your books at page 75, please.
2 . . . . so much noise, please. I'd like you all to be quiet for a moment.
3 . . . . your name at the top of the test paper.
4 . . . . out of the window when I'm talking to you.
5 Please . . . . the room quietly when you go.
6 . . . . the door behind you, please.

10   19 • Inversion after a negative phrase

21 Getting people to do things

► Finder 11B–C

Find a more polite way of getting people to do things. Use the word in brackets and say *please*.

► lend me a pen. (can)
  Can you lend me a pen, please? . . . .

1 Bring me a coffee. (have)
  . . . .

2 Hold my bag for a minute. (mind)
  . . . .

3 Give me a clean glass. (could)
  . . . .

4 Move your bicycle out of the way. (could)
  . . . .

5 Give me a receipt. (can)
  . . . .

6 Sit over here. (like)
  . . . .

22 Other uses of the imperative

► Finder 11D

Write down the use of each sentence. Choose from these uses: an advertisement, a piece of advice, an instruction, an invitation, a slogan, a warning, wishing someone well.

► Mind the wet paint.   *a warning* . . . .
1 Insert the CD and click on the icon.   . . . .
2 Always do what you know is right.   . . . .
3 Have a wonderful time.   . . . .
4 Just look at our prices!   . . . .
5 Feed the world!   . . . .
6 Do join us for dinner.   . . . .

23 Imperative + question tag

▶ Finder 11E–F

Look at the pictures and put in the right sentence from the table. Sometimes there is more than one possible question tag.

Don't drop those plates, Enjoy your game, Pass me the sugar, Let's play mini-golf, Shut the window, Turn it down,	can you? can't you? could you? shall we? will you? won't you? would you?

▶ . . . *Pass me the sugar, could you?* . . .
1 . . . .
2 . . . .
3 . . . .
4 . . . .
5 . . . .

24 Exclamations

▶ Finder 12B

Complete the conversations. Put in *how*, *what*, or *what a*.

▶ Jodie has been in a car accident. She's in hospital. ~ Oh, . . *how* . . terrible!

1 I'm doing secret work for the government, you know. ~ Oh, ... stories you tell!
2 I've fixed that computer program for you. ~ Oh, thank you. . . . . clever you are!
3 I'm afraid we've missed the train. ~ Oh no! . . . . nuisance!
4 It's raining again. ~ I know. . . . . awful weather we've been having lately.
5 We've decorated this room. ~ Yes, I can see. . . . . it's changed! It looks very different.
6 Do you remember Adam's party? ~ Of course I do. . . . . great party it was!

25 The use of questions

▶ Finder 13

A detective called Steve is questioning a suspect called Terry. Write down the use of each question. Choose from these uses: asking for information (3x), a complaint, an offer, a request (2x).

Steve:	Where were you on Friday afternoon?	▶ *asking for information*
Terry:	I told you. I was at home.	
Steve:	Can you tell me the truth, please, Terry?	▶ *a request*
Terry:	I am telling you the truth.	
Steve:	What have you done with the money?	1 . . . .
Terry:	I haven't got any money.	
Steve:	Would you like a cup of tea, Terry?	2 . . . .
Terry:	No, thanks. I want to go home.	
	I haven't done anything wrong.	
	Why can't you just let me go?	3 . . . .
Steve:	You'll go when you've told me the truth.	
	When were you last in prison?	4 . . . .
Terry:	Not long ago. You know when.	
Steve:	You'll soon be back if you don't talk.	
	Now, will you help me, Terry?	5 . . . .

26 Question forms

▶ Finder 14A–B

Put the words and phrases in the right order to form a question. Decide if it is a yes/no question or a wh-question and write it in the correct group.

- ▶ is/on time/the train
- ▶ did/say/what/you
1 be/fine/it/tomorrow/will
2 does/start/the film/when
3 everyone/is/laughing/why
4 bring/did/some money/with you/you
5 are/feeling/how/you
6 can/park/the car/we/where
7 anything/are/doing/tonight/you
8 a holiday/had/have/this year/you
9 did/on your mobile/ring/you/who
10 anything interesting/happened/has/lately

Yes/no questions
. . *Is the train on time?* . . . .
. . . .
. . . .
. . . .
. . . .
. . . .
. . . .

Wh-questions
. . *What did you say?* . . . .
. . . .
. . . .
. . . .
. . . .
. . . .

27 Question words

▶ Finder 15A

Read the true story and then write the questions.

A couple called Michael and Kate, who lived in Hereford in England, booked a holiday using the Internet. They thought they were going to Gerona in Spain. When they arrived after their flight, they were puzzled because they saw Italian flags everywhere. When a bus driver refused their pesetas, they realized something was wrong. Michael and Kate only spoke English, so they asked another British couple for help. That was when they discovered that they were in Genoa in Italy. Their mistake was that they had clicked the wrong box.

Questions	Answers
▶ . *What were the names of the two people?* . .	Michael and Kate.
1 . . . . live?	In Hereford.
2 . . . . holiday?	They used the Internet.
3 . . . . going?	To Gerona.
4	They flew.
5	Because of all the Italian flags.
6	When someone refused their pesetas.
7	Another British couple.
8	They told them they were in Italy.
9	The wrong one.

28 *Who, what,* etc as subject and object

▶ Finder 15B

What questions are suggested here?

▶ Tom beat someone at tennis, but I don't know who.   *Who did Tom beat at tennis*

▶ Someone beat Sarah, but I don't know her name.   *Who beat Sarah?*

1 Someone broke the world record. . . . .

2 Mark has broken something. I wonder what. . . . .

3 Someone called the police, but I don't know who. . . . .

4 Susan keeps something in the safe, but she won't tell me what. . . . .

5 Something made Susan late for work. I'm not sure what. . . . .

6 Emma mailed someone or other for advice. . . . .

7 Someone mailed Emma with some advice. . . . .

8 The police are interviewing a man. . . . .

9 We've spent a lot of money, but I'm not sure how much. . . . .

10 A lot of people are coming, but I couldn't say how many. . . . .

11 Something happened. I don't know what. . . . .

12 Leanne met someone. Maybe a new boyfriend? . . . .

29 Prepositions in questions

Instead of a yes/no question, ask a wh-question with a similar meaning. The question should end with a preposition.

► Are you thinking about your trip?
....*What are you thinking about?*....

1 Are those people looking for Andrew?
....

2 Has Laura decided on her next move?
....

3 Is the picture frame made of wood?
....

4 Did Sarah dance with anyone?
....

5 Are you worried about something?
....

6 Could people object to anything?
....

7 Was Sam apologizing for being late?
....

30 *Who, what,* and *which*

► Finder 16A–C

Complete the questions. Put in *who, what,* or *which*.

► ..*Who*.. told you the news? ~ My brother.
► ..*What*.. time did you go to bed? ~ Oh, after midnight.

1 .... are you doing at the weekend? ~ Nothing.

2 I know Peter's sister. ~ .... sister? He's got two.

3 .... of these colours do you like best? ~ They're all nice.

4 .... about some music? ~ I'll put a CD on.

5 .... was Mark talking to just now? ~ That was Gemma.

6 Nicola has applied for a job. ~ .... job? There aren't any jobs, are there?

7 One of these sculptures is worth a lot of money? ~ .... one is that?

8 .... of your friends lives in London, did you say? ~ Oh, that's Louise.

9 .... kind of music do you like to listen to? ~ Heavy metal.

10 .... drew this silly picture, I wonder? ~ I have no idea.

29 • Prepositions in questions   15

31 *How* and *what*

▶ Finder 16C–D, 16F

Complete each conversation. Put in these words or phrases: *how, how long, how much, how often, how old, what, what about, what colour, what else, what kind, what time*.

1 Adam: . . . . was the party?
   Rick: Oh, it was great.
   Adam: . . . . did you get home?
   Rick: About two in the morning.

2 Nicola: I'm looking for our visitor, Mrs Green.
   Martin: . . . . does she look like?
   Nicola: She's tall and slim.
   Martin: . . . . is her hair?
   Nicola: It's dark.

3 Sarah: I've nearly finished packing.
   Alan: That suitcase looks pretty full. . . . . are you going to take?
   Sarah: I might take this microscope,
   Alan: . . . . will you need that for?

4 Lisa: . . . . is your brother?
   Karen: He's 25. He's working in America at the moment.
   Lisa: . . . . is he there for?
   Karen: I'm not sure. He's been there three years now.
   Lisa: . . . . do you see him?
   Karen: About twice a year.

5 Travel agent: . . . . of holiday are you thinking of?
   Lucy: A skiing holiday. In Europe. . . . . the one in this
              brochure? . . . . does that one cost?
   Travel agent: The prices are here at the bottom, look.

32 Review of questions

▶ Finder 14–16

A girl called Kirsty has disappeared on her way to school. A detective inspector is answering reporters' questions. Write the questions.

▶ Reporter: . . *How old is Kirsty?* . .
   Inspector: She's thirteen years old.

1 Reporter: . . . .
   Inspector: She's short with fair hair. We've got a photo here.
2 Reporter: . . . .
   Inspector: She was last seen at half past eight yesterday morning.
3 Reporter: . . . .
   Inspector: She was in Carlton Road, near the newsagent's.
4 Reporter: . . . .
   Inspector: We don't know, but it's possible. Someone may have kidnapped her.
5 Reporter: . . . .
   Inspector: No. As far as we know, she isn't in trouble.

6 Reporter: . . . .
 Inspector: No, never. This is the first time she's ever gone missing.
7 Reporter: . . . .
 Inspector: Everywhere. We're looking everywhere in the area.
8 Reporter: . . . .
 Inspector: Yes, we would. We'd certainly like people to help.
9 Reporter: . . . .
 Inspector: Optimistic? Well, I'm trying to be.
10 Reporter: . . . .
 Inspector: How do they feel? Well, they feel very worried about their daughter of course.

33 Review of questions ▶ Finder 14–16

What questions did reporters ask to find out the information in **bold** type?

▶ The two leaders are meeting **next week**.
 When are the two leaders meeting?

▶ **Yes**, United's manager has resigned.
 Has United's manager resigned?

1 Scientists have discovered **a new element**.
 . . . .

2 **Four** people were killed in the accident.
 . . . .

3 **Yes**, National Bank is in crisis.
 . . . .

4 The fires have been burning **for three days**.
 . . . .

5 The new building cost **£20 million**.
 . . . .

6 New houses should be built **in rural areas**.
 . . . .

7 **No**, the Prime Minister doesn't speak French.
 . . . .

8 The government has decided **to raise taxes**.
 . . . .

9 The factory will close down **in June**.
 . . . .

10 The workers are protesting **because they will lose their jobs**.
 . . . .

34 Indirect questions ▶ Finder 17

Here are some typical questions from tourists. Make them a bit less abrupt by using indirect questions with the words in brackets.

▶ How much does a ticket cost? (tell)
 Could you tell me how much a ticket costs?

1 What time does the next guided tour start? (wonder)
 I was . . . .

2 How can I get to City Airport? (you/know)

. . . .

3 Do I need a visa? (try/find out)

. . . .

4 Where are the toilets? (tell)

. . . .

5 Is the palace open today? (need/know)

. . . .

6 Can I buy these goods tax-free? (try/find out)

. . . .

35 Negative questions

▶ Finder 18A–B

What negative questions could you ask in these situations? Use the words in brackets.

▶ Your friend has been to an all-night party and is in college at nine the next morning. (tired)
You: . . *Aren't you tired?* . . .

1 Sarah is telling you how she walked out of the cinema halfway through a film. (like)
You: . . . .

2 Amy wants to make a phone call, but she is telling you that she can't find a phone box. (mobile)
You: . . . .

3 Robert wants to get some money from a cash machine. He is wondering what his PIN number is. (remember)
You: . . . .

4 You are talking to an English person who knows nothing about the sights of London. (never)
You: . . . .

5 Steve has got a bicycle. He says he doesn't need it any more. (why/sell)
You: . . . .

36 Negative questions

▶ Finder 18B

There are some problems in class today. What questions does the teacher ask in order to solve them? Write the questions and begin with *who*, *what*, or *which*.

▶ Maria hasn't got one of the texts.
. . *Which of the texts haven't you got, Maria?* . . .

1 Carlos couldn't find something in the dictionary.

. . . .

2 Someone hasn't given in their homework.

. . . .

3 Christian can't understand one of the words.

. . . .

4 Something doesn't make sense to Isabel.

. . . .

5 Sven won't be able to attend one of the lessons.

. . . .

37 Review of questions

▶ Finder 14–18

Each of these questions is incorrect. Write them correctly.

▶ ~~Whom left all these boxes here?~~ ~ Simon did.
    Who left all these boxes here?

1 ~~At what are you looking?~~ ~ The map.

. . . .

2 ~~Watched you the football on TV?~~ ~ Yes, it was good, wasn't it?

. . . .

3 ~~Do you know what time does the shop open?~~ ~ Half past nine, I think.

. . . .

4 ~~Who's coat is this?~~ ~ Louise's.

. . . .

5 ~~What foot did you drop your bag on?~~ ~ My right foot.

. . . .

6 ~~Who other have you told the news to?~~ ~ No one.

. . . .

7 ~~Is not it time we started?~~ ~ Yes, OK.

. . . .

8 ~~Should have we checked the timetable first?~~ ~ Yes, I suppose so.

. . . .

9 ~~What on ever were you thinking of?~~ ~ I don't know.

. . . .

10 ~~What type phone should we buy?~~ ~ What about a cordless one?

. . . .

People are asking you questions. Look at the information in brackets and give your answer.

▶ Jessica: What time is the concert?
You: . . *Eight o'clock.* . . . . .
(The concert is at eight o'clock.)

▶ Paul: Have you won the lottery?
You: . . *No, I haven't, unfortunately.* . . .
(You haven't won the lottery, unfortunately.)

1 Lauren: Is it a public holiday tomorrow?
You: . . . .
(It is a public holiday tomorrow.)

2 Louise: Can I sit down?
You: . . . .
(Of course Louise can sit down.)

3 Tim: What's the matter?
You: . . . .
(You are worried about your exam.)

4 Emily: Why aren't you coming out with me?
You: . . . .
(You are sorry you aren't going out with Emily. You've got a headache.)

5 Simon: How many computers have you got?
You: . . . .
(You've got two computers.)

6 Peter: Would you like a cup of coffee?
You: . . . .
(You would like a cup of coffee.)

7 Sarah: Did you buy a newspaper?
You: . . . .
(You didn't buy a newspaper. You forgot.)

8 Jodie: Can I use your calculator?
You: . . . .
(Jodie can't use your calculator. It isn't working.)

39 Question tags

Complete the conversations. Put in the question tags.

▶ There's plenty of time, . . . *isn't there?* . . ~ Yes, there's no hurry.
▶ You haven't seen Martin, . . *have you?* . . ~ No, sorry. Not recently.

1 I really enjoyed the film. ~ Yes, it was good, ...

2 They won't catch the burglars, ... ~ No, not a chance.

3 We've been here before. ~ Yes, we came here last year, ...

4 I can't play with right-handed golf clubs. ~ Oh, so you're left-handed, ...

5 Matthew's exam results are excellent. ~ Yes, he's done well, ...

6 You aren't going to move from here, ... ~ I don't know. I might do.

7 There's no electricity, ... ~ No, it's off. They're doing some repairs.

8 These strawberries are nice. ~ Yes, they taste delicious, ...

9 Tim wants to know if Louise will be at the party. ~ He fancies her, ... I didn't know that.

10 Why don't you come to Greece with us? ~ I promised to go walking in Scotland with Steve. I can't let him down, ...

40 Echo tags

► Finder 21B

Say if the replies express interest, disbelief, or agreement.

▶ I can't read without glasses. ~ Oh, can't you?   . *interest* . . . .

1 I live next door to Madonna. ~ You don't, do you?   . . . .

2 I've just been to Australia. ~ Oh, have you?   . . . .

3 My mother swam the Atlantic. ~ She didn't, did she?   . . . .

4 This is a beautiful view. ~ Isn't it?   . . . .

5 The evening was a great success. ~ It was, wasn't it?   . . . .

6 I never watch television. ~ Don't you?   . . . .

39 • Question tags   21

41 Review of questions and answers

▶ Finder 16–21

Decide which answer goes where.

▶ How are you?	a) Yes, certainly.
1 Would you like a drink?	b) Good idea.
2 The computer isn't working.	c) Fine, thanks.
3 Do you repair bicycles?	d) It's quite interesting.
4 Isn't this music awful?	e) I'm afraid I do.
5 How about a game of cards?	f) Yes, please.
6 What's that book like?	g) Yes, it's lovely.
7 Isn't this a nice park?	h) No, it's nice.
8 I often smash plates.	i) No. It's interesting, is it?
9 Do you feel unwell?	j) Isn't it?
10 Have you read this book?	k) You do what?

▶ c)	3	6	9 . . . . .
1	4	7	10 . . . . .
2	5	8	

42 Review of questions and answers

▶ Finder 13–21

What would be the most likely answer?

▶ How often do you come here?
a) ☑ About once a month.   b) ☐ After work.   c) ☐ On the bus.

1 Are you ready to go?
a) ☐ Now.   b) ☐ Yes, I am.   c) ☐ Yes, I am ready to go.

2 I'm going to travel round the world.
a) ☐ Are you really?   b) ☐ I'm interested in what you say.   c) ☐ Round the world, is it?

3 What time is the game?
a) ☐ An hour and a half.   b) ☐ Half past seven.   c) ☐ Tomorrow.

4 Didn't you fill the form in?
a) ☐ I didn't fill it in.   b) ☐ No, I forgot.   c) ☐ Yes, I forgot.

5 It's a beautiful day, isn't it?
a) ☐ No.   b) ☐ Oh, why not?   c) ☐ Yes, it's lovely.

6 Who did you interview?
a) ☐ I interviewed the DJ.   b) ☐ The DJ interviewed me.   c) ☐ The DJ did it.

7 Can I help you?
a) ☐ All right. What is it?   b) ☐ Yes, please.   c) ☐ You can.

8 What make is your computer?
a) ☐ I play games on it.   b) ☐ It's an Apple Mac.   c) ☐ It's quite an old one.

43 Leaving out and replacing words

▶ Finder 22A

Look at this conversation in a supermarket.

Paul: I don't like this supermarket much. It's too big.
Sarah: Oh, do you think so?
Paul: I always get lost in here. I like the one in the High Street better.
Sarah: You get more choice here.
Paul: I'm looking for apples.
Sarah: There are some over here.
Paul: Oh those look nice.

Say what the words in **bold** mean in the conversation.

▶ **It**'s too big   it =   . . *this supermarket* . .

1 Oh, do you think **so**?   so = ...
2 the **one** in the High Street.   one = ...
3 There are **some** over here.   some = ...
4 **those** look nice.   those = ...

44 Leaving out nouns

▶ Finder 23

Look at this conversation and then cross out the nouns that can be left out.

Nicola: Have you seen my photos?
Laura: Oh, no, I haven't.
Nicola: These ~~photos~~ are the ones I took on our holiday in Spain.
Laura: That holiday was great, wasn't it? We had a wonderful time. I've been dying to see the photos.
Nicola: There are sixty photos here if you've got time to look at them.
Laura: I took some photos too, but not as many photos as you did. Oh, yes, they're good. There we are on the beach.
Nicola: I think this one is the funniest photo. We were sitting by the pool.
Laura: Let me see. Oh no! Look at me!
Nicola: I think I'd just told you a joke.
Laura: I can't remember which one it was. You told a few jokes, didn't you?

45 Leaving out words after the auxiliary

▶ Finder 24

Look at this conversation.

Adam:	Where's Peter? Isn't he supposed to meet us?
Kate:	He said he would. But I don't think he's coming now.
Adam:	He might be soon.
Kate:	I don't think we'll see him tonight. But if I do, I'm going to tell him what I think of him.
Adam:	I could try to get him on his mobile.
Kate:	I already have. Most people keep their phones switched on, but Peter doesn't of course. He has to be awkward.
Adam:	Well, maybe he had to stay late at work.
Kate:	No, he just can't be bothered. He doesn't keep his promises, you know. Other people do, but Peter never does.

Complete the sentences using the information in the conversation.

▶ Peter told Kate that he would . . *meet her and Adam.* . . . . .

1 Adam thinks Peter might be . . . . soon.
2 Kate is going to be angry with Peter if she . . . . tonight.
3 Kate has already . . . .
4 The problem with Peter's phone is that he doesn't . . . .
5 Kate says that Peter never . . . .

46 Other structures where we leave out words

▶ Finder 25A–B

Decide which answer goes where.

▶ Someone cheated in the exam.
1 Tom was going to do a bungee jump.
2 Why didn't you join in the fun?
3 They've closed all the roads into town.
4 Something delayed the train.
5 Will you be surfing next week?
6 I can't climb to the top.
7 You're a real optimist, you know.
8 I shouldn't have stayed in the sun so long.
9 I can sell you a ticket really cheap.

a) Am I?
b) Well, I hope to be.
c) I warned you not to.
d) And did he?
e) How much?
f) Who?
g) What did?
h) I didn't want to.
i) Are you afraid to?
j) Why?

▶ *f)* . . . . . . 1 . . . . . 4 . . . . . 7 . . . . .
                2 . . . . . 5 . . . . . 8 . . . . .
                3 . . . . . 6 . . . . . 9 . . . . .

47 Leaving out the first word

▶ Finder 26

Look at this conversation.

	Rick:	Hi. How are you?
▶	Simon:	Fine, thanks. You?
1	Rick:	I'm all right, thanks. Keeping busy?
2	Simon:	Yes, I am. Lots to do at the office. Big panic on at the moment.
3	Rick:	Oh, dear. Sorry to hear that.
4	Simon:	Doesn't bother me. Loving it, actually. Well, must dash. Call me some time.
5	Rick:	OK. See you again.

Write the missing sentences in full.

	Rick:	Hi. How are you?
▶	Simon:	*I'm fine, thanks. How are you?*
1	Rick:	I'm all right, thanks. ....
2	Simon:	Yes, I am. ....
		....
3	Rick:	Oh, dear. ....
4	Simon:	....
		Call me some time.
5	Rick:	OK. ....

48 *Too* and *either*

▶ Finder 27A

Put in *too* or *either*.

▶ I don't like this programme. ~ I don't *either.*

1 I've got a video camera. ~ I have ....

2 You can't do maths. ~ Well, you can't ....

3 My boyfriend is always calling me on my mobile. ~ Mine is ....

4 You got home very late last night. ~ You did ...., didn't you?

5 I won't have any pudding. ~ I won't .... I'm full.

6 I hate this really hot weather. ~ Me ....

49 So and *neither/nor*

▶ Finder 27B

Use the information to write sentences with *so*, *neither* and *nor*.

▶ Andrew and Robert both have beards. (so)
 . . *Andrew has a beard, and so has Robert.* . . .

▶ My brother and sister stayed in last night. (neither)
 . . *My brother didn't go out last night, and neither did my sister.* . . .

1 Alan and his father are both out of work. (neither)

. . . .

2 The hotel and the beach were both nice. (so)

. . . .

3 Karen and James both dislike jazz. (nor)

. . . .

4 The students and the teachers all enjoyed the trip. (so)

. . . .

5 My mother and father are both unable to speak French. (neither)

. . . .

6 Laura and I will both be absent from school tomorrow. (nor)

. . . .

7 Cars and planes both cause pollution. (so)

. . . .

8 Gemma and her boyfriend are both ill. (nor)

. . . .

50 Contradicting

▶ Finder 27C

Contradict what people say here.

▶ We can go in the back way. ~ . . *We can't.* . . The door's locked.

▶ I don't want to go out. ~ Yes, . . *you do.* . . You can't stay in on your own.

1 We didn't see the others in the park. ~ . . . . They waved to us.

2 I'm not very good at English. ~ . . . . You're brilliant at it.

3 My English hasn't improved. ~ Oh, ... It's getting better all the time.

4 I won't pass the exam. ~ I'm sure . . . .

5 This dress looks awful. ~ . . . . It looks lovely.

6 It's left here to go to the club. ~ No, ... It's right and then left.

7 Kate was upset. ~ . . . . She was pretending to be.

51 *I think so, I hope not*, etc

▶ Finder 28A–B

Complete these short conversations. Put in structures with *so* or *not* and use the word in brackets.

▶ Martin: Are we going to win the game? (think)

Paul: . . *I don't think so.* . . All our best players are injured.

▶ Karen: Are you still dating Melanie? (guess)

Adam: . . *I guess not.* . . . It seems like she's had enough of me.

1 Sam: Don't you think you need a new car? (suppose)

Emily: . . . . This one is falling to pieces, isn't it?

2 Alice: Will you be going away on holiday? (expect)

Mark: . . . . I can't afford it, really.

3 Simon: My bicycle has been stolen. I suppose I should have left it locked up. (tell)

Nicola: Well, ... didn't I? But you wouldn't listen.

4 Lisa: Has David gone back to America? (hope)

Jodie: . . . . He owes me fifty pounds.

5 Sarah: Have they finished digging up the road? (seem)

Laura: . . . . They're putting the equipment back in the lorry.

6 Leanne: Does a Mr Perkins live in this building. (believe)

Mr Foot: Yes, ..., although I don't actually know him.

7 Tom: Will you have time to help us? (afraid)

Lucy: . . . . I'm very busy at the moment.

8 Louise: Is Steve going to move to the new flat, did he tell you? (say)

Rick: I don't know. But then he never tells me anything.

52 *Do so, do it*, and *do that*

▶ Finder 29A

Complete the sentence by putting in the two missing words. Use a form of *do,* and *so, it,* or *that.* Sometimes there is more than one possible answer.

▶ The conjuror sawed a woman in half, and we have no idea how he . . *did it.* . . .

1 You were told to leave the building, and the manager wishes you to . . . . immediately.

2 We've won the Cup! We've . . . . !

3 The aircraft will be allowed to take off only if it is safe for it to . . . .

4 Would you like me to peel some potatoes? ~ It's OK. I'm just . . . . now.

5 'On the couch' will psychoanalyse you! No other computer program can . . . .

6 The soldiers told the driver to get out of the car, and he . . . . at once.

53 Structures with *so*, *not*, *the same*, and *that way*

▶ Finder 28–29

Complete the sentences. Put in *so*, *not*, *the same*, or *that way*.

▶ Are they going to build new houses here? ~ Well, . .*so*. . it appears.

1 Do we have to pay to go in? ~ I hope . . . . I haven't got any money.
2 Steve really likes Nicola, but she doesn't feel . . . . about him.
3 My grandfather went to university. He was the first person in our family to do . . . .·
4 I always wash up after a meal. Other people should do . . . .·
5 The atmosphere on the streets is peaceful just now, and the police want it to stay . . . .·
6 I hope I can pay by credit card. If . . . ., I'll have to get some cash from the machine.
7 Who's got the key? ~ You have, haven't you? ~ Oh, ... I have. It's here in my pocket.
8 The people seem content, but how long will they remain . . . .?

54 Note style

▶ Finder 30D

Read the postcard and then write the full sentences.

Hi Sophie,

Arrived here Sunday.
All having marvellous time.
Weather perfect. Writing
this on beach. Children
playing in sea. Water nice
and clean. Going on tour
of island tomorrow.

Love,
Melissa

Ms Sophie Wilson

3 Oaks Drive

Chesterfield

Derbys

S42 3VA

We arrived here . . . .
. . . .
. . . .
. . . .
. . . .
. . . .

55 Review of leaving out and replacing words ▶ Finder 25–29

Write these answers in the right place.

And did you?	So do I.	Yes, I am.
I guess not.	So they say.	~~Yes, I think so.~~
Neither do I.	Thanks. Same to you.	You shouldn't do that.
Of course not.	Well, I hope to.	
Oh, so I have.	Who did?	

▶ Are you sure you've made the right decision? ~ ..*Yes, I think so.*...
1 I love this music. ~ ....
2 Feeling fit? ~ ....
3 Did you steal that watch? ~ ....
4 Someone climbed up onto the roof. ~ ....
5 You've got mail, look. ~ ....
6 I don't like horror films. ~ ....
7 Have a nice weekend, won't you? ~ ....
8 Thirteen is an unlucky number, isn't it? ~ ....
9 Will you be going to university? ~ ....
10 We wanted to go to the concert. ~ ....
11 I often walk out of restaurants without paying. ~ ....
12 You can't wear trainers to a wedding, can you? ~ ....

56 Review of leaving out and replacing words ▶ Finder 24–29

Andrea and Carlos are studying at a college in Britain. Look at their conversation and help them to improve their English by leaving out or replacing words in the underlined parts.

Andrea: You were late this morning.	
Carlos: (▶) Yes, I'm afraid I was late. My bus was late.	..*Yes, I'm afraid so.*...
Andrea: The buses aren't very reliable, are they?	
Carlos: (1) No, they aren't very reliable.	....
Andrea: I cycle to college, so I don't have that problem.	
Carlos: (2) I can't cycle to college, really.	....
(3) I'd like to cycle to college, but there isn't a very good route from where I'm staying. The main road is too dangerous.	....
Andrea: (4) Yes, I suppose the main road is too dangerous.	....
Carlos: Sometimes my landlady gives me a lift in her car.	
Andrea: (5) Oh, does she give you a lift in her car? That's handy.	....
Carlos: She's very nice, my landlady.	

Andrea:	(6) <u>Mine is very nice too.</u> But she doesn't work in town, unfortunately. (7) <u>And her husband doesn't work in town.</u>	. . . .
Carlos:	Well, no one will mind if you're late once or twice.	
Andrea:	(8) <u>I hope they won't mind.</u> Actually, no one would notice if I missed the first lesson every day.	. . . .
Carlos:	(9) <u>You mustn't miss the first lesson.</u> You'd soon fall behind with your studies.	. . . .

57 Review of leaving out and replacing words ▶ Finder 23–29

Correct the sentences.

▶ I'm meeting my friend, but I've forgotten ~~what time am I~~.
. . . I'm meeting my friend, but I've forgotten what time. . . .

1 The kitchen is in a mess, and is the living-room.
. . . .

2 My friends all rode on the roller-coaster, but I couldn't do so.
. . . .

3 Which way is the quickest way?
. . . .

4 I went to the party, although I didn't really want.
. . . .

5 You don't need to tell me I'm late because I know so.
. . . .

6 I'm not certain the trains are running, but they should.
. . . .

7 The women sat on one side of the room, and the men sat other side.
. . . .

8 The weather is lovely, and it's going to stay so all weekend.
. . . .

9 My girlfriend doesn't like sport, but I like.
. . . .

10 I didn't get here as quickly as got you.
. . . .

11 The book isn't very funny, and the film either.
. . . .

12 There could be problems, but I don't hope so.
. . . .

Put each group of sentences into the most sensible order and create a short text. It will help if you look for links between the sentences.

1 An atom consists of even smaller particles. Around this nucleus a number of electrons are in constant orbit. Everything in the world is made up of tiny particles. There is a nucleus in the middle of each atom. These particles are called atoms.

THE ATOM

Everything in the world . . . .
. . . .
. . . .
. . . .

2 All this is making me very depressed. He never tells me where he is, and he's out late most nights. I'm really fed up at the moment. It's because of my boyfriend. Last night he went to a club with some friends, but he didn't want me there.

FED UP

. . . .
. . . .
. . . .
. . . .
. . . .

3 His route through the country is on a map pinned on his bedroom wall. Mike Roots, a 57-year-old teacher from Colchester in Essex, is cycling round the world. The next country he will be passing through is Sierra Leone. This began in Norway, and he has now reached West Africa. But 'cycling' means that Mr Roots rides an exercise bike at home and uses maps to plot his imaginary journey.

JOURNEY ROUND THE WORLD

. . . .
. . . .
. . . .
. . . .
. . . .
. . . .
. . . .

59 Word order in a text

▶ Finder 31–34

This student composition isn't very easy to read. Rewrite each sentence changing the word order so that the sentence begins with a different phrase.

OUR HOUSE

In King Street is our house. Quite old are the houses in this street. On two floors is our house. We've got a living-room, dining-room, kitchen and bathroom downstairs. There are three bedrooms upstairs. At the front is my bedroom. Quite a big garden is behind the house. My mum's hobby is the garden. Looking after it she spends a lot of time. In summer it looks beautiful. We like to sit there on sunny days. Under the apple tree we usually sit.

OUR HOUSE

Our house is . . . .

. . . .

. . . .

. . . .

. . . .

. . . .

. . . .

60 Linking the subject

▶ Finder 33

Add a sentence from the box to each of the sentences below. Each time there are two sentences which make sense. Choose the sentence where the subject makes the best link with what has gone before.

People of all ages enjoy the story.
The story appeals to people of all ages.

It attracts thousands of visitors.
Thousands of people visit it.

Someone built them in the summer.
They were built in the summer.

The delay caused us to miss our connecting flight.
We missed our connecting flight because of the delay.

A panel of experts will discuss the prospects for world government.
This topic will be discussed by a panel of experts.

The new Olympic Stadium is the biggest in the country.
The country has nothing else as big as the Olympic Stadium.

The price includes the battery.
You get a free battery with it.

▶ There's a new shopping mall. . . . . . *It attracts thousands of visitors.* . . .

1 The phone costs £20. . . . .
2 Do we need a world government? . . . .
3 The city is ready for the Games. . . . .
4 These houses are new. . . . .
5 The plane was two hours late. . . . .
6 It's a wonderful book. . . . .

61 An adverbial in front position.

▶ Finder 34A

Complete each sentence using the information in brackets. Put the adverbial at the beginning of the clause.

▶ (He heard an explosion suddenly.)
Tom was sitting doing his homework when . . . *suddenly he heard an explosion.* . . .

1 (News came through on Friday.)
I was in suspense all week until . . . .

2 (We eat at home sometimes.)
Sometimes we go out to eat, and . . . .

3 (Everyone knows you in a village.)
In a city you're anonymous, but . . . .

4 (I missed the turning, stupidly.)
I wasn't concentrating on the driving, and . . . .

5 (We should go home perhaps.)
It's getting rather late, so . . . .

62 Inversion

▶ Finder 34

Put the words into the right order and add another sentence. Where possible, start with something that links to the previous sentence. Sometimes there is inversion and sometimes not.

▶ is / a big attraction / the new theme park
There's lots going on here. . . . . . *A big attraction is the new theme park.* . . .

1 a man in uniform / at the entrance / stood
The taxi stopped outside the hotel. . . . .

2 I have to do / right now / this
I can put off some things. But . . . .

3 were celebrating / people/ everywhere
The victory had thrilled the whole town. . . . .

4 comes / here / the bus
Oh, look. At last. . . . .

5 I wouldn't/ Marcus/ trust
Tim and Marcus are a strange pair. . . . .

6 one slight problem / the lack of time / was
Things went more or less to plan. . . . .

7 goes / it / there
The plane is taking off. . . . .

8 a message in code / on the screen / was
The computer was switched on. . . . .

63 The empty subject *there*

▶ Finder 35

Write sentences of similar meaning using *there*.

▶ The shopping mall has a multi-screen cinema in it.
. . . . . *There's a multi-screen cinema in the shopping mall.* . . .

▶ We have seen a sharp increase in the cost of living.
. . . . . *There has been a sharp increase in the cost of living.* . . .

1 The safe might have something valuable in it.

. . . .

2 Lots of people were on the beach.

. . . .

3 Soon a further difficulty arose.

. . . .

4 Life after death – does it exist?

. . . .

5 A hotel has to have fire doors in it.

. . . .

6 No other messages have come for you.

. . . .

7 A parade took place last week, didn't it?

. . . .

8 It seems we have a problem with the heating.

. . . .

9 Someone should be waiting for me at the airport.

. . . .

10 Will we have time for a proper discussion?

. . . .

11 A gust of wind blew some tiles off the roof.

. . . .

12 A number of people have been mugged in this area recently.

. . . .

64 The empty subject *it*

▶ Finder 36

Some of these sentences are correct, and some have the word *it* missing from them. If a sentence is correct, put a tick (✓) after it. If it is incorrect, put *it* in the right place.

▶ Today is the 16th. ✓ ▶ Lisa, ^*it* was wonderful to see you again.

1 For most of the game looked as if we were going to lose.
2 What time is now?
3 We found the questions very easy to answer.
4 This program will make possible to access the data more quickly.
5 Look, really is a beautiful day.
6 Luckily, appears that the bomb warning was a false alarm.
7 What happened next came as a shock.
8 Actually, amuses me to sit here and watch people go by.
9 Don't you think is terrible not having any friends?
10 I consider absolutely ridiculous that we have to fill these forms in.

65 *There* or *it*   ▶ Finder 37

Complete the conversations. Put *there* or *it* in each space.

▶ Was . . *there* . . someone at the door earlier? ~ Yes, . . *it* . . was the postman.

1 . . . .'s raining really hard now. ~ . . . .'s a phone box over there. We could shelter until it stops.

2 How far is . . . . to Leeds? ~ Oh, I'd say . . . .'s about forty miles from here.

3 . . . .'ll be the start of the holiday in three weeks. ~ I haven't really thought about that. . . . .'s so much work to do.

4 . . . .'s quarter to eight. Adam is late again. ~ Yes, I don't think . . . .'s any point in waiting.

5 Is . . . . any butter in the fridge? ~ No, but . . . .'s some margarine.

6 Is . . . . something wrong? ~ Well, yes. Sarah said something quite nasty to me, and . . . . really upset me.

66 Emphasis in the verb phrase   ▶ Finder 38C

Complete the conversation. Put in sentences with the emphatic form.

▶ Louise: There are lots of rumours about you, James. They say your father's a multi-millionaire.
  James: Well, ... *he is a multi-millionaire.* . . . .
▶ Louise: Oh, really? And there's a story about you owning a yacht.
  James: Yes, actually . . . . . *I do own a yacht.* . . . .

1 Louise: Someone told me you're an American citizen.
  James: That's right. . . . .

2 Louise: So it isn't true that your parents live in Australia?
  James: Yes, in fact . . . . But they're American.

3 Louise: And is it true that your sister works at the Kennedy Space Center?
  James: Yes, ... there.

4 Louise: And I suppose she's orbited the earth?
  James: Yes, in fact . . . . many times.

5 Louise: She must be famous then. Someone said you know lots of famous people.
  James: Yes, actually . . . .

6 Louise: They say you once met the President.
  James: Yes, it's true. . . . . And it was the proudest moment of my life.

67 Emphasis with *it* and *what*

▶ Finder 38D–E

Rewrite the sentences in a way that emphasizes the bold part. Start each sentence with the word in brackets.

▶ The World Trade Center was destroyed **in 2001**. (it)
  It was in 2001 that the World Trade Center was destroyed, ... not 2000.

▶ In the evenings we usually **watch TV**. (what)
  We don't go out much. *What we usually do in the evenings is watch TV.* . . . . . .

1 I'm worried about **the money**. (what)
. . . . Where are we going to get it from?

2 I was complaining about **the poor service**. (it)
The food was OK. . . . .

3 Kate expected **a friendly welcome**. (what)
. . . . But she didn't get one.

4 We went to Greece **four years ago**. (it)
. . . . wasn't it? Not three.

5 **Charles Dickens** wrote *Oliver Twist*. (it)
. . . . It wasn't Thomas Hardy.

6 I want **some peace and quiet**. (what)
No, no music, please. . . . .

7 Earlier **Paul and Steve had an argument**. (what)

. . . .
That's why they weren't speaking to each other.

8 We saw *Titanic* **in London**. (it)
No, ... , not *Pearl Harbor*.

9 Lewis and Clark **explored the American West**. (what)

. . . .

10 I first felt ill **after I'd been jogging**. (it)

. . . .

11 **I** did all the work. (it)
. . . . , you know.

12 **The fact that no one offered to help** really annoyed me. (what)
. . . .

68 Review of word order and emphasis

▶ Finder 34–38

Write the correct sentences.

▶ People were strolling along the sea front. ~~On the beach were playing some children.~~
  On the beach some children were playing. . .

▶ We hoped to hear some nice music. ~~That we actually heard it was a horrible noise.~~
  What we actually heard was a horrible noise. . .

1 Everything was quiet. ~~But then it was a sudden shout.~~

. . . .

2 No, I didn't forget to lock the door. ~~I did locked it.~~

. . . .

3 I can't find my bag. ~~Oh, here is it.~~

. . . .

4 My English isn't very good. ~~I find hard understand English people~~.

. . . .

5 Those are my college friends. ~~Who we saw just now aren't students~~.

. . . .

6 Are we locked in? ~~Seems be no way out of the building~~.

. . . .

7 To our right we saw pine trees. ~~To our left steep cliffs were~~.

. . . .

8 No, the town hasn't got a theatre. ~~But two cinemas are~~.

. . . .

9 You've had time to answer the letter. ~~Two weeks ago were that you received it~~.

. . . .

10 Mark ate the vegetables. ~~The meat left he on his plate~~.

. . . .

11 The music had stopped. ~~There looked as if the party was over~~.

. . . .

12 I think everything's OK now. ~~Any more problems shouldn't be~~.

. . . .

69 Introduction to verb tenses ▶ Finder 39

Read this true story about a man in hospital.

AFTERNOON OUT

A hospital patient enjoyed an afternoon in bed in a beer garden while the police were searching everywhere for him. Malcolm Storey's friends had wheeled him quietly out of Southampton General Hospital and into a waiting van. Malcolm had been feeling extremely bored after twelve days in hospital with a broken spine following a motorcycle accident. The hospital management have been discussing the matter, and they are taking it very seriously, although they have admitted that the staff find it highly amusing.

Write one verb from the story in each space.

▶ Present simple: *find* . . . .

1 Present continuous: . . . .
2 Present perfect: . . . .
3 Present perfect continuous: . . . .
4 Past simple: . . . .
5 Past continuous: . . . .
6 Past perfect: . . . .
7 Past perfect continuous: . . . .

70 Present simple and present continuous ▶ Finder 40B, 41B

Which time expression is the correct one in these sentences? Cross out the wrong one.

▶ We ~~already~~/often go to the park at weekends.

1 I'm making good progress always/now.
2 My friend just now/sometimes visits me.
3 Louise is living alone at the moment/every day.
4 Do you ever/tonight stay up all night?
5 I do physical exercises at the moment/three times a day.
6 We're just/sometimes discussing a few details.

71 Present simple or present continuous? ▶ Finder 40–42

One day Tom happens to meet his old friend Sarah in the street. Complete their conversation by putting in the correct form of each verb in brackets. Use the present simple or present continuous.

Tom: Hello, Sarah.
Sarah: Tom! (▶) . . *I don't believe* . . (I/not/believe) it!
Tom: How are you? And what (1) . . . . (you/do) these days?
Sarah: Oh, I'm fine. (2) . . . . (I/work) at a bank at the moment.
        But (3) . . . . (I/not/think) I'll be there for very long.
        Anyway, Tom, where (4) . . . .(you/go)?
Tom: To the library. (5) . . . . (I/take) this book back.
Sarah: (6) . . . . (I/go) to the travel agent's. But I'd love a cup of
        coffee and a chat.
Tom: Great. But have you got time?
Sarah: Yes, (7) . . . . (I/not/work) today. I've got the day off.
        (8) . . . . (I/suggest) we go to that little café in the town
        hall. (9) . . . .(they/serve) really good coffee there.
Tom: But (10) . . . .(you want) to go to the travel agent's first?
Sarah: No, it (11) . . . . (not/matter). Anyway,
        (12) . . . . (I/want) to ask them some questions, and
        (13) . . . . (it/always/take) ages in there. Let's have a
        coffee first.
Tom: What time (14) . . . . (the café/open)?
Sarah: (15) . . . . (I/not/know), but it must be open soon. It's
        nearly ten o'clock.

72 Present simple or present continuous?

► Finder 40-42

Write a second sentence so that it has a similar meaning to the previous one. Use the verb in brackets in the present simple or present continuous.

► The car is our neighbour's. (belong) ..*The car belongs to our neighbour.*...
► Gemma is at the computer now. (use) ..*Gemma is using the computer.*...

1 My journey to work is usually by train. (go) . . . .
2 I can hear the telephone. (ring) . . . .
3 There are nuts in this cake. (contain) . . . .
4 I'm on a journey to India. (travel) . . . .
5 The children are fond of ice-cream. (like) . . . .
6 In my opinion it's a lovely painting. (think) . . . .
7 My sister is halfway through that book. (read) . . . .
8 The movement of hot air is always upwards. (rise) . . . .
9 Nicola is a vegetarian. (eat) . . . .

73 Present simple or present continuous?

► Finder 42A–B

Complete the conversations. Put each verb in brackets into the present simple or present continuous.

► Anna: They've got some special offers at Computer World this week. ..*They're selling*.. (they/sell) some good games really cheap.
Simon: Oh, ..*I never go*.. (I/never/go) there. ..*I always buy*.. (I/always/buy) computer things by mail order.

1 Katie: My cousin is really clever. . . . . (he/speak) five languages.
Oliver: That's pretty good. (I/only/speak) two, and one of those not very well.
Katie: He's in the travel business, so . . . . (he/travel) to lots of different places. . . . . (he/travel) around the Far East at the moment.

2 Emma: How is your mother?
Peter: Oh, ... (she/improve) slowly. . . . . (she/hate) being in bed all the time. But these things . . . . (always/take) a long time, so we have to be patient.

3 Jodie: What . . . . (you/do)?
Alan: . . . . (I/just/put) this beer mat in my pocket. . . . . (I/collect) beer mats, and it's one I haven't got.
Jodie: What a strange hobby.

4 Sophie: . . . . (you/go) to evening classes every week?
Jake: Yes, ... (I/do) yoga this year.
Sophie: I might do a course next term. How much . . . . (it/cost)?
Jake: Well, it depends on the subject.

74 Present simple or present continuous?

▶ Finder 42

Put each verb in brackets into the present simple or present continuous. Then look in the box and find a phrase which gives a clue about the choice of tense. Write the phrase under the sentence.

an action in a story	a performative verb	a timetable
an instant action	a permanent routine	annoyingly often
an instruction	a state	reporting the written word
in the middle of something	a temporary routine	

▶ My father . . *owns* . . (own) three racehorses.
. . *a state* . .

1 This book . . . . (tell) an amazing story.
. . . .

2 Sorry, I can't talk now because . . . . (I/drive).
. . . .

3 You're quite right. I must say . . . . (I/agree) with you.
. . . .

4 Owen . . . . (shoot)! And it's a goal!
. . . .

5 . . . . (I/live) in a caravan at the moment.
. . . .

6 The train . . . . (arrive) at four tomorrow afternoon.
. . . .

7 . . . . (you/click) on this icon, look. That's how to do it.
. . . .

8 That man never shuts up. . . . . (he/always/talk)
. . . .

9 . . . . (I/usually/get) up at about seven on weekdays.
. . . .

10 Juliet . . . . (find) Romeo dead at her side.
. . . .

75 The past simple

▶ Finder 43A

Complete the story. Put in the past simple forms of the verbs in brackets.

This is the true story of three-year-old Cameron Munro, who once (▶) ..*had*.. (have) an exciting adventure. Cameron, his mother and his younger sister Annie (1) . . . .(be) at a beauty spot in the Highlands of Scotland when Cameron suddenly (2) . . . . (disappear) among the trees. His mother (3) . . . . (run) after him but Cameron (4) . . . . (not come) back. They (5) . . . . (not know) where he had gone. Mrs Munro (6) . . . . (ring) the police. Police officers and local people (7) . . . . (begin) searching for the boy. But soon the police (8) . . . . (call) off the search for the night. Cameron (9) . . . . (spend) the night in the woods as the temperature (10) . . . . (fall) to almost freezing. Early the next morning a rescue dog called Rosie (11) . . . . (find) Cameron. She (12) . . . . (race) back to her handler, Dave Riley, and he (13) . . . . (follow) her back to where Cameron (14) . . . . (be). Fortunately the boy (15) . . . . (not seem) hurt or upset. Mr Riley (16) . . . . (phone) for an ambulance, which (17) . . . . (take) Cameron to hospital in Inverness. Doctors (18) . . . . (give) him some toast and then (19) . . . . (allow) his mother to take him home. 'I (20) . . . . (want) to look for dinosaurs,' (21) . . . . (say) Cameron. I (22) . . . . (see) two, a big one and a small one. But I (23) . . . . (have) a stick. I (24) . . . . (scare) them away with my stick.'

76 The present perfect

▶ Finder 44A

Complete the conversations using the present perfect.

▶   .. *Have you sent* .. (you/send) your sister a birthday present? ~ No, .. *I haven't even decided* ..(I/not/even/decide) what to buy her yet.

1 This rain . . . . (not/stop) for three days now.
   ~ I know. . . . . (you/ever/see) anything like it?
2 How long . . . . (we/have) this television?
   ~ . . . . (we/have) it at least five years.
3 Oh no, ... (I/forget) my mobile. Can I use yours, please?
   ~ Sorry, ... (I/not/bring) mine with me.
4 . . . . (anyone/ever/jump) off this cliff?
   ~ I don't know. . . . . (I/never/hear) of anyone doing that.

77 Past simple or present perfect?

▶ Finder 43–45

Complete the news report about a village with a by-pass. Put in the past simple or the present perfect of the verbs in brackets.

The village of Greyford (▶) .. *has been* .. (be) largely traffic-free since its by-pass (▶) .. *opened* .. (open) a year ago. Yesterday on the first anniversary of the new road, villagers (1) . . . . (hold) a street party to celebrate the event. 'We (2) . . . .(have) peace and quiet here for a year now,' said Mrs Debbie Groves, who (3) . . . . (organize) the campaign for the by-pass. 'Ever since the traffic stopped coming through here, it (4) . . . . (be) wonderful. Before that we (5) . . . . (suffer) for years, and all that time we (6) . . . . (campaign) for our by-pass. I'll never forget the day when the work finally (7) . . . . (start), or the day when it (8) . . . . (finish). We (9) . . . . (have) the party yesterday because we (10) . . . . (want) to celebrate. Everyone here (11) . . . . (enjoy) themselves. And now we (12) . . . . (decide) to hold one every year.' But not everyone is happy.

The pressure group People Before Cars (13) . . . . (just/complete) a survey of traffic in the area. 'Traffic levels are higher than they (14) . . . . (be) a year ago,' said a spokesperson. 'Traffic (15) . . . . (increase) since the opening of the by-pass. It's true that things are better now in Greyford. The situation (16) . . . . (improve) there. But other places are now worse off than before. The road (17) . . . . (simply/move) the traffic problems to other villages which a year ago (18) . . . . (not have) much of a problem. New roads mean more traffic. We (19) . . . . (tell) the government time and time again, but they never listen.' Some of the villages (20) . . . . (now/ask) the government if they too can have a by-pass, but so far they (21) . . . . (not/receive) a reply.

78 Past simple or present perfect?　　　　　▶ Finder 43-45

Complete the conversation. Put in the past simple or the present perfect of the verbs in brackets.

Polly: Someone (▶) . . *told* . . (tell) me last week that (▶) . . *you've given* . . (you/give) up your job, Justin.

Justin: That's right. (1) . . . . (I/give) it up in March. For the last six months (2) . . . . (I/have) a job as a hospital porter.

Polly: Oh, really. And why (3) . . . . (you/decide) to take a job like that?

Justin: (4) . . . . (I/get) fed up with my old job in the City.
(5) . . . . (it/be) well paid, of course, but
(6) . . . . (I/not/believe) I was playing a useful role in society. So then (7) . . . . (I/decide)
to start a new life and do something socially useful.
So (8) . . . . (I/apply) for the job in a hospital, and
(9) . . . . (they/give) it to me. And so far
(10) . . . . (it/be) a great success.
(11) . . . . (I/not/regret) it for one moment. It's marvellous to be helping other people.

Polly: Well, I'm amazed, Justin. You simply aren't the person
(12) . . . . (I/know) last year.

Justin: (13) . . . . (I/change) since then. I'm a different person now. That's because I'm a member of the Church of Goodness.

Polly: Eh? What's that?

Justin: I'm not surprised (14) . . . . (you/not/hear) of it. It's quite small, but it's growing. (15) . . . . (it/double) its membership over the last six months.

Polly: And how long (16) . . . . (you/be) a member?

Justin: (17) . . . . (I/join) earlier this year, before
             (18) . . . . (I/leave) my old job. Look, Polly, why don't you
             come along to our church on Sunday?
Polly: Sorry, Justin. (19) . . . . (I/just/remember) an appointment.
             I must dash. See you.

79 Reporting news

▶ Finder 45D

Give the news using the present perfect and the past simple. You will need to add extra
words, but do not change the order of the words in the notes.

▶ the US President / resigned / health reasons / announce / decision / a few minutes ago
  The US President has resigned for health reasons. He announced his decision a
  few minutes ago.

1 inflation / rise / again / prices / go up / 4 per cent / last year
  . . . .
  . . . .

2 the firemen / decide / return to work / tomorrow / earlier today / the union / accept /
  improved offer
  . . . .
  . . . .

3 four climbers / die / an accident / the Alps / fall / 200 metres/ when / a rope / break
  . . . .
  . . . .

4 a new traffic scheme / start / Manchester / come into operation / seven o'clock this morning
  . . . .
  . . . .

5 the England football captain / break / his leg / receive / the injury / a match at Newcastle /
  earlier this evening
  . . . .
  . . . .

80 Adverbials of time

▶ Finder 46

Complete the conversation. Put in these missing words: *already, ever, for, just, last, once,
recently, since, this.*

▶ Have you eaten out . . *recently* . . ? ~ Yes, we had a Chinese last week.

1 I've been to America twice. ~ Oh, I've only been there . . . .
2 Are you going to send the fax? ~ I've . . . . done it this minute.
3 Have you taken an exam lately? ~ No, I was about eighteen when I . . . . took one.
4 Are you still friends with Sarah? ~ I suppose so, but I haven't seen her . . . . months.
5 Have you . . . . appeared on television? ~ No, never.
6 Do you want to see this film? ~ No, I've . . . . seen it actually.
7 Where's Steve? ~ I don't know. I haven't seen him . . . . week.
8 Are you hungry? ~ You bet. I haven't eaten anything . . . . seven o'clock this
  morning.

81 Adverbials of time

▶ Finder 46

Choose the best answer.

▶ Kate: I've been very busy this morning. It's been non-stop.
Kate is speaking a) ☑ around the end of the morning b) ☐ in the afternoon.

1 Peter: No chocolate for me, thanks. I've given it up. It's a month since I've eaten any.
Peter doesn't want any chocolate because a) ☐ he's had too much in the last month
b) ☐ he stopped eating it a month ago.

2 Lucy: I never have enough energy. I felt really tired at work today.
Lucy is speaking a) ☐ at work b) ☐ after work.

3 James: I had a holiday in Portugal once. I had a really good time.
The holiday was probably a) ☐ quite a long time ago b) ☐ very recent.

4 Lisa: I'm doing a course here at the college. I'm here for six weeks.
Lisa a) ☐ arrived at the college six weeks ago b) ☐ is on a six-week course at the college.

5 Matthew: The meeting isn't this afternoon, you know. It was this morning.
Matthew is speaking a) ☐ in the morning b) ☐ in the afternoon.

6 Rick: I can't play tennis. I haven't played for years.
Rick can't play because a) ☐ he hasn't practised for long enough b) ☐ he last played
a long time ago.

82 Past simple and present perfect

▶ Finder 45–46

Write a second sentence so that it has a similar meaning to the previous one. Use the word
in brackets.

▶ Prices are higher now. (increased)
  . *Prices have increased.* . .

1 This house has always been my home. (lived) ·
. . . .

2 Weeks passed as Karen lay in hospital. (for)
. . . .

3 I switched the computer on a few seconds ago. (just)
. . . .

4 As a child I had a hatred of school. (hated)
. . . .

5 The parcel is here. (arrived)
. . . .

6 The parcel has been here for two hours. (arrived)
. . . .

7 And Anderson is the winner of this year's Grand Prix! (won)
. . . .

8 My grandfather was the winner of three Olympic medals. (won)
. . . .

9 The last time I flew was in April. (since)
. . . .

10 By the time he was twenty, the young entrepreneur was already a millionaire. (had)
. . . .
. . . .

83 The past continuous

► Finder 47

Choose the best answer.

► While Alice was packing the groceries, someone stole her handbag.
Which took longer, a) ☑ the packing or b) ☐ the theft?

1 When I woke, the phone was ringing.
Did I wake a) ☐ before or b) ☐ after the phone started ringing?
2 We were living in a bungalow at the time.
Does it sound as if the bungalow was a) ☐ a temporary home or b) ☐ a permanent home?
3 I was dialling 999 when I heard a shout.
Which took longer, a) ☐ the dialling or b) ☐ the shout?
4 When the music started, everyone stood up.
What happened first? Did a) ☐ the music start or did b) ☐ everyone stand up?
5 We sat down at a table next to four men who were playing cards.
Did we sit down a) ☐ before, b) ☐ during, or c) ☐ after the game?
6 I had to hurry because I was seeing the doctor at ten thirty.
Does 'was seeing' refer to a) ☐ an action over a long period, b) ☐ a routine, or
c) ☐ an arrangement?
7 As I was drilling the hole, I felt a sudden pain in my back.
Did a) ☐ the drilling interrupt the pain or b) ☐ the pain interrupt the drilling?
8 When I looked out of the window, I saw that someone was cutting the grass.
Which happened first, a) ☐ I looked out of the window or b) ☐ someone started cutting the grass?

84 Past continuous and past simple

► Finder 47C

Find the second part of each sentence. Put both verbs into the correct form. Use the past continuous for the longer action and the past simple for the shorter one.

► When we (arrive) at the party,	when suddenly we (notice) a police car behind us.
► As I (cut) the glass,	while he (swim) in the lake.
1 When Alice (ride) the pony,	~~it suddenly (break) into two pieces.~~
2 We (drive) along	as he (run) towards the net.
3 Someone (steal) Adam's clothes	~~everyone (dance).~~
4 When Tom (wake) up,	when I (discover) a dead insect in it.
5 The player (drop) his racket	she (have) a bad fall.
6 I (eat) a yoghurt	sunlight (stream) in through the curtains.

► When we arrived at the party, everyone was dancing.
► As I was cutting the glass, it suddenly broke into two pieces.

1 ....
2 ....
3 ....
4 ....
5 ....
6 ....

85 Past continuous and past simple

▶ Finder 47B–E

Put in the correct form of the verb in brackets. Use the past continuous or the past simple.

▶ I . .*was reading*. . (read) on the sofa yesterday evening when suddenly all the lights
. .*went*. . (go) out.

1 I'm sorry I couldn't stop when I . . . . (see) you the other day.
I . . . . (catch) a train, so I was in a hurry.

2 Mark . . . . (not understand) the instructions, so he . . . .
(give) up trying to make the machine work.

3 I . . . . (injure) my leg when I . . . . (play) basketball.
I . . . . (fall) awkwardly.

4 When Richard . . . . (marry) Amy, he only . . . . (have)
a temporary job. He . . . . (work) for a building company at the time.

5 When I was younger, I . . . . (hate) going out and meeting people. When I
was with other people, I . . . . (think) they . . . . (laugh)
at me.

6 When the phone . . . . (ring), Matthew . . . . (pick) it up at once.
Joanna . . . . (listen) to music and . . . . (not seem)
to hear it.

86 The present perfect continuous

▶ Finder 48A–B

Write a sentence for each situation. Use the present perfect continuous with *for* or *since*.

▶ There seems no end to the civil war in Silonia, which began three years ago. The two sides are
still fighting.
The two sides have . .*been fighting for three years.*. . .

1 Paul is trying to set a new world record for playing the piano. He started 32 days ago, and he's
still playing.
Paul has been . . . .

2 The police have arrested a man. They began questioning him early this morning, and they are
continuing to do so.
The police have . . . .

3 That dog is a real nuisance. It began barking half an hour ago, and it hasn't stopped since.
That dog . . . .

4 Our friends are going on holiday to India soon. Their preparations started months ago.
Our friends . . . .

5 The government can't decide what they should do about rising crime. It's a big problem.
Discussions began last year and have not yet finished.
The government . . . .

87 Present perfect or present perfect continuous?

► Finder 48C

Put these sentences in the right place.

There are none left, I'm afraid.	I just couldn't stop turning the pages.
I feel a bit stiff.	I'm about halfway through.
He can already say a few words.	They're delicious.
He can speak it perfectly.	We sometimes have to sit in the dark.
I didn't come on the train.	We're in the dark now.

▶ I've been driving. . . . *I feel a bit stiff.* . . .

1 I've driven here. . . . .
2 I've read this book. . . . .
3 I've been reading this book. . . . .
4 They've cut off the power. . . . .
5 They've been cutting off the power. . . . .
6 Steve has learned Welsh. . . . .
7 Steve has been learning Welsh. . . . .
8 I've eaten the chocolates. . . . .
9 I've been eating the chocolates. . . . .

88 The past perfect

► Finder 49A–B

Put in the past perfect form of these verbs: *count, destroy, expect, pay, receive, see, sleep, stop, teach.* Sometimes the verb is negative.

▶ Oliver greeted me like a long-lost friend he . . *hadn't seen* . . for years.

1 I knew there were exactly fifty names on the list because I . . . .
them carefully.

2 I was feeling quite tired because I . . . . very well the night before.

3 As the rain . . . . at last, we decided to leave the shelter and walk on.

4 We were getting worried because five days after the letter was posted to us, we still . . . . .
. . . . it.

5 Terry knew how to read a map. The army . . . . him to do that.

6 I got into trouble with the authorities because I . . . . my taxes for
some time.

7 The journey didn't look far on the map, but actually it took much longer than
I . . . .

8 There was nothing left of the town. The earthquake of the previous
year . . . . it completely.

89 Past simple and past perfect

▶ Finder 49C

Put the verbs into the past simple or past perfect.

▶ I couldn't ring home because I . . *had forgotten* . . (forget) my mobile.

1 When the man . . . . (fall) from the window,
he . . . . (land) on the roof of a car.

2 We were late. When we arrived, the show . . . . (start).

3 We were the guests of honour, so they were all waiting for us. As soon as we arrived, the
show . . . . (start).

4 It's a brilliant film, you know. I . . . . (see) it last Saturday.

5 When the guard . . . . (inspect) the bag,
he . . . . (hand) it back to Mark.

Do the same with this paragraph.

6 When Adam . . . . (wake), it was light. A new
day . . . . (dawn). He . . . . (look) around
him and . . . . (see) that he was in hospital.
How . . . . (he/get) there? Obviously, someone . . . .
(take) him there, presumably in an ambulance. But he wasn't in pain.
He . . . . (feel) all right. He . . . .
(not think) he . . . . (suffer) any major injuries.
He . . . . (try) to remember the events of the previous evening, but
they . . . . (disappear) from his memory.

90 The past perfect continuous

▶ Finder 50A–B

Find the sentence that follows on and put the verb into the past perfect continuous.

▶ The hiker was soaked.	He (search) everywhere for them.
1 Nicola was exhausted.	~~He (walk) in the rain.~~
2 Andrew finally found his keys.	He (wait) all day.
3 The soldiers were filthy.	She (eat) chocolates all evening.
4 Karen suddenly felt sick.	She (work) hard all day.
5 Our friends were still in fancy dress.	They (crawl) through the mud.
6 The reporter was finally allowed a short interview with Madonna.	They (wear) it at a party.

▶ . . *The hiker was soaked. He'd been walking in the rain.* . .

1 . . . .
2 . . . .
3 . . . .
4 . . . .
5 . . . .
6 . . . .
. . . .

91 The past perfect continuous and other tenses

▶ Finder 50B-C

Complete the conversations. Put the verb into the right tense: past continuous, past perfect, present perfect continuous or past perfect continuous.

▶ Laura seemed rather upset last night. ~ That was because . . *she'd been arguing* . . (she/argue) with her boyfriend most of the evening.

1 You look hot. ~ I am hot. (I/cook).

2 Didn't you see me when . . . . (you/drive) to work this morning?
~ No, I didn't notice you. ~ . . . . (I/wait) for the bus. But I would have liked a lift.

3 Did you enjoy your trip to California? ~ It was wonderful. . . . . (I/look) forward to going there for a long time, and I wasn't disappointed.

4 I saw some people you know in the park yesterday. ~ Oh, who was that? ~ Peter and Kate. (they/play) tennis, so I stopped and watched them for a while.

5 Have you seen Peter and Kate lately? ~ Yes, I saw them yesterday. They were coming out of the park. They had their tennis rackets with them, so I suppose . . . . (they/play) tennis.

6 You weren't at the club last night. ~ I was too tired. . . . . (I/look) at flats all day. (I/see) about a dozen, and none of them were any good.

92 Action verbs and state verbs

▶ Finder 51A-C

Complete each conversation by choosing the correct form of the verb.

▶ This dog is quite heavy, isn't he? ~ Yes, he weighs/~~he's weighing~~ 20 kilos.

1 Who's going to win the big game tonight? ~ No idea. Actually I don't care/I'm not caring who wins.

2 Are you ready to go? ~ No, not yet. I still have/I'm still having breakfast.

3 Did you notice anything unusual in the way your boss behaved? ~ No, he appeared/was appearing perfectly normal.

4 This chocolate is nice. ~ It tastes/It's tasting delicious. And it didn't cost/wasn't costing much.

5 We have to pay a toll if we go on the motorway. ~ Not again! This holiday costs/is costing us a fortune. ~ Yes, but we enjoy/we're enjoying ourselves.

6 What are you doing/do you do? ~ I fit/I'm fitting this new shelf. I have to make sure that it fits/it's fitting this space exactly.

7 Do you think/Are you thinking Angela is going to pass her exams? ~ I don't expect/I'm not expecting so. She doesn't seem/isn't seeming to be working very hard.

8 What do you look/are you looking at? ~ That building. I always think it looks/it's looking like a wedding cake.

93 *See, hear*, etc

▶ Finder 51E

Put in a form of *see, hear,* or *feel*. Sometimes you need to use *can* or *could*.

▶ Oh, look. I . . *can see* . . . an elephant over there.

1 I . . . . a very funny joke yesterday.
2 I've got a full diary today. I . . . . a number of important customers.
3 Steve was sitting on the ground, and he . . . . his leg as if he thought there was something wrong with it.
4 It was a quiet night. Our footsteps were the only thing we . . . .
5 We . . . . that film in London last year.
6 Alan hasn't got a job, but he doesn't need one. His parents are billionaires.
   ~ Oh, I . . . .
7 As I lay there on the ground, I . . . . the sun beating down.

94 The main uses of the tenses

▶ Finder 52

Decide which meanings go with which sentences.

▶ I believe in God.
1 I've had toothache for two days.
2 We've been playing mini-golf.
3 I'm repairing this chair.
4 He's living here for the moment.
5 I've closed the windows.
6 I visit my mother every weekend.
7 We've played the game lots of times.

a) in the middle of an action
b) a permanent routine
c) a series of actions up to the present
d) a state up to the present
e) a present state
f) a short action in the period up to the present
g) an action over a period up to the present
h) a temporary routine

▶ . *e*) . . 2 . . . . . 4 . . . . . 6 . . . . .
1 . . . . . 3 . . . . . 5 . . . . . 7 . . . . .

Now do the same with these.

8 Something strange happened.
9 The last train had already gone.
10 I had been asleep ten hours.
11 All that year I'd been wasting time.
12 I caught the bus every morning.
13 We all knew the answer.
14 People were going home from work.

i) a state before a past time
j) a past state
k) a series of past actions
l) an action in the past
m) an action over a period of past time
n) an action before a past time
o) an action over a period up to a past time

8 . . . . . 10 . . . . . 12 . . . . . 14 . . . . .
9 . . . . . 11 . . . . . 13 . . . . .

95 The main uses of the tenses

▶ Finder 52

Put each verb in brackets into the correct tense. Sometimes there is more than one possible answer.

Hannah: What's that (▶) *you're reading* (you/read)?

Phil: It's a news article about that accident at the crossroads last month.

Hannah: Yes, (1) . . . . (I/remember).

Phil: The police (2) . . . . (complete) their enquiries now. Apparently the van (3) . . . . (do) fifty at the time of the accident. It (4) . . . . (not/slow) down at the crossroads at all. It (5) . . . . (crash) straight into a car and (6) . . . . (kill) two people. The driver of the van was only sixteen and (7) . . . . (take) drugs regularly for at least a year. And the van (8) . . . . (be) in an accident before.

Hannah: Oh, that's terrible. Completely irresponsible.

Phil: Mind you, that crossroads is dangerous. (9) . . . . (I/see) some near misses there before now. (10) . . . . (I/think) they should put traffic lights there. It says here that (11) . . . . (they/put) up warning signs only a week before the accident, but that obviously wasn't enough.

Hannah: (12) . . . . (I/usually/take) another route if I can. (13) . . . . (I/not/like) going that way.

Phil: Last year when (14) . . . . (I/have) that job in town, (15) . . . . (I/go) that way every day.

Hannah: (16) . . . . (they/dig) up the road by the park at the moment, so more traffic than usual (17) . . . . (come) through the crossroads.

Phil: There's too much congestion. Journey times (18) . . . . (get) slower and slower over the last few years.

Hannah: But we still have accidents, unfortunately.

96 Review of verb tenses

▶ Finder 39–52

Write the correct sentences.

▶ They've repaired the heater. ~~They've done it yesterday.~~
. . . . . . *They did it yesterday.* . . .

1 It wasn't me. ~~I no took the money.~~

. . . .

2 I'm ready now. ~~I was ready for ten minutes.~~

. . . .

3 Sorry, but you phoned at a bad moment yesterday. ~~I cooked the supper.~~

. . . .

4 Where have you been? ~~I wait here for twenty minutes.~~

. . . .

5 I have to go to the town hall. ~~Know you where it is?~~

. . . .

6 Yes, I've washed the dishes. ~~I had done them ages ago.~~

. . . .

7 Is this enough potatoes? ~~I've been peeling about twenty.~~

. . . .

8 Nicola felt very pleased with herself. ~~She achieved all her aims.~~

. . . .

9 There's something wrong with this computer. ~~It not working properly.~~

. . . .

10 Maybe I'll throw this old sweater out. ~~I had it for ages.~~

. . . .

11 Are you busy? ~~What you do now?~~

. . . .

12 Let's go to a restaurant. ~~We didn't eat out since your birthday.~~

. . . .

13 They're decorating my office. ~~So I work in here this week.~~

. . . .

97 Review of verb tenses ▶ Finder 39–52

Complete this newspaper report. It tells a true story. Put each verb in brackets into the correct tense. Sometimes there is more than one possible answer.

Rats (▶) . . *aren't* . . (be not) really very popular animals. But now a rat called Fido
(1) . . . . (do) something to improve their image. The young rat, who
(2) . . . . (live) in Torquay with the Gumbley family, (3) . . . . (lie)
in his cage in the middle of the night when an electric heater (4) . . . . (start) a fire
on the ground floor of the house. Fido (5) . . . . (notice) that someone
(6) . . . . (forget) to shut his cage door properly, so he (7) . . . .
(jump) out, (8) . . . . (run) upstairs and (9) . . . . (scratch) at the
door of the bedroom where Lisa Gumbley and her two daughters (10) . . . .
(sleep). Nine-year-old Megan (11) . . . . (wake) up. When she
(12) . . . . (open) the bedroom door, she (13) . . . . (see) Fido. As
she (14) . . . . (carry) him back down to his cage, she (15) . . . .
(see) the smoke and flames. But the fire (16) . . . . (only just start) – it
(17) . . . . (not burn) for long. When mum, Megan and three-year-old
Shannon (18) . . . . (get) safely out of the house, they (19) . . . .
(call) the fire brigade, which soon (20) . . . . (bring) the fire under control. 'We
(21) . . . . (owe) our lives to Fido,' said Lisa. 'He (22) . . . . (not
run) away. He (23) . . . . (save) us, and we (24) . . . . (love) him. At
the moment (25) . . . . (he/have) a special chocolate treat.
(26) . . . . (we/make) a fuss of him all day.' One firefighter said
(27)' . . . . (we/hear) of dogs and cats doing this but never a rat before.'

98 Review of verb tenses

▶ Finder 39–52

Complete the second sentence so that it has a similar meaning to the previous one. Sometimes you need to put in one word and sometimes more than one.

▶ We're in the middle of an important discussion.
We're .. *discussing* .. something important.

1 The freezing point of water is 0°C.
Water . . . . at 0°C.

2 It was last summer when Lisa first learned the secret.
Lisa . . . . the secret since last summer.

3 You started sending text messages half an hour ago, and you're still doing it.
You've . . . . text messages for half an hour.

4 Those kids very often make a noise.
Those kids . . . . always . . . . a noise.

5 Laura is an early riser.
Laura . . . . up early.

6 My mother is the author of two books.
My . . . . written . . . .

7 We were in the middle of a picnic lunch.
We . . . . at lunch time.

8 His death came after a long illness.
When . . . . , he . . . . for a long time.

99 Introduction to the future

▶ Finder 53A–B

This article is about the results of the Advanced Level exams, which are taken by 17- and 18-year-old pupils in England.

A-LEVEL SUSPENSE

Two hundred and sixty thousand 18-year-olds **are waiting** anxiously for the big day. Months of worry and suspense **will come** to an end when they **get** their A-level results next Thursday. Most pupils **have taken** three A-levels in subjects of their choice, and the results **will be** important for career prospects and especially for university entrance. Of course, some people **are going to be** disappointed if they **don't get** good enough grades. But help **will be** at hand. Many schools **are to bring** in counsellors who **have had** special training to help pupils talk over their problems.

Pupils **are warned** not to worry too much. 'There **are** more important things in life than exams,' **says** counsellor Mary Ruddock. 'A poor result **won't ruin** your life. You**'ll be able to do** something positive about it, such as re-sitting your exams.'

Pupils without the grades they need for their chosen university **will have** the chance to get a place at another university. They can do this by going through the 'clearing system', which **begins** on the Wednesday of next week. Last year this system **found** places for thirty thousand pupils. Plenty of up-to-date information **will be** available on teletext, and from next Thursday the BBC **is broadcasting** several hours of news and information on both television and radio. And most universities and colleges **have** websites and **will be running** Telephone Helplines.

Look at the forms in **bold type**. Which ones refer to the future, and which ones refer to the present or the past? Write the verb forms in the correct group.

Future time: *will come*, ...

Present or past time: *are waiting*, ...

100 *Will* and *shall*   ▶ Finder 54

Complete the conversations. Put in *'ll, will, won't*, or *shall*. Sometimes there is more than one possible answer.

▶ . . *Shall* . . we go out somewhere at the weekend? ∼ I'm not sure if I can. I . *'ll* . . ring you tomorrow to tell you if I'm free.

1 . . . . I carry this bag for you? ∼ Oh, thank you.
2 Can't we get across the river here? ∼ No, they're repairing the bridge. The road . . . . be closed for about six weeks. It's a real nuisance.
3 Are you watching this film? ∼ No, not really. ∼ Well, I . . . . switch it off then.
4 . . . . the photos be ready later today, do you know? ∼ No, they can't do them today. They . . . . be ready until tomorrow morning.
5 What time . . . . we meet, do you think? ∼ Half past seven outside the cinema? ∼ Fine. I . . . . see you then.
6 Can I call in to see you tomorrow? ∼ I'm afraid I . . . . be out tomorrow. . . . . Thursday be OK? ∼ Yes, that's fine.
7 What's the problem? ∼ The machine . . . . accept this 50p coin. ∼ I . . . . see if I've got one. Yes, I have. Here, try this one.
8 The warning light is on. We . . . . be out of petrol soon. ∼ OK. I . . . . stop at the next filling-station.
9 I'm just going out. ∼ How long . . . . you be? ∼ Oh, I . . . . be long. I'm just popping round the corner.
10 I . . . . just clean up this mess. ∼ Don't bother. The cleaners . . . . do that.
11 . . . . we have a cup of coffee? ∼ It's a bit early. The café isn't open yet. It . . . . be open until ten.
12 Would you like something to eat? ∼ Thank you. I . . . . have one of these sandwiches.

101 *Be going to*   ▶ Finder 55

Comment on each situation using *be going to*. The word in brackets will help you.

▶ Mr and Mrs Newman are in a car showroom. They're looking at the cars. (buy)
    They're going to buy a car. . . . . . .
1 Tom has invited some friends for a meal this evening. He's looking at a recipe. (cook)
    . . . .
2 The train is approaching a station. The driver is putting the brakes on. (stop)
    . . . .
3 It's a really warm day, and Matthew has gone out in his coat. (hot)
    . . . .

4 Emily is doing a geography exam. She isn't very good at geography, and she hasn't done any revision. (fail)

. . . .

5 Nicola and Joanna are walking to the tennis court. They've got their rackets with them. (play)

. . . .

6 Sarah can see three masked men running out of the bank. She is taking her mobile out of her bag. (police)

. . . .

102 Present tense forms for the future ▶ Finder 56

Complete the conversation with verbs in the present continuous or the present simple.

Emma: What (▶) . . _are you doing_ . . (you/do) at the weekend?
Simon: (1) . . . . (I/go) to the rugby international - England against France at Twickenham. Some people from the local rugby club
(2) . . . . (travel) on a special coach which
(3) . . . . (go) from here at ten on Saturday morning.
Emma: And (4) . . . . (you/come) back on Saturday?
Simon: Yes, the match (5) . . . . (finish) at about half past four, and the coach (6) . . . . (leave) Twickenham at five. I'll be back on Saturday evening. What about you? (7) . . . . (you/do) anything this weekend?
Emma: Not on Saturday. (8) . . . . (I/visit) a friend on Sunday.

103 *Will, be going to*, and present tense forms ▶ Finder 56–57

Complete this paragraph from a letter. With each verb in brackets, use *will, be going to* or a present tense form. Usually there is more than one possible answer.

Next month (▶) . . _we're going_ . . (we/go) to Arizona. (1) . . . . (we/visit) some friends of Andrew's. I'm sure (2) . . . . (it/be) a lovely break for us, and the kids are looking forward to it. (3) . . . . (we/take) a trip to the Grand Canyon. (4) . . . . (that/be) a wonderful experience. The kids (5) . . . . (do) some whitewater rafting, too. Their school term (6) . . . . (end) on the 6th, and (7) . . . . (we/fly) out on the 7th. I can't wait.

104 *Will* and *be going to* ▶ Finder 57

Complete the conversations. Put in *'ll* or a form of *be going to*.

▶ It's quite cold, isn't it? ~ Yes, I suppose it is. I _'ll_ . . put the heating on.
▶ Have you made any plans for the weekend? ~ Yes, I _'m going to_ . . visit my sister.

1 We . . . . have a party next weekend. Would you like to come?
~ Yes, I'd love to. Thank you.
2 Look at Sophie. ~ Her eyes are closing. She . . . . fall asleep.
3 I'm busy getting things ready at the moment. ~ We . . . . help you if
you like.
4 What's Jane doing these days? ~ She's studying medicine. She . . . . be
a doctor.
5 This car is making a funny noise. ~ Yes, we . . . . break down at any
moment.
6 I'm having next week off, so I . . . . see you the week after.
~ OK. Have a nice break.
7 Your brother is always reading computer magazines. ~ He . . . . buy a
new computer, so he needs to find out about all the latest models.
8 Would you like something to drink? ~ Er, I . . . . have a cola, please.
9 What's the matter? ~ Quick! The ladder . . . . fall!
10 Are you doing anything tonight? ~ Yes, I . . . . work on my project. I have
to finish it soon.

105 *Be to*   ▶ Finder 58A–B

Some of these sentences give news of an event which has been officially arranged, and
some are instructions to do or not to do something. Complete each sentence by putting in
the missing word.

▶ The last coal mine in Wales . . *is* . . to close next month, putting 200 people out of work.
▶ The computers are not to . . *be* . . taken out of this room.

1 This ticket is . . . . be shown to any inspector who wishes to see it.
2 Bicycles are . . . . to be left in front of this window.
3 The tax . . . . to be reduced by one per cent from next month, bringing it down to
fifteen per cent.
4 The fee is to . . . . paid in full before the goods can be delivered.
5 New rules on the transport of live animals . . . . to be introduced next April by the
Ministry of Agriculture.
6 The Foreign Secretary is . . . . discuss a number of issues with ministers from the
other EU countries in Brussels tomorrow.
7 This fire door . . . . to be kept shut at all times.

Then say which sentences are about a future event and which are instructions.

Future events: numbers . . . .
Instructions: numbers . . . .

106 *Be about to* and *be on the point of*   ▶ Finder 58C

Write a second sentence so that it has a similar meaning to the previous one. Use the word
in brackets.

▶ They're going to serve lunch now. (about)
. . . *They're about to serve lunch.* . . .

1 The company is very close to going bankrupt. (point)

. . . .

2 The football season begins very soon. (about)

. . . .

3 The country will very shortly join the European Union. (about)

. . . .

4 I think our boss is going to resign at any moment. (point)

. . . .

5 I'm going home in just a moment. (about)

. . . .

107 The present simple in a sub-clause ▶ Finder 59

The Prime Minister is going to watch a football match. A team of security guards are being told what to do. Combine each pair of sentences using the word in brackets. Use the present simple in the sub-clause.

▶ You will search the stadium. Then the public will be allowed in. (before)
. . *You will search the stadium before the public are allowed in.* . . .

1 You will receive a warning. The PM will be five minutes away. (when)

. . . .

2 You will be given a second warning. The PM will enter the stadium. (as soon as)

. . . .

3 You will be on full alert. The PM will get out of his car. (when)

. . . .

4 You will stay on alert. The PM will be in the stadium. (while)

. . . .

5 You will be responsible for taking care. Nothing must happen. (that)

. . . .

6 You must take action immediately. There may be trouble. (if)

. . . .

7 You must stop people. They may try to get too close to the PM. (who)

. . . .

8 After the match you will wait. Everyone will leave first. (until)

. . . .

108 The future continuous and future perfect ▶ Finder 60–61

Put in the future continuous or the future perfect of these verbs: come, dry, not finish, ~~not go~~, ~~learn~~, pass, play, revise, spend, use, not wear.

▶ Lisa has had a big argument with Rick. She says she . . *won't be going* . . out with him again.

▶ I'm enjoying the course. I *'ll have learned* . . a lot by the time I've completed it.

1 This paint is still wet, but it . . . . by tomorrow morning.

2 These jackets are going out of fashion now. People . . . . them much longer.

3 I've got an exam tomorrow, so I can't come out tonight. I . . . .
   all evening.

4 I haven't got much money left. If I go on at this rate, I . . . . it
   all soon.

5 Lucy never misses a disco. She . . . . to the one here tomorrow
   evening, I expect.

6 I'm late with my project. I . . . . it by the time we're supposed to
   hand it in.

7 Gemma's leg is all right now, so she . . . . volleyball with us later.

8 I use this car quite a lot. It . . . . the 20,000-mile mark before I've
   had it a year.

9 How much longer . . . . the video recorder?

109 The future perfect

Here is some information about a woman who loves walking. Answer the questions about
Jodie at the end of her journey. Be careful – one answer needs the continuous form.

Jodie loves walking. Over the next two months she's going to walk the length of Britain, from
Land's End to John O'Groats. And she won't be walking in a straight line. She's going to walk 25
miles a day, and the journey will take 64 days. She's going to eat two bars of chocolate and drink a
litre of milk every day. Each pair of socks that she takes will last her eight days, and then she'll
throw them away. She's going to take a camera with her, and she's decided to take about twelve
photos each day.

▶ How far will Jodie have walked?
   When she gets to the end, *she'll have walked 1,600 miles.*

1 How much milk will she have drunk?
   By the time she finishes, ...
2 How many bars of chocolate will she have eaten?
   When she finally gets there, ...
3 How many pairs of socks will she have worn out?
   By the end of the walk, ...
4 If one film will take 36 photos, about how many films will she have used?
   Altogether . . . .
5 How long will Jodie have been walking?
   At the end of her journey, ...

110 *Was/were going to*

Rewrite the sentences using *was going to* or *were going to.*

▶ Carl intended to do his homework, but he had a headache.
   Carl was going to do his homework, but he had a headache.

1 Adam had decided to have a bath, but there was no hot water.

. . . .

2 The girls had planned to look round the museum, but there was no time.

. . . .

3 Tony intended to buy some flowers, but he forgot.

. . . .

4 We had agreed to play golf, but then it started to rain.

. . . .

5 Linda decided to take some photos, but she didn't have a film.

. . . .

6 It was Gary's intention to take driving lessons, but he couldn't afford it.

. . . .

7 We had planned to work in the library, but it was closed.

. . . .

111 *Was going to, would, was to*, etc ▶ Finder 62

Complete the sentences. Put one of these words in each space: *about, going, seeing, to, was, would, wouldn't.*

▶ I was going . . *to* . . tidy my room, but then I couldn't be bothered.
1 All the players were ready, and the game was . . . . to start.
2 I was in a hurry yesterday. I was . . . . the doctor at eleven.
3 We went to a night club, but for some reason the doorman . . . . let us in.
4 I was . . . . to be a lawyer, but unfortunately I failed the exams.
5 We wondered what our new boss would be like. She . . . . to start the next day.
6 The family had decided to emigrate. It was a decision that . . . . change their lives.

112 Review of the future ▶ Finder 53–62

Decide which answer is correct.

▶ My brother . . *is going to* . . get up early tomorrow.
  a) goes to   b) is going to   c) will go to

1 The letter . . . . here tomorrow.
  a) is   b) shall be   c) will be

2 I haven't got much homework. . . . . it by eight o'clock.
  a) I do   b) I'll have done   c) I've done

3 I think . . . . the game tomorrow.
  a) we'll win   b) we're winning   c) we win

4 . . . . a party here next Saturday.
  a) We have   b) We're about to have   c) We're having

5 Look at that car! It's out of control! . . . . crash!
  a) It'll   b) It's going to   c) It's to

6 The caretaker retires next year. He'll . . . . here for 25 years.
  a) be working   b) have been working   c) work

7 This time next week . . . . in the Highlands.
   a) I'll be walking   b) I'll walk   c) I'm walking

8 Please note that all visitors are . . . . to the office.
   a) report   b) reporting   c) to report

9 I'll give you the photos when . . . .
   a) we'll meet   b) we meet   c) we're meeting

10 I was . . . . signing the document when my mobile rang.
   a) due to   b) just about for   c) on the point of

11 Where . . . . we go for our holidays? Any ideas?
   a) are   b) shall   c) will

12 I . . . . have an early night, but some friends called round.
   a) was going to   b) will   c) would

113 Review of the future

▶ Finder 53–6

Write a second sentence of similar meaning using the word in brackets.

▶ I've decided to buy a new bike. (going)
  . . . *I'm going to buy a new bike.* . . .

1 This time tomorrow we'll be in the air over the Atlantic. (flying)
  . . . .

2 I'm sure you'll pass the test. (definitely)
  . . . .

3 We intended to get up at six in the morning. (going)
  . . . .

4 The ferry leaves at ten thirty tonight. (due to)
  . . . .

5 They're going to close the flight in a minute. (about)
  . . . .

6 I've arranged to have next week off work. (I'm)
  . . . .

7 We'll probably get a message on our arrival at the hotel. (when)
  . . . .

8 None of the guests will still be here tomorrow. (all)
  . . . .

9 When I finally go into hospital, I'll have had a ten-month wait. (been)
  . . . .

10 The government refuses to comment on the affair. (not)
  . . . .

114 Review of the future

▶ Finder 53–62

Complete the news report using the correct forms to express the future. Usually there is more than one possible answer.

OLD PEOPLE HAVE TO PAY UP

Mavis Pearce (▶) _will be_ (be) 82 years old next Tuesday. She is a widow who can no longer look after herself, and so (1) . . . . (she/move) into a nursing home. Although the home costs £450 a week, much more than Mrs Pearce's pension, her local Council is refusing to pay for her. It says (2) . . . . (she/have to) sell her house, which is worth about £250,000, in order to pay for her care. Mrs Pearce is angry. 'When I was younger I never realized that anything like this (3) . . . . (happen),' she says. 'But they say there aren't enough hospital beds for old people who need nursing care. So (4) . . . . (I/have to) go into a private home. It's not right, you know. And (5) . . . . (I/tell) you something else – it's not fair on my daughter, either. (6) . . . . (I/leave) the house to her, but now I can't.'

Mrs Pearce's daughter, Alison Davis, is worried about her mother. 'We've done our best to look after her, but she needs care 24 hours a day,' she says. 'It's wrong that she has to sell her house. From now on (7) . . . . (she/pay) all that money week after week. In a couple of years, (8) . . . . (she/spend) all her money. And what then? (9) . . . . (they/throw) her out of the nursing home when the money (10) . . . . (run) out? My husband and I are really worried.'

The problem of old people and their care (11) . . . . (not/disappear). In future more people (12) . . . . (find) that they have to sell the house they had hoped to leave to their children. The government is worried, and ministers (13) . . . . (meet) next week to discuss the problem. But the numbers of old people needing care (14) . . . . (continue) to rise, and it is hard to see how the government (15) . . . . (be able to) find the huge sums of money necessary to pay all their costs.

115 Auxiliary verbs and ordinary verbs

▶ Finder 64

What kind of verbs are the ones in **bold** type? Put a tick in the right place.

				Auxiliary verb	Ordinary verb
Mr Price:	It**'s** getting dark early, isn't it?	▶		✓	
Mrs Green:	Yes, the days **are** shorter now.	1			
Mr Price:	I **do** hate this time of year.	2			
	It**'s** dark at five o'clock.	3			
Mrs Green:	And it**'s** feeling colder.	4			
	It **was** really cold this morning.	5			
Mr Price:	It's **been** very wintry this last week.	6			

	Auxiliary verb	Ordinary verb
Mrs Green: We've switched our heating on. 7		
Mr Price: Oh, we **did** that some time ago. 8		
We've **had** ours on a couple of weeks. 9		
Mrs Green: What **did** the forecast say? 10		
Mr Price: Oh, it'll **be** even colder tomorrow. 11		
Snowstorms have **been** forecast. 12		

116 The ordinary verb *be*

▶ Finder 65A–C

Complete each sentence with a form of *be*. Use a pronoun if you need to.

▶ Did you attend the concert? = . . *Were you* . . at the concert?

1 We've had lots to do. = ... very busy.
2 Does this bank card belong to you? = ... this bank card yours?
3 The business didn't succeed. = The business . . . . a success.
4 We had enjoyed the party. = The party . . . . very enjoyable.
5 This knife doesn't cut properly. = This knife . . . . very sharp.
6 I support United. = ... a United fan.
7 You're acting very cautiously. = You're . . . . very cautious.

117 *Be* in the continuous

▶ Finder 65C

Comment on these situations using *be* in the continuous.

▶ Emily said hardly a word to our visitors yesterday. She seemed very shy.
. . . *She was being very shy.* . . .

1 The children are all playing in the garden. They're doing something very noisy.

. . . .

2 You never know what to expect with Paul. Yesterday evening he was behaving in a very unpleasant manner. . . . .

3 Mark is thinking only of himself. His behaviour is rather selfish.

. . . .

4 A customer in the supermarket was arguing with the cashier. She was making things awkward for him. . . . .

5 I don't know what those people are doing. They're behaving in a very secretive manner.

. . . .

6 People didn't seem to mind waiting. They were standing there patiently.

. . . .

118 *Gone* or *been*

▶ Finder 65D

Complete the conversation. Put in *gone* or *been*.

Leanne: Have you seen Simon this week?
Karen: No, he's (▶) . . *gone* . . to Greece.
Leanne: There seems to be no one here at the moment. Everyone has (1) . . . .
on holiday.
Karen: I know. Louise has (2) . . . . to Italy. We've just had a postcard from her.
Leanne: And what about Rick?
Karen: Oh, he's here. He got back yesterday. He's (3) . . . . to Cuba.
Leanne: Cuba? I've never (4) . . . . there. Is it nice?
Karen: I don't know. I've never (5) . . . . there either. Why don't you ask Rick?
He's (6) . . . . to the post office, but he'll be back soon.

119 *Have* and *have got*

▶ Finder 66B–D

Put in the sentences.

▶ **Short form**: Who's got the tickets? **Long form**: *Who has got the tickets?* . . . . . .
▶ **Statement**: I've got everything. **Question**: *Have I got everything?* . . . .
1 **Question**: Did Emma have the money? **Statement**: . . . .
2 **Long form**: They have got time. **Short form**: . . . .
3 *Have*: We don't have the address. *Have got*: . . . .
4 **Present**: Lisa has a cat. **Past**: . . . .
5 **Positive**: Mark has a cold. **Negative**: . . . .
6 **Statement**: I had an umbrella. **Question**: . . . .
7 *Have got*: Has Sarah got a bike? *Have*: . . . .
8 **Past**: I didn't have a map. **Present**: . . . .
9 **Present**: They've got the best seats. **Present perfect**: . . . .

120 *Have* and *have got*

▶ Finder 66B–E

Put in a form of *have* or *have got*. There is usually more than one possible answer.

Jessica: I'm thinking of buying a car.
Martin: Really? (▶) . . *Have you got* . . (you) enough money?
Jessica: Well, (1) . . . . (I/not) enough to buy one right away, but I
can borrow part of the money.
Martin: But why bother? (2) . . . . (you) friends who can give you a
lift. (3) . . . . (I/never) a car in my life, but I still manage to
get around.
Jessica: Yes, but sometimes it's a nuisance (4) . . . . (not) a car. Like
last weekend after the party. The last bus had gone, and (5) . . . .
(I/not) enough money for a taxi. Luckily (6) . . . . (I) my
mobile with me, so I rang my brother, and he came and drove me home.

121 *Have* and *have got*

Look at these sentences and decide if the word *got* needs to be crossed out or not. If it is incorrect, cross it out. If the sentence is correct, put a tick.

> ▶ Julie has got some photos to show us. ✓
> ▶ We've had ~~got~~ this television for years.

1 Do you have got a pound coin?
2 It's our daughter's great wish to have got a pony of her own.
3 If they don't know the way, they might have got lost.
4 The radio didn't have got batteries with it.
5 Have you got any stamps? ~ Sorry, no, I haven't got.
6 All the walkers had got rucksacks.
7 Have you had got this computer long?
8 We're lucky to have got these seats at the front.

122 *Have* and *have got*

▶ Finder 66

Complete each sentence so that it has a similar meaning to the previous one. Include a form of *have* or *have got*.

> ▶ There's a girl with green hair over there.
> That girl over there . . *has got green hair.* . . .

1 Matthew bought his motor-bike two years ago.
Matthew . . . . for two years now.

2 My tooth was hurting.
. . . . toothache.

3 There's a CD with the magazine.
The magazine . . . . with it.

4 A man with a suitcase got on the bus.
The man who got on the bus . . . .

5 I think that's my umbrella in your hand.
I think . . . . umbrella.

6 The material is very strong.
. . . . great strength.

7 There's a pond at the end of the garden.
The garden . . . . end of it.

64 121 • *Have* and *have got*

123 The ordinary verb *have*

▶ Finder 67

Write the sentences using the ordinary verb *have*.

▶ Tell someone that you experienced an awful journey.
. . . *I had an awful journey.* . . .

1 Ask Paul's friend if Paul received a letter this morning.
. . . .

2 Tell someone that you are going to drink some water.
. . . .

3 Ask someone what she ate for breakfast.
. . . .

4 Explain that you never experience dreams.
. . . .

5 Tell your friend that you have received an invitation.
. . . .

124 *Have* and *have got*

▶ Finder 66–67

Choose the correct words.

▶ Good morning. ~~You've got~~ /You've had a long sleep.

1 We cook in the evening. At lunch time I usually have/I've usually got a sandwich.
2 Steve is an only child. He doesn't got/He doesn't have any brothers or sisters.
3 This is a super party. We have/We're having a great time.
4 It looks a bit full in here. Are you having/Have you got room for me?
5 It rained all weekend. We didn't have/We hadn't got a very good time.
6 Do you have a guitar? ~ No, I don't./No I haven't got.

125 The ordinary verb *do*

▶ Finder 68A

Complete the conversations. Put the correct form of *do* in each space.

▶ We're having a really lazy holiday. We've . . *done* . . absolutely nothing so far.
~ We aren't . . *doing* . . much either.

1 When are you going to . . . . your project?
~ I'm . . . . it now.
2 Have you . . . . any cycling lately?
~ Yes, I have. I . . . . fifty miles yesterday.
3 I think we've . . . . as much as we can now. Everything seems to be ready.
~ There's nothing else to . . . . for the moment.
4 Adam knows all about cars. He . . . . all the repairs.
~ I'm hopeless with cars. I couldn't . . . . anything like that.

126 Do and *make*

Put in the correct form of *do* or *make*.

► I'm never bored. I've always got lots to . . *do* . .
► Don't keep looking at your watch. You're . . . *making* . . . me nervous.

1 Terry always . . . . his best for the team, but he isn't really a very good player.
2 My son . . . . this model aircraft when he was a little boy.
3 Lucy . . . . lots of mistakes, but she never seems to learn from them.
4 Don't just stand there. You could . . . . something to help.
5 I'm checking everything again. I'm just . . . . sure we haven't forgotten anything.
6 My brother is at university now. He's . . . . an engineering degree.
7 I wasn't there when the argument started. It was nothing to . . . . with me.
8 Do you think this lamp would . . . . a nice present for someone?
9 What experience have you had? Have you . . . . this kind of work before?
10 The comedian was great. He . . . . us all howl with laughter.

127 Have a look, make a start, etc

► Finder 69

Complete the sentence so that it has a similar meaning. Use an idiom consisting of a verb + object.

► Can I look at your photos, please?
. . . *Can I have a look* . . . at your photos, please?
► These figures will indicate roughly the size of the problem.
These figures . . *will give a rough indication of the size* . . of the problem.

1 I usually swim before breakfast.
. . . . before breakfast.

2 I'd better wash quickly before I go out.
. . . . before I go out.

3 Your friend suggested something rather silly.
Your friend . . . .

4 The victim was able to describe his attacker.
The victim . . . .

5 The government should act immediately.
The government . . . .

6 Why don't you use the Internet facilities here?
Why don't you . . . . here?

7 The students contributed significantly to the discussion.
The students . . . . the discussion.

8 The new development will affect our business adversely.
The new development . . . . our business.

66   126 • *Do and make*

128 Review of *be, have, do,* etc

▶ Finder 64–69

Complete each sentence by putting in one of these words: *been, being, did, didn't, doing, done, go, got, had, has, have, having, is, made, make, makes.*

▶ A robot . . .*is* . . doing my old job now.

1 We've . . . . a problem here.
2 Shall we . . . . for a walk?
3 I'm just . . . . a few odd jobs.
4 What time . . . . you get here this morning?
5 I wasn't happy, so I . . . . a complaint.
6 I couldn't ring you because I . . . . have my mobile.
7 We're . . . . lunch at the moment.
8 I've . . . . careful not to do any more damage.
9 On the next day we . . . . a look at some of the sights.
10 What have you . . . . with the calculator?
11 Do you mind if I . . . . a suggestion?
12 The share price . . . . fallen again today.
13 That kind of behaviour always . . . . me angry.
14 I felt at the time that the official was . . . . rather unhelpful.
15 It would be nice to . . . . a flat of our own.

129 Introduction to modal verbs

▶ Finder 70

Read this news item about women being accepted on commando training courses with the marines.

TOUGH WOMEN WANTED

The Royal Marines have decided that in future women can take their green beret commando training course. Those who pass could get places in commando units. They would carry arms and might operate in battle situations, which at present they are not allowed to do.

The marines' commando courses are famously tough. A successful recruit has to reach a high standard. Recruits must show, for example, that they can run 200 metres carrying another soldier. They also have to do a nine-mile march in full kit in 90 minutes. A Royal Marine spokeperson said that it may take some time to find women who were able to complete the 30-week course.

The decision to admit women will please campaigners for equal rights, who believe this should have happened years ago, but there are others whom it will not please at all. One Major General said, 'You must be joking. This isn't going to work. It's ridiculous to think that women should be put in these situations. It's obvious they aren't physically strong enough.'

1 Read the text again. Write down the first six modal verbs and the verbs that follow them.

▶ *can take*   a) . . . .   c) . . . .   e) . . . .
▶ *could get*   b) . . . .   d) . . . .   f) . . . .

2 Find phrases from the text with similar meanings to modal verbs. Write down each phrase and the verb that follows it.

▶ can't do =   *are not allowed to do* . .

a) must reach = ...
b) must do = ...
c) could complete = ...

3 Find these structures in the text and write down the words.

a) modal verb with the continuous: . . . .
b) modal verb with the perfect: . . . .
c) modal verb with the passive: . . . .
d) modal verb with a negative: . . . .

▶ Finder 70C

130 Negatives and questions with modal verbs

Write a shorter version of these sentences.

▶ I don't think I can carry this suitcase.
   I can't carry this suitcase.
▶ Did someone say we should wait here?
   Should we wait here?

1 Do you think I could have a lift?

. . . .

2 I wonder what time the guests will arrive.

. . . .

3 I don't think you should do anything illegal.

. . . .

4 Is it a fact that all birds can fly?

. . . .

5 It just isn't true that a new computer would be a waste of money.

. . . .

6 I wonder how long the journey would take.

. . . .

7 I just don't believe the plan will work.

. . . .

8 It might be true that there aren't any tickets.

. . . .

131 Modal verbs and time ▶ Finder 70D

Say if the underlined words in these sentences refer to the present, the past, or the future.

▶ I got in free. I <u>didn't have to pay</u>. .....*past*.......

1 There <u>may be</u> some changes soon. . . . .
2 The police <u>weren't allowed to question</u> the patient. . . . .
3 Julia <u>can't be</u> at home. Her car hasn't been here all day. . . . .
4 I haven't brought the photos. I'm afraid I <u>couldn't find</u> them. . . . .
5 I <u>must phone</u> my parents this evening. . . . .
6 It's midnight. Peter <u>will be</u> in bed now. . . . .
7 I really <u>had to hurry</u> to get here in time. . . . .
8 Tom <u>might</u> already <u>know</u> what the plans are for tomorrow. . . . .
9 The weather <u>should get</u> better later in the week. . . . .
10 Someone <u>may have taken</u> the coat by mistake. . . . .

132 *Must* and *have to* ▶ Finder 71

Complete the conversation. Put in *must, have to, has to, had to,* or *having to*. You will need to use some of them more than once.

Anna: This novel is really good.
Jake: What is it? *A Suitable Boy* - it looks very long. What's it about?
Anna: It's about an Indian girl, a student called Lata. Her mother says she (▶) ...*has to*... get married, so they (1) . . . . find someone suitable.
Jake: It doesn't sound very exciting.
Anna: Oh, it's good. You (2) . . . . read it. There are lots of characters. I can't explain it all. You'll (3) . . . . find out for yourself.
Jake: I (4) . . . . study novels when I did my English exam. I don't like (5) . . . . analyse them. I just want to enjoy reading them.
Anna: You'll enjoy this. You can have it when I've finished.
Jake: I'll (6) . . . . wait a long time then. You've got another 500 pages to go.
Anna: I (7) . . . . hurry up and finish it. I want to know who Lata marries in the end.

133 *Have to*

Complete the sentence about each situation. Use *have to, has to, don't have to, doesn't have to, didn't have to, 'll have to,* or *won't have to.* Sometimes more than one answer is correct.

▶ Students can get advice from the Careers Office any time. They can call in without making an appointment.
They . . . *don't have to make* . . . an appointment.

1 Matthew failed his exam. He wants to get the qualification, but this means retaking the exam.
He . . . . the exam.
2 When Katie went back to New York, she was able to renew her visa rather than applying for a new one.
She . . . . a new one.
3 I usually get up early because I live a long way from my work. But fortunately tomorrow is a public holiday.
I . . . . early tomorrow.
4 Sophie's garage has an automatic door. She can open it without getting out of the car.
She . . . . the car.
5 You and your friends want to watch a TV show at a studio. You can only do this if you book tickets in advance.
We . . . . tickets in advance.
6 Ed hates painting. He's having some new plastic windows put in. They don't need painting.
In future he . . . . his windows.

134 *Have to* and *have got to*

▶ Finder 72

Look at these sentences and decide if the word *got* belongs in the sentence or not. If it is incorrect, cross it out. If the sentence is correct, put a tick.

▶ The bill doesn't have ~~got~~ to be paid right away, I hope.
▶ Have you got to clean up all the mess? ✓

1 You didn't have got to wait for us, you know.
2 I've got to go now, I'm afraid.
3 My friend won the lottery, so he hasn't got to work for a living.
4 We regret to have got to inform you that you have been unsuccessful.
5 Do we have got to apply in writing?
6 What time have we got to be at the meeting?
7 For most of last month I was having got to get up early every day.

135 *Needn't, mustn't,* and *don't have to*

▶ Finder 73A–B, D

Put these sentences in the right place.

We mustn't stop here.
We don't need to stop here.
We mustn't ring her now.
We don't need to ring her now.
~~You mustn't stay any longer.~~

You needn't stay any longer.
He mustn't clean it.
He doesn't have to clean it.
You mustn't shout.
You needn't shout.

▶ There'll be trouble if someone finds you here. *You mustn't stay any longer.*

1 I can hear you quite clearly. . . . .
2 Tom's flat looks perfectly clean. . . . .
3 Emma is expecting an important call about now. . . . .
4 There's another garage a few miles further on. . . . .
5 If Tom tries to clean the picture, he'll damage it. . . . .
6 This place isn't safe. . . . .
7 You can go home now if you like. . . . .
8 I told Emma I'd ring her some time in the next few days. . . . .
9 You'll disturb everyone. . . . .

136 *Needn't have done* and *didn't need to do*

▶ Finder 73C

Complete the sentences using *needn't have* or *didn't need to* and these verbs: *buy*, ~~*cook*~~, ~~*do*~~, *put*, *take*, *wait*, *water*.

▶ I've already had a hot meal today. You *needn't have cooked* anything for me.
▶ The car was all right, so fortunately the garage *didn't need to do* any repairs.

1 The postman came and collected all the parcels, so we . . . .
   them to the post office.
2 It's been raining all night. Louise . . . . the garden yesterday.
3 I thought someone might want a cool drink, but no one did. I . . . .
   this bottle in the fridge.
4 The sales assistant kindly pointed out that the clock already had a battery in it, so I . . . . .
   . . . . one separately.
5 Alan was able to see the doctor right away. He . . . . long.

137 *Should* and *ought to*

▶ Finder 74A

Comment on these situations using the modal verbs in brackets.

▶ Angela isn't very well, but she doesn't take her medicine. She just pours it down the sink.
   (ought, should)
   She ought to take her medicine. She shouldn't pour it down the sink.
▶ Simon promised to help, and now he's sunbathing. He isn't helping. (should, should)
   He shouldn't be sunbathing. He should be helping.
▶ Louise lent Gemma a book. Gemma found a £20 note in the book, and she kept it. She didn't
   give it back to Louise. (should, ought)
   She shouldn't have kept it. She ought to have given it back to Louise.

1 Paul has got exams next week, and he hasn't done any work for them. And now he's chatting
   to his friends. He isn't studying. (should, should)

   . . . .

2 Karen has to decide about her career soon. She never makes her mind up. She puts off the
   decision. (ought, should)

   . . . .

3 It was Steve's sister's birthday, and he didn't send her a card. He forgot. (should, should)

. . . .

4 Alison is running in a marathon next month, but at the moment she's lying in bed. She isn
doing a practice run. (should, should)

. . . .

5 My friends went on holiday and the hotel was awful. But they didn't complain. They suffere
in silence. (should, should)

. . . .

6 Nicola isn't a very thoughtful person. She just bursts into other people's rooms. She never
knocks. (should, ought)

. . . .

138 *Should, ought to, had better*, and *be supposed to*

▶ Finder 74

Complete the sentences. Put two words in each space.

▶ If this letter is urgent, you'd . . *better post* . . it right away.

1 Your trousers have got all muddy. . . . . to change them.
2 You can't have two main courses. You're . . . . have soup and a
   main course.
3 Be careful with that glass. You'd better . . . . it on the floor.
   Someone might knock it over.
4 I don't know why I'm just sitting here. I ought . . . . some work.
5 I love chocolate. And it's . . . . be good for you, too.
6 If you're going out in this rain, you'd . . . . an umbrella.
7 You made one mistake. You . . . . looked in the mirror before you
   stopped the car.
8 Why did you show Tom those photos yesterday? . . . . supposed to
   see them.

139 Asking permission

▶ Finder 75A

These people are all asking permission. What are they saying? Use one of these words i
each sentence: *come, down, photo, ~~trousers~~, umbrella*. Begin each sentence with *can I,
could I,* or *may I.* (All these are possible.)

▶  1  2

3  4

► .. Could I try on these trousers? ..

1 ....
2 ....
3 ....
4 ....

140 Talking about permission

► Finder 75C

Complete the sentences. Use a form of *be allowed to* and a following verb.

► Lorries used to drive right through the town centre, but nowadays .. *they aren't allowed to drive* .. into the central area.

1 Anita's friends all stay out late, but Anita's parents don't approve.
She . . . . out after midnight.
2 Lots of shops open for a few hours on Sundays now. Years
ago . . . . on Sundays.
3 Students can use the library. I'm still a student,
so . . . . it.
4 They're going to ban photography at the exhibition next week, so don't bother to take your
camera. . . . . photos.
5 It's terrible that they don't let us hold parties here. The place where we lived before wasn't so
strict. . . . . parties there.
6 The professor is going to explain his theory to a group of us. But what we want to know is
this. . . . . questions?

141 Permission

► Finder 75

Write a sentence for each situation. Use *can, could, may,* or *be allowed to*. (Sometimes there is more than one possible answer.)

► Ask someone's permission to look at his/her magazine.
. . *Can I look at your magazine, please?* . .

1 Say that you have permission to take photos because you are a professional photographer.
. . . .
2 Ask if under the rules it will be possible for you to take a dictionary into the exam.
. . . .
3 Tell someone it is OK for them to watch TV in your room if they want to.
. . . .
4 Say you hope to get permission to interview Robbie Williams.
. . . .
5 Ask to borrow someone's bicycle.
. . . .
6 Point out that a century ago it was permissible for people to travel around Europe without a passport.
. . . .
7 Explain that so far no one has had permission to use the new machine.
. . . .

8 Explain that when you were young, you didn't have permission to go out alone.

. . . .

9 Explain that your brother swam in the river. (He had permission.)

. . . .

10 Refuse someone permission to use the computer just now. You are using it yourself.

I'm afraid . . . .

142 *Must* and *can't*   ▶ Finder 7(

Look at the information and answer the questions using *can't* and *must*.

▶ Hamsters and mice are rather similar, but a
hamster has a short tail, and a mouse has a
long one. Are these hamsters or mice?
They can't .. *be mice* .. because they've got
.. *short tails* .., so .. *they must be hamsters.* ..

1 British postage stamps have never had the words
'Great Britain' on them. This looks like an old
British stamp. But is it real, or is it a fake?
It can't . . . . because it's got . . . .
So . . . .

2 Lacrosse is a game where players carry sticks with
nets on them to catch the ball. Netball is a game
where players try to throw a ball through a ring with
a net on it. Are these girls playing lacrosse or netball?
. . . . because . . . .
So . . . .

Nights of Terror(18)
Disney Fun(U)

3 'U' film means 'universal' – it's for everyone. '18'
means that you must be 18 to watch it.
Which film have the boys seen? . . . .

. . . .

4 A London minicab looks like any other car,
   but the famous black taxi certainly doesn't.
   Is this a minicab or a taxi? . . . .
   . . . .

5 Leanne has been to both the Netherlands and
   Switzerland this year. This is a photo of her. But
   where was it taken? (Remember that there are no mountains in one of these countries.)
   . . . .
   . . . .

143 *Should*   ▶ Finder 74A, 77

Choose a) or b), whichever is closer in meaning to the previous sentence.

▶ I've just seen the weather forecast. It should be fine tomorrow.
   a) ☐ I hope it will be fine tomorrow.
   b) ☑ It looks as if it will be fine tomorrow.

1 I've made a fruit salad. It should be enough for four people.
   a) ☐ I think it's enough for four people.
   b) ☐ I want the four people to eat less.

2 On Sunday there shouldn't be much traffic on the roads.
   a) ☐ It would be better if people didn't drive on Sunday.
   b) ☐ On Sunday there probably won't be much traffic.

3 You always spend your money. You should try to save some of it.
   a) ☐ I expect you save some of it.
   b) ☐ It would be a good idea if you saved some of it.

4 You can usually walk straight through Customs. You shouldn't have any problems.
   a) ☐ Please don't cause any problems.
   b) ☐ You aren't likely to have any problems.

144 *May* and *might*   ▶ Finder 78A–B

**Complete the conversation between two people in an office. Use *may* or *might* (either is
possible) and the correct form of the verb in brackets.**

James: I'm looking for a letter – a handwritten note. It was on my desk a couple of days ago. I
          thought (▶) . . *you might have seen* . . (you/see) it.
Alison: No, I haven't. (1) . . . . (it/be) in the files. Your
          secretary (2) . . . . (file) it.

James:	No, I don't think so. It's just a note. It's personal actually, very personal. I'm rather worried someone (3) . . . . (take) it from my desk. (4) . . . . (they/show) it to all their friend at this very moment.
Alison:	Oh, I'm sure no one would do that. (5) . . . . (it fall) on the floor. (6) . . . . (it/throw) in the waste-paper basket. (7) . . . . (you/find) it in one of the dustbins outside. Why don't you go and take a look?
James:	Oh, no. I think that (8) . . . . (make) me look even more ridiculous.

145 *May, might, can,* and *could*   ▶ Finder 78–7*

Decide which answer is correct.

▶ Are you having a holiday this year? ~ I'm not sure. We . . *might* . . go to Greece.
  a) can   b) maybe   c) might

1 The old garage suddenly collapsed one day. Luckily the owner wasn't in there or
  he . . . . killed.
  a) can have been   b) could be   c) could have been

2 I think Phil's got lots of money. He just pretends to be poor. ~ Do you think so? Well,
  you . . . . be right.
  a) can   b) may   c) possibly

3 That woman in the flat next door to mine is really miserable. She never even says hello to m￼
  ~ Oh, she . . . . be quite nice sometimes, I've found.
  a) can   b) may   c) might

4 This film seems familar. ~ It seems familiar to me, too. We . . . . it befor￼
  a) might see   b) might be seeing   c) might have seen

5 Is this music too loud for you? ~ Yes. . . . . you turn it down a bit, please?
  a) Could   b) May   c) Might

6 Can't you get through to Julie? ~ No, she's switched her mobile off. She . . . .
  a shower or something.
  a) can have   b) may have   c) may be having

7 Haven't you finished this decorating yet? ~ No, and I do think you . . . . help m￼
  instead of just standing around.
  a) may   b) might   c) please

8 I think I might go into politics. ~ You're joking, aren't you? You . . . . be seriou￼
  a) can't   b) may not   c) mightn't

9 I'm not enjoying this holiday at all. ~ Well, in that case we . . . . go hom￼
  a) can as good   b) may so well   c) might as well

10 No one will give me a job. What can I do? ~ Well, you . . . . go to an agenc￼
  a) could   b) may   c) perhaps

146 *May, might, can,* and *could*

▶ Finder 78–79

Write a second sentence so that it has a similar meaning to the previous one. Use the word in brackets.

▶ Perhaps I'll go out. (may)
..*I may go out.*..

1 I suggest we take a taxi. (could)

. . . .

2 It's possible Louise is waiting for us at the airport. (may)

. . . .

3 It's impossible for the story to be true. (can't)

. . . .

4 I wish you would take off your wet shoes before you come in. (might)

. . . .

5 Perhaps the others are looking for us now. (could)

. . . .

6 Maybe Matthew forgot all about it. (might)

. . . .

7 Sometimes Polly is very rude. (can)

. . . .

8 Please fill in this form. (could)

. . . .

9 It's possible we won't have enough money. (might)

. . . .

10 I had the chance to do a parachute jump, but I was too scared. (could)

. . . .

147 *Could* and *was/were able to*

▶ Finder 80C

Put in *could* or *was/were able to*. Sometimes either is possible. Use a negative if necessary.

▶ I was sitting at the back, and I . . *couldn't* . . hear the speaker.

1 The car broke down, but fortunately we . . . . get it going again.

2 There was a big fire at a warehouse. People . . . . see the smoke ten miles away.

3 I've always loved the water. I . . . . swim when I was quite young.

4 Adam didn't have enough money for a taxi, but luckily he . . . . borrow some from a friend.

5 We'd forgotten our keys, so we . . . . get in the building.

148 *Can, could,* and *be able to*

▶ Finder 80

Each of these sentences is incorrect. Write the correct sentence.

▶ I couldn't to open the window.

.. I couldn't open the window. ..

1 I simply can not understand it.

. . . .

2 Are you able study with the TV on?

. . . .

3 I can played the piano when I was five.

. . . .

4 I was able to go to the party, but I was just too tired.

. . . .

5 I'll can retake the exam next year.

. . . .

6 I am afraid we able not help you.

. . . .

149 *Can, could,* and *be able to*

▶ Finder 80

Comment on these situations. Use *can, could,* or a form of *be able to*. Sometimes there is more than one possible answer.

▶ Michael has had a few games of poker, and he knows the rules.
He .. can play .. poker.

1 We thought there had been a traffic accident. Police sirens were audible in the distance.
We . . . . in the distance.

2 The shot went straight to the goalkeeper, so it was easy for him to save it.
He . . . . it.

3 Amy once knew the address, but now it's gone from her memory.
Amy . . . . the address.

4 David always faints at the sight of blood. It would be impossible for him to be a doctor.
He . . . . a doctor.

5 Hannah's dress looks very striking, but it will be right out of fashion next year.
She . . . . next year.

6 My friends had the chance to go on the excursion, but they turned it down.
They . . . . the excursion.

7 For several years Mr and Mrs Chapman have been too unwell to go on holiday.
They . . . . on holiday.

8 My grandfather was a good runner. He ran a mile in four minutes many times.
He . . . . minutes.

9 When they're buying a new car, people like to have a choice of colour.
They like . . . . the colour.

150 Uses of *would*

▶ Finder 81

Complete each of these sentences so that it has a similar meaning to the previous one.

▶ Could you wait a moment?
Would you mind . . *waiting a moment* . .?

1 I want to go home now.
I'd . . . .

2 Sarah would prefer us to leave early.
Sarah would rather . . . .

3 I can imagine everyone laughing at me if I wore that hat.
People . . . .

4 I want to see the parade.
I wouldn't . . . .

5 Working in this place would be terrible.
I'd . . . .

151 *Like* and *would like*

▶ Finder 81C

Put in *I like*, *I want*, or *I'd like*.

▶ . . *I like* . . skiing. I've been on several skiing holidays in Austria and Switzerland.

1 Can I help you?
~ Yes, ... some information on flights to New York, please.

2 My boyfriend and . . . . walking. We often go for long walks in the country.

3 . . . . a biscuit.
~ Well, if you ask nicely, you might get one.

4 . . . . a shower. Would you mind?
~ No, of course not. I'll just get you a towel.

5 Who's your favourite composer?
~ I'm not sure. Mostly . . . . to listen to Beethoven while I'm ironing.

152 *Used to*

▶ Finder 82B

Complete the sentences with *used to* and either the infinitive or ing-form of a verb.

▶ I .. *used to read* .. a lot of novels, but nowadays I only read newspapers and magazines.
▶ Richard feels very lonely now that his girlfriend is no longer with him. He isn't . *used to* . *being* . on his own.

1 We're always hard up, but we never worry about it. I suppose we've got . . . . poor.

2 We live in London now, but we . . . . in Manchester.

3 The country seemed so quiet after living in the town. We couldn't hear any traffic. We'd got . . . . it all day in town.

4 Joanna has moved to the right in her politics. She . . . . Labour, but now she votes Conservative.

5 My grandmother is getting absent-minded. Nowadays she forgets lots of things. I'm sure she . . . . things.

6 Making decisions isn't always easy, but as a manager, I'm . . . . them.

7 The new job is OK, but I hate starting at seven o'clock. I'll never get . . . . so early.

8 These days even students have got mobile phones. It was different in my day. We . . . . them when I was at college.

153 *Dare*

▶ Finder 83

Write a sentence with *dare* so that it has a similar meaning.

▶ I'm too scared to go up on the roof.
. . *I daren't go up on the roof.* . . .

1 No one has the courage to argue with the President.
. . . .

2 We're afraid to go out after dark.
. . . .

3 People were too frightened to resist the invaders.
. . . .

4 Are you brave enough to step into the unknown?
. . . .

5 You have no right to come in here without knocking!
. . . .

154 Modal verb + phrase
▶ Finder 84

The following sentences are written in a rather formal style. Can you express the meaning in everyday English? Use words from this table.

will should ought to may might	have to be allowed to be able to

▶ One can predict a future necessity for radical changes.
   There . . *will have to be radical changes.* . .

1 It is desirable that students be permitted to take a short break.
   Students . . . .
2 It will be necessary for candidates to possess a driving licence.
   Candidates . . . .
3 There is a possibility that research students will be granted permission to see the documents.
   Research students . . . .
4 It is probable that visitors will experience no difficulty in finding accommodation.
   You . . . .
5 It is possible that applicants will be required to prove their identity.
   Applicants . . . .

155 The use of modal verbs
▶ Finder 70–85

Put in a positive or a negative modal verb such as *can* or *wouldn't*. Sometimes there is more than one possible answer.

▶ . . *Can* . . I give you a hand with these bags? ~ Oh, thank you.

1 . . . . I borrow your pen for a moment?
2 You . . . . remind me. I haven't forgotten, you know.
3 Your library books are always overdue. You . . . . take them back at the right time.
4 Emma owns five houses, so she . . . . be rich.
5 I tried to lift the stone, but it was so heavy I . . . .
6 We're thinking of having a holiday. We aren't sure, but we . . . . go to Italy.
7 It's a serious matter. You . . . . laugh.
8 What shall I do? ~ I don't know. In your situation, I . . . . have any idea what to do.
9 We don't give enough money to charity. We . . . . to give more in my opinion.
10 It's not your fault that Justin is so annoyed. He . . . . be very unreasonable sometimes.
11 My parents were always very strict. I . . . . even go out on my own.
12 Ann has just started work as a shop assistant. She . . . . earn very much money.

156 Review of modal verbs

▶ Finder 70–8[

Decide which descriptions go with which sentences.

▶ I might go out later on.
1 You must wait in the queue.
2 I'd rather cycle than walk.
3 Yes, of course you can borrow my bike.
4 We ought to write a letter of thanks.
5 We could all meet up next weekend.
6 I daren't look down.
7 This phone number must be wrong.
8 Shoes must not be worn in the gym.
9 The café should open soon.
10 Could you dry these dishes?

a) giving permission
b) making a suggestion
c) making a request
d) saying something will probably happen
e) saying something is necessarily true
f) expressing an uncertain intention
g) saying what is the right thing to do
h) forbidding something
i) saying you are afraid to do something
j) saying you prefer one thing to another
k) ordering someone to do something

▶ . . f) . . 3 . . . . . 6 . . . . . 9 . . . .
1 . . . . . 4 . . . . . 7 . . . . 10 . . . . .
2 . . . . . 5 . . . . . 8 . . . . .

157 Review of modal verbs

▶ Finder 70–8[

Each of these sentences is incorrect. Write the correct sentence.

▶ My sister can to ride a motorbike.
. . . . My sister can ride a motorbike. . . . .

1 I'm afraid the photos don't might be ready.

. . . .

2 You'll must renew your visa soon.

. . . .

3 We ought visit Phil in hospital.

. . . .

4 Someone must take your bike last night.

. . . .

5 Does Charlotte would be willing to help?

. . . .

6 That old man used be a professional boxer.

. . . .

7 I would love to can sing, but I just can't.

. . . .

158 Review of modal verbs

▶ Finder 70–85

Write a second sentence so that it has a similar meaning to the previous one. Use the word in brackets.

▶ It's possible that Amy is ill. (may)
   .. *Amy may be ill.* ...

1 I have permission to use this room. (allowed)

. . . .

2 I'm afraid to go out on my own. (dare)

. . . .

3 It was unnecessary for you to leave a tip. (didn't)

. . . .

4 At one time I played tennis regularly. (used)

. . . .

5 The best decision would have been for you to accept the offer. (ought)

. . . .

6 We expect the parcel to arrive soon. (should)

. . . .

7 It was necessary for Mark to go to hospital. (had)

. . . .

8 It's obvious that the child has run away. (must)

. . . .

159 Introduction to the passive

▶ Finder 86

Read the sentences and answer the questions.

   The prisoners were playing football.
▶ Is the sentence active or passive? .. *active* ..
1 What is the agent? . . . .

   The prisoners were released.
2 Is the sentence active or passive? . . . .
3 Is the agent mentioned? . . . .

   The kids ate all the ice-cream.
4 Is the agent the subject or the object? . . . .
5 Is the sentence active or passive? . . . .

   All the ice-cream was eaten by the kids.
6 Is the agent the subject? . . . .
7 What word comes just before the agent? . . . .

160 Active and passive tenses

▶ Finder 87A

Read the story and then write one of the verbs in each space.

The most expensive airline meal in history **was eaten** on a flight from London to Moscow. After take-off, the first drinks **were being served** when suddenly the captain made an announcement. He told the passengers that the main course **had been left** behind at Heathrow when the plane **had taken** off. Several hundred chicken portions **were** still **waiting** there. They would have to go back and fetch them. 'Most of our fuel **will be jettisoned** over the sea before we **land**,' he said. The plane landed, and the crew took the meals on board. The plane then took off again three hours late. 'The needs of our passengers **are** always **given** top priority,' said a spokesman for the British airline, 'so we had to go back for the food.' 'I **have** never **heard** anything so silly in all my life,' said one of the passengers. The cost **has not been revealed** by the airline.

▶ Present simple (active) . . _land_ . . ▶ Present simple (passive) . . _are given_ . .
1 Present perfect (active) . . . .
2 Present perfect (passive) . . . .
3 Past simple (passive) . . . .
4 Past continuous (active) . . . .
5 Past continuous (passive) . . . .
6 Past perfect (active) . . . .
7 Past perfect (passive) . . . .
8 Future (passive) . . . .

161 Active and passive verb forms

▶ Finder 87A–C

Complete the news article by putting in the correct active or passive form of the verb in brackets. Sometimes there is more than one possible answer.

NOISIER AND NOISIER

For the last ten years, engineers (▶) . . _have been measuring_ . . (measure) noise levels in Britain's cities. The study (▶) . . _has just been completed_ . . (just/complete), and it (1) . . . . (show) that there is more noise than ever before. More and more people (2) . . . . (drive) mad by the sounds of the city. Complaints about noise (3) . . . . (increase) constantly over the last twenty years. Last year almost 300,000 complaints (4) . . . . (make). The least favourite sources of noise (5) . . . . (include) loud music, barking dogs, mobile phones, car alarms and home improvements. We are all familiar with the problems. How is it that a car alarm (6) . . . . (can/hear) by everyone except the owner of the car? Why (7) . . . . . electric drills . . . . (have to/use) early on Sunday morning? Why (8) . . . . . arguments . . . . (carry) on with the windows wide open? 'Noise (9) . . . . (still/increase),' said a member of the research group. These days traffic (10) . . . . (start) earlier in the morning, and shops and clubs (11) . . . . (stay) open later. The problem (12) . . . . (must/tackle). People (13) . . . . (can/drive) to commit suicide because of noise. So why (14) . . . . . nothing . . . . (do) about the problem? Up to now the government (15) . . . . (pay) little attention to it, but now action (16) . . . . (need). We all hope that the results of our study (17) . . . . (not/ignore).

162 *Was broken*: action or state?

► Finder 87E

Look at the words in **bold type** and say if they express an action or a state.

► When the bomb threat was received, the road **was closed** by the police. . . *action* . .
► We went to the Tourist Office, but it **was closed** for the day. . . *state* . .

1 The goods **were damaged** in the accident. . . . .
2 The goods **were damaged** deliberately. . . . .
3 These chairs **are sold** in all our stores. . . . .
4 I'm sorry, but those chairs **are sold**. . . . .
5 It was starting to get dark. I **was frightened**. . . . .
6 The animal **was** too **frightened** to come out of its nest. . . . .
7 The carpet **was stained** where someone had spilt wine on it. . . . .
8 The carpet **was stained** when someone spilt wine on it. . . . .

163 Passive verb forms

► Finder 87

Complete the second sentence so that it has a similar meaning to the previous one. There is no need to use a phrase with *by* in your passive sentences.

► They might change the rules.
The rules . . *might be changed.* . .

1 People don't respect politicians.
Politicians . . . .
2 The grass is being cut.
Someone . . . .
3 They're going to repair the phone.
The phone . . . .
4 They had lost the document.
The document . . . .
5 Has anyone corrected the mistakes?
Have . . . .
6 The door should have been locked behind us.
We . . . .
7 They will broadcast the programme on Sunday.
The programme . . . .
8 Someone had torn the page.
The page . . . .
9 We have to do the shopping.
The shopping . . . .
10 We're looking into the matter.
The matter . . . .
11 People just laugh at my suggestions.
My suggestions . . . .
12 Something must have delayed your visitors.
Your visitors . . . .

164 The use of the passive

▶ Finder 88

Look at these pairs of sentences and answer the questions about them. Put a tick by the right answer.

▶ Which of these sentences could be made passive?
   a) ☑ Lots of famous people wear these jackets.
   b) ☐ That style of jacket really suits you.

1 Which of these is more informal?
   a) ☐ People are playing football in the park.
   b) ☐ Football is being played in the park.

2 Which one of these sentences is correct?
   a) ☐ The company is belonged to my cousin.
   b) ☐ The company is owned by my cousin.

3 The coast of Brazil was explored by Amerigo Vespucci.
   Is this sentence more likely to occur in
   a) ☐ a fact file on Brazil, or
   b) ☐ a fact file on Vespucci?

4 Which one of these sentences could be made passive?
   a) ☐ The parcel weighs two kilos.
   b) ☐ I've weighed the parcel.

5 Which of these is more impersonal?
   a) ☐ You should keep this information in a safe place.
   b) ☐ This information should be kept in a safe place.

6 Which of these sentences is more likely?
   a) ☐ People make soap from vegetable oils.
   b) ☐ Soap is made from vegetable oils.

165 The form and use of the passive

▶ Finder 87–88

Look at the information in brackets and then add the information to the next sentence. Begin with *it, they,* or *which*. Decide if the sentence has to be active or passive.

▶ (The X-ray machine scans the bags for weapons.)
   The bags go through an X-ray machine, *which scans them for weapons.*
▶ (People developed the steam engine in the 18th century.)
   A key invention was the steam engine. *It was developed in the 18th century.*

1 (Someone invented ice-hockey in Canada.)
   Ice-hockey is a popular game, ...
2 (The owners have completely renovated the house.)
   The house looks magnificent. . . . .
3 (The project cost millions of pounds.)
   The project was very expensive. . . . .

4 (We can mix the primary colours to make other colours.)
   The primary colours are red, yellow and blue. . . . .
5 (People listen to the BBC World Service all over the world.)
   The BBC World Service is well known. . . . .
6 (The company has taken over its main competitor.)
   The company is expanding. . . . .
7 (The stadium lacks proper facilities.)
   International matches cannot be played at the stadium, ...

166 The agent in passive sentences

Write passive sentences with *by*.

Sherlock Holmes	(build)	Alexander Graham Bell
Jurassic Park	(~~create~~)	~~Sir Arthur Conan Doyle~~
The Harry Potter books	(direct)	the Egyptians
The telephone	(invent)	J.K. Rowling
The pyramids	(write)	Steven Spielberg

► . . *Sherlock Holmes was created by Sir Arthur Conan Doyle.* . .

1 . . . .
2 . . . .
3 . . . .
4 . . . .

167 The agent in passive sentences

► Finder 89

If the phrase with *by* adds important information, write *yes*. But if it can easily be left out,
write *no* and cross it out.

► We were driven home by a friend of ours. . . *yes* . .
► We were driven home in a taxi ~~by a taxi driver~~. . . *no* . .

1 TV programmes are broadcast all night by the TV companies. . . . . .
2 The programme was seen by 8 million viewers. . . . . .
3 The windows of the office are cleaned regularly by a window cleaner. . . . . .
4 In the storm several trees were blown down by the wind. . . . . .
5 The gang have all been arrested by the police. . . . . .
6 The man was arrested by a 23-year-old female police officer. . . . . .

168 The passive with *get*

► Finder 90

Put in a form of *get* and the passive participle of these verbs: *change, kill, leave, lose,
marry, start, ~~stop~~, throw*.

► I was driving too fast, and I . . *got stopped* . . by the police.

1 If you try to walk across a motorway, you'll probably . . . .

2 Not only have I got a boyfriend, but we're . . . . next month.
3 I can't go out in these clothes. I must . . . . first.
4 When the coach continued its journey, two members of the group . . . .
behind by mistake.
5 Andrew is no good at map-reading. He's always . . . .
6 Would you like to eat up some of this food before it . . . . away?
7 We've got all this housework to do, so let's . . . ., shall we?

169 The passive with *give, send*, etc ▶ Finder 91

Rewrite the sentences putting the part in **bold type** at the beginning. You may need to change from active to passive or from passive to active.

▶ We found **jobs** for most of the students.
. . *Jobs were found for most of the students.* . . .
▶ They've offered **Sophie** a place at university.
. . *Sophie has been offered a place at university.* . .

1 You should show **this photo** to the police.
. . . .
2 This jumper was given to me by **my grandmother**.
. . . .
3 The boss has promised **Polly** a rise.
. . . .
4 You can feed **the leftover meat** to the dogs.
. . . .
5 Simon was handed the receipt by **the shop assistant**.
. . . .
6 Large fees are paid to **the lawyers**.
. . . .
7 A handsome instructor is going to teach **our group** skiing.
. . . .

170 The passive with verbs of reporting ▶ Finder 92A

Combine each pair of sentences. Begin with *it* and a passive verb.

▶ We know something about the Prime Minister. He has bought a holiday home.
. . *It is known that the Prime Minister has bought a holiday home.* . . .

1 There's a rumour about the company. It is in difficulties.
. . . .
2 People believed in the Emperor. To them he was a god.
. . . .
3 Someone reported on the fighting. It had just begun.
. . . .
4 The figures will show us something about poverty. It is increasing.
. . . .
5 The official estimate is 200 people. They were killed by the pollution.
. . . .

6 An agreement was reached about wages. They would be raised by five per cent.

. . . .

7 They have made a decision about the project. It will have to be cancelled.

. . . .

8 There was a suggestion about the tickets. They should cost five pounds.

. . . .

171 ... *said to be ...* ▶ Finder 92B

Rewrite the first six sentences of Exercise 170 using a passive verb and a to-infinitive.

▶ *The Prime Minister is known to have bought a holiday home.*
1 The company . . . .
2 The Emperor . . . .
3 . . . .
4 . . . .
5 . . . .

172 Passive verb + to-infinitive or active participle ▶ Finder 93

Combine each pair of sentences using a passive verb + a to-infinitive or active participle.

▶ The team members have to work together. That's what the boss told them.
   The team members were told to work together.
▶ The old man was wandering around the streets. The police found him.
   The old man was found wandering around the streets.

1 The workers have accepted lower wages. The company has persuaded them.

. . . .

2 Two young men were fighting. We saw them.

. . . .

3 The victims may take legal action. That's what their lawyers have advised them.

. . . .

4 The children had to pick up all the litter. The teacher made them do it.

. . . .

5 The woman was smuggling cigarettes into the country. Customs officers caught her.

. . . .

6 The refugees can't get a job. The government won't let them.

. . . .

7 £50,000 on decorating the ballroom – that's what they spent.

. . . .

8 You shouldn't have driven so fast. I warned you not to.

. . . .

173 Some patterns with *have* and *get*

▶ Finder 94B–C

Write a sentence about each situation using a structure with *have* or *get* + a passive verb.

▶ Paul is at the dry-cleaner's. They've cleaned his jacket.
   Paul has had his jacket cleaned.

1 The decorators are at Angela's. They're working on her flat.
   . . . .

2 Some vandals damaged Lisa's car last week.
   . . . .

3 Your friends got some builders to build a house for them.
   . . . .

4 You really must finish your homework soon.
   . . . .

5 The bank has withdrawn Mark's credit card.
   . . . .

6 You're wondering: where did Tom go for that haircut?
   . . . .

7 Someone is coming to Karen's place tomorrow. They're going to clean her carpets.
   . . . .

174 The passive to-infinitive and gerund

▶ Finder 95

Complete these sentences, which are set in a business context. Use a passive to-infinitive or ing-form of the verb in brackets. Sometimes you need to use a perfect form.

▶ It's important for the figures *to be updated* (update) regularly.
▶ Rick ignored the problems despite *having been warned* (warn) about them.

1 The men wanted to avoid . . . . (see) on security cameras.
2 Alice is hoping . . . . (promote) soon.
3 The goods ought . . . . (deliver) two weeks ago.
4 The system was adopted without . . . . (test) at all.
5 I'd like the money . . . . (transfer) immediately, please.
6 The Chief Executive insists on . . . . (inform) of every detail.
7 I'm afraid the documents seem . . . . (mislay).
8 As well as . . . . (move) to a less important job, Emily had suffered a drop in salary.

175 Active verbs with a passive meaning

▶ Finder 96

Choose the correct words.

▶ We've got some work to do/~~to be done~~.
1 The table has to lay/to be laid.
2 The grass wants to cut/cutting.
3 There's so much to do/to be done on a Club Sun holiday!

4 Our latest range of computers <u>are selling</u>/<u>are being sold</u> really well.
5 I had several letters <u>to write</u>/<u>to be written</u>.
6 This puzzle isn't very easy <u>to solve</u>/<u>to be solved</u>.
7 These instructions are too difficult <u>to understand</u>/<u>to be understood</u> by a child.
8 These brakes don't work very well. They need <u>see to</u>/<u>seeing to</u>.

176 The passive

▶ Finder 86–96

Put the one missing word in each sentence.

▶ No one can find the place. Everyone . . *gets* . . lost.

1 I'm . . . . my hair cut tomorrow.
2 The pilot is thought . . . . have lost control of the aircraft.
3 These boxes are to . . . . moved away from the door.
4 Last week we . . . . a man come and dig the garden for us.
5 I can't wear my red sweater. It's . . . . washed at the moment.
6 It's a great film. The main character is played . . . . Tom Hanks.
7 Matthew is furious about . . . . been tricked out of his money.
8 On the bank's security video, the man was . . . . waving a gun around.
9 The picture isn't in the shop window now. It might have . . . . sold.
10 People shouldn't smoke because . . . . is known that smoking causes cancer.
11 James had forgotten his electric razor, so he couldn't . . . . shaved.
12 How many times . . . . you get burgled at your last house?

177 The passive

▶ Finder 86–96

Put in the correct active or passive form of the verbs.

The last train (▶) . . *stopped* . . (stop) at Wellbury Station twenty years ago, and since then the country branch line(▶) . . *has been left* . . (leave) to fall into disuse. But five years ago the old station buildings (1) . . . . (sell) to a young couple, Alan and Sarah Pickford. Immediately the Pickfords (2) . . . . (apply) to the local Council and (3) . . . . (promise) a sum of money to help them with their project. Months (4) . . . . (spend) planning all the details. Then their plans (5) . . . . (have to/approve). After that the way was clear. The Pickfords (6) . . . . the house completely . . . . (renovate) by local builders. They themselves also (7) . . . . (create) a beautiful garden around it. They certainly had lots (8) . . . . (do). The task (9) . . . . (seem) hopeless at first because everything was in such a poor condition, but today the old station (10) . . . . greatly . . . . (admire), and it (11) . . . . (say/be) the best of its kind in the country. Many authentic railway details (12) . . . . (preserve), and an old railway carriage (13) . . . . (now/use) as a greenhouse. The station house (14) . . . . (can/visit) by the public on weekend afternoons and holidays, but visitors (15) . . . . (ask/not/come) at other times as the Pickfords are not keen on (16) . . . . (disturb) during the week.

178 The passive

▶ Finder 86–96

Rewrite each sentence so that it ends with the information in **bold type**.

▶ Someone will **weigh** our suitcases.
. . .*Our suitcases will be weighed.*. . .

1 We got someone to **remove** the rubbish.

. . . .

2 **A new bus shelter** has been put up.

. . . .

3 **An American architect** designed the building.

. . . .

4 I always have to **prepare** meals.

. . . .

5 It's terrible when people **ignore** you.

. . . .

6 They're going to **publish** the story.

. . . .

7 Do we have to **print out** the document?

. . . .

8 **An Oscar** was awarded to the actress.

. . . .

179 Introduction to the infinitive

▶ Finder 97B

For each sentence tick one or two of the boxes. Choose only those words which describe the to-infinitive.

	simple	perfect	continuous	passive	negative
▶ We decided not to take part.	✓				✓
1 I'd like to have seen the show.					
2 You're supposed to have been practising.					
3 I hate to be stared at.					
4 It's time to be going.					
5 It's annoying not to have received an invitation.					

180 Infinitive clauses

▶ Finder 98

Put the words in the right order to form an infinitive clause.

▶ see / the fireworks / to
We wanted . . *to see the fireworks.* . .

1 on holiday / to / go
Amy is keen . . . .

2 about / think / to
We've got something . . . .

3 an e-mail / to / send
I'm going . . . .

4 be / better / to
I expected the weather . . . .

5 from / to / fly
It's quite a convenient airport . . . .

181 *It* and to-infinitive clauses

▶ Finder 99A

Match the two halves of each sentence. Then write the sentences beginning with *it* and putting the to-infinitive clause at the end.

▶ To keep the jewels in a bank	is a basic human right.
1 To hitch-hike on your own	costs a great deal of money.
2 To have an education	~~would be safer.~~
3 To visit Mecca	is not easy.
4 To fully understand the theory of relativity	might be dangerous.
5 To keep a racehorse	is the duty of every Muslim.

▶ . . *It would be safer to keep the jewels in a bank.* . . .

1 . . . .

2 . . . .

3 . . . .

4 . . . .

5 . . . .

182 The to-infinitive expressing purpose

▶ Finder 100A

Add a to-infinitive clause to explain the purpose of the action. Use these words: *celebrate, fit, get rid of, keep in, parcel, protect.*

▶ The team are doing a lap of honour . *to celebrate their victory.* . .
1 Louise is going to the post office . . . .
2 Terry is wearing gloves . . . .
3 We bought a cat . . . .
4 The farmer put up an electric fence . . . .
5 Steve and Karen go jogging . . . .

183 The to-infinitive used as an adverbial

▶ Finder 100

Complete each sentence with a clause from the box. Say if the clause expresses purpose (A), an outcome (B), a comment (C), or an explanation for a wrong idea (D).

to be honest	to provide information
to fall at the last fence	to see the pictures
to find an angry crowd	to stay awake
to hear him talk	to warm them

▶ The company set up a website . *to provide information.* . . . .(. A .) . .
1 Police officers arrived . . . . (. . . .)
2 I put the plates in the oven . . . . (. . . .)
3 I'd rather just go home now, ... (. . . .)
4 . . . . , you'd think a child had painted them. (. . . .)
5 . . . . , we drank strong coffee. (. . . .)
6 The horse took the lead, only . . . . (. . . .)
7 You'd think Tom was an expert . . . . (. . . .)

184 Verb + to-infinitive

▶ Finder 101A

Write sentences from the table. Put the verb into the correct to-infinitive form.

▶ Maybe we should offer	(be) Julius Caesar in an earlier life.
1 Our neighbours threatened	~~(pay) part of the cost.~~
2 MPs have voted	(apologize) for something I haven't done.
3 Those people seem	(call) the police.
4 I refuse	(change) the law.
5 The man claims	(argue) about something.

▶ .....*Maybe we should offer to pay part of the cost.*.....

1 ....

2 ....

3 ....

4 ....

5 ....

185 Verb + to-infinitive or verb + gerund?

▶ Finder 101B–C

Complete this newspaper article about a successful business executive. Choose the to-infinitive or the gerund of the verbs in brackets.

Sandra King had agreed (▶) ...*to meet*... (meet) me in her office in central Manchester. The head of Greenway Supermarkets, a smart 40-year-old woman, gave me a big smile of welcome. You can't help (▶) ..*liking*.. (like) Sandra King. 'Greenway expects (1) .... (make) a big profit again this year,' she told me. The company has never failed (2) .... (do) well since she took over five years ago. In fact she has managed (3) .... (avoid)(4) .... (lose) customers at a time when others have seen their profits fall. 'I enjoy (5) .... (solve) problems,' she says. Next year Greenway plan (6) .... (open) ten new supermarkets, and they have also offered (7) .... (buy) the Lo-Price Stores group. Sandra King hopes (8) .... (have) discussions with Lo-Price boss Steven Weyman soon. You can't afford (9) .... (relax) in this job,' she told me. 'You can never give up (10) .... (think) about how you can do things better. That's what you have (11) .... (do) if you want (12) .... (be) successful.'

186 Verb + to-infinitive or verb + gerund?

▶ Finder 102

Complete the sentence so that it has a similar meaning to the previous one.

▶ I have finally realized the secret of happiness.
I have come ..*to realize the secret of happiness.*..

1 I wouldn't like to work nights.
I don't fancy ....

2 Our team is winning, apparently.
Our team seems . . . .

3 Several people heard gunshots, they said.
Several people reported . . . .

4 We usually stay in and watch TV.
We tend . . . .

5 We haven't got enough money. We can't start a business.
We can't afford . . . .

6 It seems that things are improving.
Things seem . . . .

7 Someone appears to have trodden on this radio.
This radio appears . . . .

8 Singing isn't allowed in this pub.
This pub doesn't . . . .

9 It's OK – I'll wait for you.
I don't . . . .

10 You must show me the photos. I can't wait.
I'm dying . . . .

187 Verbs taking either a to-infinitive or a gerund

▶ Finder 10.

If a sentence is correct, put a tick. If you can use a different form, then write the verb -
to-infinitive or verb + gerund after the tick. If the sentence is incorrect, cross out the
two verbs and write them correctly.

▶ We intend keeping the project a secret.
▶ I'd love visiting Australia one day.

✓ *intend to keep*
love to visit

1 I hate to hear you talk like that.
2 The street lights were starting coming on.
3 I like having my teeth checked every few months.
4 The protestors continued throwing stones.
5 I would like welcoming all our visitors.
6 We prefer to do the journey in two days.

. . . .
. . . .
. . . .
. . . .
. . . .
. . . .

188 Verb + to-infinitive/gerund with a change in meaning

▶ Finder 10.

Complete the conversations. Choose either the to-infinitive or the gerund of the verbs
in brackets.

1 Laura: I'm having problems with this computer again. With all the trouble it's given us, I
really regret (▶) . . *buying* . . (buy) it.

Karen: Does it need . . . . (repair)?
Laura: Actually I think I just need . . . . (study) the manual.
Karen: Well, stop . . . . (fiddle) around with it now, will you?

2 James: I see your favourite actress won an Oscar.
Paul: Yes, but I regret . . . . (say) she didn't make a very good speech. First she thanked lots of people who had helped her, and then she went on . . . . (tell) us her whole life story.
James: I know. She just wouldn't stop . . . . (talk).

3 Sarah: Did you remember . . . . (go) to the supermarket?
Oliver: Yes, but I forgot . . . . (get) the chicken.
Sarah: But that was the most important thing.
Oliver: I know. I'm sorry. I can remember . . . . (mean) . . . . (get) it, but then I stopped . . . . (chat) to someone, and it went right out of my head.
Sarah: Why don't you make a list next time? Or you could try . . . . (write) the word 'chicken' in large letters on your hand and see if that helps.
Oliver: Sorry, Sarah. I can go back and get the chicken now.
Sarah: No, not now. It would mean . . . . (drive) through town in the rush hour. Let's just try . . . . (decide) on something else we can have tonight.

189 Verb + object + to-infinitive

▶ Finder 105

Combine the sentences using a verb + object + to-infinitive.

▶ I played the piano. My dad encouraged me.
. . . . *My dad encouraged me to play the piano.* . . . .

1 Please come with me. I need you to.

. . . .

2 The animals do tricks. They've been trained.

. . . .

3 The police used water cannon. They were ordered to.

. . . .

4 Paul has gone on a diet. His doctor advised him to.

. . . .

5 The drug is harmful. Scientific tests have proved it.

. . . .

6 You can get a discount. This card enables you to.

. . . .

7 There must be a doctor present. The law requires it.

. . . .

8 The road was dangerous. That was well-known.

. . . .

190 Adjective + to-infinitive

▶ Finder 106

These sentences are all from a travel guide. Put the words in the right order and use a to-infinitive.

▶ exciting / explore / it is / the strange landscape
   . . It is exciting to explore the strange landscape. . . .

1 in the sea / it is / swim / too dangerous
   . . . .

2 less than an hour / lucky / wait / you'll be
   . . . .

3 are / find / hard / good restaurants
   . . . .

4 foolish / insurance / it is / not buy
   . . . .

5 are / close / for lunch / liable / the shops
   . . . .

6 an interesting / is / place / the town / visit
   . . . .

7 book / in advance / important / it is
   . . . .

8 a / it is / journey / make / on foot / too long
   . . . .

9 not carry / too much cash / wise / would be / you
   . . . .

10 attract / dramatic enough / is / thousands of visitors / the view
   . . . .

191 Noun phrase + to-infinitive

▶ Finder 107A

Rewrite the sentences using a noun phrase + to-infinitive.

▶ Tom tends to say what he thinks, which sometimes offends people.
   . . Tom's tendency to say what he thinks sometimes offends people. . . .

1 People desire to breathe clean air. This has led to a flight from the city.
   . . . .

2 The company failed to modernize, and this caused its decline.
   . . . .

3 Matthew had decided not to take the exam, which is quite understandable.
   . . . .

4 Simon was reluctant to spend any money, and this annoyed Emma.
   . . . .

5 The President promised to end the war, which surprised everyone.
   . . . .

6 Is the government able to run the country? That is seriously in doubt.
   . . . .

192 Question word + to-infinitive

▶ Finder 108

Comment on the situations. Each of your sentences should contain the word in brackets and a question word + to-infinitive.

▶ Lisa is thinking 'How can I explain things?' (worry)
Lisa is _worrying about how to explain things._

1 James was thinking 'Who shall I ask for help?' (wonder)
James was . . . .

2 Justin is asking 'Where should I put the flowers?' (know)
Justin wants . . . .

3 Nicola was wondering 'How much money should I take with me?' (not sure)
. . . .

4 Adam is wondering 'Should I accept the offer or not?' (no idea)
. . . .

5 Lucy was thinking 'What shall I do next?' (not know)
. . . .

6 Hannah is asking 'How do I download the software?' (try/find out)
. . . .

193 *For* and *of* with a to-infinitive

▶ Finder 105, 109

Express the idea using a pattern with *for* or *of*, or use a verb + object + to-infinitive.

▶ You'll have to get ready, so I'll wait.
. _I'll wait for you to get ready._ .

▶ Kate gave away our secret. That was stupid.
. . _It was stupid of Kate to give away our secret._ . .

▶ Sam hasn't signed our petition yet, but I reminded him.
. _I reminded Sam to sign our petition._ .

1 Cars come along here at top speed. It's dangerous.
. . . .

2 I rode a pony. My mother taught me.
. . . .

3 A decorator could smarten this place up. I wouldn't mind paying.
. . . .

4 Your friend has invited me to the party. That was very nice.
. . . .

5 I did a parachute jump because my brother persuaded me.
. . . .

6 They won't have updated the website yet. It takes ages.
. . . .

7 No one has to get up early tomorrow. There's absolutely no need.
. . . .

8 You didn't speak to my friends. That was very rude.
. . . .

9 People will recognize my genius. That's my ambition.
. . . .

194 The infinitive without *to*

► Finder 11(

Choose the correct form.

► You should take/~~to take~~ an interest in current affairs.

1 It's late. We'd better hurry/to hurry.
2 I saw the balloon land/to land in a field.
3 I got my sister lend/to lend me some money.
4 I can let you have/to have the book when I've finished with it.
5 You really ought be/to be more careful.
6 Our teacher made us copy/to copy the whole page.
7 Would you rather have/to have tea or coffee?
8 The reporters wouldn't leave us alone. They forced us answer/to answer their questions.
9 Those students do nothing but lie/to lie in bed all day.

195 Infinitive forms

► Finder 97, 11(

Put in a verb in the correct infinitive form.

► The doctor won't let me . . . *eat* . . . sweets.
► I'm afraid the bus is likely . . . *to have left* . . . already.

1 This phone doesn't work, so I'm going . . . . it back to the shop.
2 I'm not sure what Martin is doing just now. He might . . . . ches:
   with someone.
3 Why are you sitting here when you ought . . . . some work.
4 You'd better . . . . your best suit at the job interview.
5 We had a trip on the river yesterday, but I'd rather . . . . round
   the museum.
6 Where are we? We seem . . . . our way.
7 When I saw Peter, he was standing at the bus stop. He must . . . .
   for a bus.

196 The infinitive

► Finder 97–11(

Some of these sentences are correct, and some have a word which should not be there. I
a sentence is correct, put a tick (✓). If it is incorrect, cross the unnecessary word out of th
sentence and write it in the space.

► We hope to see you soon.   . . . . ✓ . . . . . .
► I like to ~~be~~ play basketball.   . . . *be* . . . . . .

1 I won't be able to afford to go to New Zealand.   . . . .
2 We need a table to put the projector on it.   . . . .
3 No one knows of how to get to the meeting place.   . . . .
4 The man claimed to have been trying to break up the fight.   . . . .
5 It was clever of you to spot that mistake.   . . . .
6 The driver stopped for to get some petrol.   . . . .
7 Would anyone like to meet the professor?   . . . .
8 These packets aren't very easy to open them.   . . . .
9 The customs officials made everyone to wait half an hour.   . . . .

Correct the sentences.

▶ Steve has asked I help him.
   Steve has asked me to help him.

1 You must have forgotten locking the door.
   . . . .

2 I want that you trust me.
   . . . .

3 We set off really early not to be late.
   . . . .

4 It was kind for you to make me feel so welcome.
   . . . .

5 There are some important rules for follow them.
   . . . .

6 I'm not sure if to buy this CD.
   . . . .

7 The builders accepted to do the work all over again.
   . . . .

8 That joke Tom told really made me to laugh.
   . . . .

9 I'd love to did meet Albert Einstein.
   . . . .

10 It was amazing the Grand Canyon to fly over.
   . . . .

11 That's a too difficult question to answer.
   . . . .

12 There are picnic tables for people sit at them.
   . . . .

198 The infinitive ▶ Finder 97–110

Complete each sentence so that it has a similar meaning. Use an infinitive form.

▶ I may succeed in interviewing Bill Gates.
   I may get . . . *to interview Bill Gates.* . . .

1 Where can we go on holiday? We can't decide.
   We can't decide . . . .

2 Keep the audience happy. That's the main thing.
   The main thing . . . .

3 Shall we walk? I think I'd rather.
   I think I'd . . . .

4 You can't walk. It's too far.
It's too . . . .

5 Anita is moving to Ireland soon. That's the plan.
Anita is planning . . . .

6 The police can't arrest people without reason. They don't have the power.
The police don't have . . . .

7 I can get around OK in my wheelchair.
My wheelchair enables . . . .

8 A product has to be advertised if it's going to sell.
For . . . . it has to be advertised.

9 By chance we travelled on the same train.
. . . . travel on the same train.

199 Introduction to the gerund

▶ Finder 111

Read the conversation and then write the gerunds.

Lucy: That woman over there is Chloe Barker.
Alan: Who?
Lucy: Chloe Barker. She's famous for having sailed round the world single-handed. It was a
         great achievement. She kept going despite having been injured in a terrible storm and
         not knowing if she would survive the journey.
Alan: Well, don't stare at her. She probably doesn't like being stared at.

▶ Simple gerund: . . _sailing_ . .

1 Simple gerund in the negative: . . . .
2 Simple passive gerund: . . . .
3 Perfect active gerund: . . . .
4 Perfect passive gerund: . . . .

200 Gerund clauses with a subject

▶ Finder 112B

Combine the two sentences using a gerund clause with a subject. Use a possessive form.

▶ You practise on the drums. It gives me a headache.
   . . _Your practising on the drums gives me a headache._ . . .

1 I do all the cooking. It isn't fair.
. . . .

2 We invited everybody to Carl's party. That wasn't a good idea.
. . . .

3 You wear these strange clothes. It amuses everyone.
. . . .

4 I'm sitting here. Does that bother you?
. . . .

201 Some patterns with the gerund

▶ Finder 113A–B

Put the words in the right order.

▶ feeling / is / it / no good / sorry for yourself
  . . *It is no good feeling sorry for yourself.* . .
▶ all your money / away / is / gambling / ridiculous
  . . *Gambling all your money away is ridiculous.* . .

1 getting / had / I / problems / to work

   . . . .

2 by train / can be / relaxing / travelling

   . . . .

3 having / it / a map / not / a nuisance / was

   . . . .

4 getting / no difficulty / there / tickets / was

   . . . .

5 Madonna / quite a thrill / seeing / was

   . . . .

6 can / fun / going out / have / to discos / we

   . . . .

7 at a computer / bad for you / can be / sitting

   . . . .

8 is / it / the machine / no use / to repair / trying

   . . . .

202 Verb + object + to-infinitive or gerund

▶ Finder 105, 113E

Complete this news article. Put in a to-infinitive or gerund.

NEW LONDON AIRPORT 'A DISASTER'

There has been a mixed reaction to the government's announcement yesterday of plans to build a new London airport. The airlines have welcomed the news, but environmental groups have declared the scheme (▶) . . *to be* . . (be) a disaster. 'It is totally wrong,' said Sue Paine of Green Transport. 'I can't imagine any sensible person (▶) . . *supporting* . . (support) this measure. Why should we tolerate the government (1) . . . . (destroy) our environment?'

The government say that the increase in air traffic has forced them (2) . . . . (build) another airport and that the new facility will enable more people (3) . . . . (fly). 'We can't stop people (4) . . . . (want) to travel,' said the Minister of Aviation. 'The growth of international travel and tourism should be welcomed, and it naturally involves new facilities (5) . . . . (construct).'

Ms Paine disagrees. 'How can you justify more aircraft (6) . . . . (cause) even more pollution?' she asks. 'We urge everyone (7) . . . . (oppose) the scheme. If we act together, we can prevent it (8) . . . . (happen). We must persuade the government

(9) . . . . (change) their minds. We would prefer them (10) . . . . (put) money into a more environmentally-friendly transport project. We resent all this money (11) . . . . . (go) to an airport. And no one should have an airport built near their house. If you have ever experienced a large aircraft (12) . . . . (fly) just 100 metres over your house, you will know what I mean.'

203 Preposition + gerund ▶ Finder 114

Write a sentence with a similar meaning. Use the word in brackets. There is no need to change the order of the clauses.

▶ Andrew went to work, but he felt unwell. (despite)
 Andrew went to work despite feeling unwell.

▶ Polly does a full-time job. And she has two children to look after. (as well as)
 As well as doing a full time job, Polly has two children to look after.

1 The prisoners escaped. They dug a tunnel. (by)

. . . .

2 My sister heard the news and immediately fainted. (on)

. . . .

3 Always look in your mirror. Then you can drive off. (before)

. . . .

4 I didn't enjoy the film. I was totally bored by it. (far from)

. . . .

5 We borrowed money. As a result we added to our problems. (in)

. . . .

6 I'm sure you'll have a great time even though I won't be there. (without)

. . . .

7 I bought this special brush. You paint ceilings with it. (for)

. . . .

8 I was mugged. I've been afraid to go out on my own. (since)

. . . .

9 Sending an e-mail is quick, but posting a letter isn't. (than)

. . . .

10 My friend is in trouble. He hasn't renewed his visa. (on account of)

. . . .

204 Verb + preposition + gerund ▶ Finder 115

Complete the conversations. Put in a preposition and gerund.

▶ Alice: Matthew lost all his savings in that Internet business that went bankrupt.
  Robert: Well, he would insist *on putting* (put) his money into it. You did warn him *against taking* (take) risks.

1 Paul: I'm really looking forward . . . . (go) on holiday next week.
        I couldn't put up . . . . (work) in that awful place a
        moment longer.
  Mark: So are you thinking . . . . (get) another job?
  Paul: Well, the pay isn't bad. That's the only thing that's keeping
        me . . . . (leave).

2 Lisa: I suppose I'd better get on . . . . (clear) up the kitchen.
  Carol: It's a pity the men don't believe . . . . (share) the work.
        They always seem to succeed . . . . (avoid) it. I really
        object . . . . (do) more than my fair share.

3 Leanne: The traffic is so bad it takes ages to drive into town. So now they're trying to
        discourage people . . . . (use) cars.
  Nicola: Yes, but you can't rely . . . . (get) to work by bus. The buses
        are hopeless. And catching one involves you . . . . (wait)
        around for ages. I think I'll settle . . . . (sit) in a traffic-jam.

4 Isabel: I can't stand my maths teacher.
  Adam: Why? What's the problem?
  Isabel: She's always criticizing me . . . . (make) mistakes. She
        never praises me . . . . (get) something right. And now
        she's accused me . . . . (cheat) in the test. And I
        wouldn't dream . . . . (try) to cheat. I feel
        . . . . (give) up the course.

205 Adjective + preposition + gerund   ▶ Finder 116

Combine the two sentences using an adjective + preposition + gerund.

▶ I'm bored. We're just sitting here.
  . . *I'm bored with just sitting here.* . . .

1 I wasn't very good. I couldn't climb the rope.
. . . .

2 The parcels are ready. We can load them into the van.
. . . .

3 I'm worried. I might forget the number.
. . . .

4 Emily is quite capable. She can photocopy the document.
. . . .

5 Jodie is responsible. She messed up the arrangements.
. . . .

6 I'm annoyed. I have to do all this work again.
. . . .

7 My friend was involved. She helped to organize the event.
. . . .

8 We're fed up. We're always told to do the boring jobs.
. . . .

206 Noun + preposition + gerund

▶ Finder 117

Combine the two sentences using a noun + preposition + gerund.

▶ United are playing at home. They have the advantage.
  .. *United have the advantage of playing at home.* ...

1 I'm going to start a new life. I'm thrilled by the prospect.
  . . . .

2 You took yesterday off. Have you got a good excuse?
  . . . .

3 I broke the bad news. I had the unpleasant task.
  . . . .

4 Why are they keeping everything secret? What's the reason?
  . . . .

5 I can fly. I've conquered my fear.
  . . . .

6 We all want to promote our products. We share your interest.
  . . . .

7 They won't find those people alive. There's no hope.
  . . . .

8 The boss chases after women. He's got a reputation.
  . . . .

9 The company dominates the market. I admire its success.
  . . . .

207 *For joining* and *to join*

▶ Finder 118B

Choose the correct form.

▶ The receptionist told me about waiting/to wait here until I'm called.

1 Meeting new people always makes me feel anxious about saying/to say the wrong thing.
2 Will you remind me of posting/to post this letter when we go past the post office?
3 I couldn't climb a tall ladder like that because I'd be afraid of falling/to fall.
4 I'm ashamed of admitting/to admit it, but I can't actually read very well.
5 Did I tell you about seeing/to see a bank robbery the other day? It was quite terrifying.
6 Simon is really into films. He's interested in making/to make a film of his own some day.
7 We have discussed your proposal, and we are pleased about accepting/to accept it.
8 I'm sorry for behaving/to behave so badly yesterday. It was thoughtless of me.
9 Children have enough to do with their school work. I don't agree with them to deliver/
  delivering newspapers before they go to school.

208 *To* + gerund and to-infinitive

▶ Finder 11*

Put in *to* + gerund or a to-infinitive.

▶ I look forward .. *to hearing* .. (hear) from you soon.

1 It turned out . . . . (be) a very enjoyable evening.

2 Do you have any objection . . . . the police . . . . (take)
your fingerprints?

3 It was such an awful moment that I came close . . . . (burst)
into tears.

4 I was persuaded . . . . (help) collect money for the homeless.

5 Surely you're opposed . . . . (have) your rights taken away?

6 It is important . . . . (read) the instructions carefully.

7 The critics say it's a brilliant show, so no one will admit . . . . (not like) it.

8 Since my marriage ended, I've been resigned . . . . (live) alone.

9 That was a dangerous thing to do. You're lucky . . . . (not kill).

209 Verb/Adjective/Noun + preposition + gerund

▶ Finder 115–117

Complete this true story. Put in the prepositions.

When Ian Johnstone decided to go travelling around Australia for a year, his girlfriend Amy Dolby
was resigned (▶) . . _to_ . . staying behind in England and trying to concentrate (1) . . _to_ . . . .
getting on with her work as a legal secretary. After spending some time in Australia, Ian was
feeling fed up (2) . . . . being on his own and ready to admit (3) . . . . being
lost without Amy. He dreamed (4) . . . . seeing her again. The fact that this involved a
journey of 11,000 miles did not deter him (5) . . . . popping back to England with the
intention (6) . . . . surprising her with a proposal of marriage. Ian is a real romantic. He
arrived at Amy's home carrying a ring, some flowers and a bottle of champagne. But Amy wasn't
at home. She had grown tired (7) . . . . waiting for him and had taken a flight to
Australia, intent (8) . . . . joining him there. In fact they had been amazingly close
(9) . . . . bumping into each other as they both changed planes in Singapore. They
were both pretty annoyed (10) . . . . having made the trip for nothing, but Ian
proposed by phone from England and was accepted. The prospect (11) . . . . seeing
each other again soon cheered them up. 'I'm looking forward (12) . . . . putting this
ring on her finger,' said Ian.

210 Determiner + gerund

▶ Finder 120

Put one of these words in each sentence: *cleaning*, *no*, *of*, *running*, *some*, *the*, *wearing*.

1 We'd better not eat our sandwiches here because it says ' . . . . picnicking'
on that notice.

2 The house is filthy. No one ever does any . . . .

3 It would be nice to do . . . . wind-surfing if we get the chance.

4 The sounding . . . . a horn is illegal when the vehicle is not moving.

5 I like playing football, but all the . . . . you have to do tires me out.

6 I don't mind cooking, but I hate doing . . . . ironing.

7 The . . . . of shoes is not permitted in the temple.

211 The gerund

Write a second sentence so that it has a similar meaning. Use the word or phrase in brackets.

▶ I admire the woman because she's got to the top in her profession. (for)
I admire the woman for getting to the top in her profession.

1 Riding in a racing-car was quite an experience. (it)

....

2 Everyone said 'Well done' to Emma for passing her test. (congratulated)

....

3 I don't remember that I wrote a cheque. (having)

....

4 Let's fish this weekend. (do some)

....

5 It's our job to analyse the figures. (have the job)

....

6 The woman is famous because she impersonates the Queen. (for)

....

7 You aren't doing any work, and that's a cause for concern. (your)

....

8 This crisis will make it necessary for me to go into the office tomorrow. (necessitate)

....

9 No boxer should go so far as to bite his opponent. (resort)

....

212 The gerund

Each of these sentences is incorrect. Write the correct sentence.

▶ ~~Tom insisted to come with us.~~
Tom insisted on coming with us.

1 ~~I'm looking forward to go away.~~

....

2 ~~There isn't worth spend a whole day in the town.~~

....

3 ~~I was aware haven't eaten for some time.~~

....

4 ~~In those days the copying books was a laborious task.~~

....

5 ~~I was sorry for hearing the bad news.~~

....

6 ~~At last we succeeded to get the car started.~~

....

7 ~~I was really annoyed at been tricked out of my money.~~

....

8 ~~I won't tolerate you tell lies about me.~~

....

108   211 ● The gerund

9 ~~I was excited by the game in spite of I was a neutral.~~

. . . .

10 ~~We haven't a hope to finish the work in time.~~

. . . .

213 Introduction to participles   ▶ Finder 121

In this paragraph from an e-mail the participles are in **bold** type. Answer the questions about them.

Unfortunately I can only type one-handed because I've **broken** my arm. I did it yesterday **playing** football. It took ages to get it **seen** to of course. **Having been taken** to hospital in a taxi, I faced a very long wait. There seemed to be quite a few people **being treated** for sports injuries. **Having sat** there patiently for what seemed like hours, I finally got some attention. I'll have to keep off the football field for a few weeks,

▶ playing	Active or passive?	*active*
1 having sat	Perfect or continuous?	. . . .
2 having been taken	Active or passive?	. . . .
3 being treated	Perfect or continuous?	. . . .
4 seen	Past or passive?	. . . .
5 broken	Past or passive?	. . . .

214 Participle clauses   ▶ Finder 122

Each of these sentences is incorrect. Write the correct sentence.

▶ ~~I noticed a lorry down the hill coming.~~
. . . *I noticed a lorry coming down the hill.* . . .

1 ~~Having been cancelled the show, we all went home.~~

. . . .

2 ~~We can hear our neighbour the piano playing.~~

. . . .

3 ~~Karen having arrived at the flat, Karen rang the bell.~~

. . . .

4 ~~By the police cornered, the gang tried to shoot their way out.~~

. . . .

215 Participle + noun

▶ Finder 123A–E

Complete this news report. Put in the correct participle form of each verb in brackets.

A large part of the north of England was hit by a (▶) _raging_ (rage) storm which swept across the country yesterday, leaving a trail of (▶) _damaged_ (damage) buildings behind it. Large numbers of (1) . . . . (injure) people were treated in hospitals or by paramedics. One man, a (2) . . . . (retire) postman who lived in Leeds, died after he was struck on the head by a (3) . . . . (fall) roof tile. The (4) . . . . (alarm) force of the (5) . . . . (howl) winds forced many people to take shelter. There was chaos on the roads as many were blocked by (6) . . . . (fall) trees. The (7) . . . . (not expect) storm now threatens to bring floods to the area, as the still (8) . . . . (rise) waters of the River Ouse have almost reached danger level.

216 Compound participle + noun

▶ Finder 123C–D

Rewrite the phrases using a compound with an active or passive participle.

▶ a task which consumes a lot of time   _a time-consuming task_

1 a scheme which saves money   . . . .
2 a movie packed with action   . . . .
3 a table with a glass top   . . . .
4 criticism that hits hard   . . . .
5 a building that looks strange   . . . .
6 a result that breaks your heart   . . . .
7 a girl with fair hair and blue eyes   . . . .

217 Verb + participle

▶ Finder 124A

For each picture, write a sentence from the table.

~~The woman~~	went	injured	at the gate.
The family	ran	racing	from the building.
People	~~sat~~	screaming	down the slope.
The player	stood	~~staring~~	on the grass.
The girls	lay	waving	~~into space.~~

▶ _The woman sat staring into space._

1

2

3

4

```
1 . . . . . . . . . . . . . . . . . . . . . . . . . . . . . . . . . . . . . . . . . . . . . . . . . . . . . . . . . . . .
2 . . . . . . . . . . . . . . . . . . . . . . . . . . . . . . . . . . . . . . . . . . . . . . . . . . . . . . . . . . . .
3 . . . . . . . . . . . . . . . . . . . . . . . . . . . . . . . . . . . . . . . . . . . . . . . . . . . . . . . . . . . .
4 . . . . . . . . . . . . . . . . . . . . . . . . . . . . . . . . . . . . . . . . . . . . . . . . . . . . . . . . . . . .
```

218 *I saw you do/doing it*

▶ Finder 125A–C

A detective is giving evidence in court. Combine his two sentences into one.

▶ I watched the man. He bumped into a woman and snatched her handbag.
  I watched the man bump into a woman and snatch her handbag.
▶ We saw a group of men outside the pub. They were fighting.
  We saw a group of men fighting outside the pub.

1 We saw a man. He threw a brick at the shop window.
. . . .

2 I heard someone. They broke down the door.
. . . .

3 I saw a young man. He was being attacked by several others.
. . . .

4 I observed a blue car. It was driving very fast towards the motorway.
. . . .

5 We heard something. People were shouting and screaming.
. . . .

6 I noticed a woman. She put two tins in her bag and left the store without paying.
. . . .
. . . .

219 Verb + object + participle

▶ Finder 125

Put one missing word in each sentence.

▶ I left your sister _sitting_ in an armchair in front of the television.

1 I wanted my hair . . . . short, I had decided.

2 Lots of people heard the bomb . . . .

3 I'm sorry if I . . . . you waiting.

4 We've . . . . a lot of money trying to make this place nice.

5 We could hear a burglar alarm . . . . in the next street.

6 Two men were caught . . . . to break into the bank.

7 Our teacher prefers the homework . . . . be saved to disk.

8 I found the vase . . . . to pieces in a corner of the room.

9 We watched the old factory . . . . knocked down.

10 The sports teacher . . . . us all doing exercises in the gym yesterday.

220 *Go swimming, do the washing, etc*

▶ Finder 124B

Rewrite the parts in **bold** type. Use *do* or *go* and an ing-form.

Hannah: I might **sunbathe for a bit** on the terrace.	▶ _do a bit of sunbathing_
Mark: Good idea? Coming, Amy?	
Amy: I need to **iron some clothes**.	1 . . . .
Mark: Amy, you're on holiday.	
Amy: Oh, all right. And I'd like to **swim** in the sea later.	2 . . . .
Mark: OK, we'll go out. I'll **drive**. I'll take you in my new car.	3 . . . .
Hannah: While we're out, we'd better **get something at the shop**. We haven't got much food.	4 . . . .
Mark: Well, we can eat out. We don't want to **cook much**, do we?	5 . . . .
Amy: No, I agree. And tomorrow I'd like to **sail somewhere in a boat**.	6 . . . .

221 Conjunction + participle

▶ Finder 126

Look at this information about a piece of computer software. Rewrite each participle clause as a finite clause.

▶ Although designed for all computers, the software may not run on older machines.
Although it has been designed for all computers, the software may not run on older machines.

1 When using this software, please be aware of the system requirements.
. . . ., please be aware of the system requirements.
2 Once opened, this product cannot be returned.
. . . ., it cannot be returned.
3 If found to be faulty, the product will be replaced.
. . . ., it will be replaced.

222 Participle clauses of time

▶ Finder 127

Put in the correct form of the verbs in brackets.

▶ . . _Having filled_ . . (fill) up with petrol, we continued our journey.

1 I broke a tooth . . . . (bite) on a nut.
2 Michael drove home from work, ... (achieve) nothing all day.
3 I just had to stand there . . . . (stare) at by all those people.
4 After . . . . (look) round the museum, we went back to our hotel.
5 Every single sandwich . . . . (eat), there was no food left.
6 The drugs entered the country . . . . (hide) in a container.
7 . . . . (search) the building, the police went away again.
8 . . . . (catch) sight of Adam across the street, she waved at him.

223 Participle clauses of reason

▶ Finder 128

Match the two parts and then rewrite the sentence using a participle.

▶ As I had been cheated out of all my money,	Simon had to ask for directions.
1 Because he didn't know his way around,	motorists have to make a long detour.
2 Since I had forgotten my watch,	~~I couldn't even pay the rent.~~
3 As she is recognized wherever she goes,	we've just had to stay indoors.
4 Because the weather is so awful,	the pop star always has a bodyguard.
5 As the road has been closed by the police,	I had no idea of the time.

▶ . . . _Having been cheated out of all my money, I couldn't even pay the rent._ . .
1 . . . .
2 . . . .
3 . . . .
4 . . . .
5 . . . .
. . . .

224 The use of participle clauses

Look at each participle clause. Does it express time, reason, result or a condition? Or is it comment on the sentence?

▶ Having lifted the receiver to her ear, Angela replaced it thoughtfully. ...*time*...

1 Generally speaking, people travel more in summer than in winter. . . . .
2 The computer crashed, destroying a whole afternoon's work. . . . .
3 Pulling up sharply, Tom leaped out of the car. . . . .
4 We were very hungry, not having eaten all day. . . . .
5 Done regularly, these exercises will improve your fitness and health. . . . .

225 Other participle clauses

▶ Finder 12

Rewrite the parts in **bold** type using a participle.

▶ Our neighbour fell off a ladder **and broke his arm.**
  Our neighbour fell off a ladder, ...*breaking his arm.*...
1 **In view of the effort we put in**, the rewards aren't very great.
  . . . ., the rewards aren't very great
2 The place was a mess. **Piles of papers were lying everywhere.**
  The place was a mess, ...
3 **If all is well**, we shall meet again next year.
  . . . ., we shall meet again next year.
4 **If you judge by Tom's attitude**, he isn't going to go along with our plans.
  . . . ., he isn't going to go along with our plans.
5 I knocked the milk over **and spilled it all over the floor.**
  I knocked the milk over, ...
6 **While we're on the subject of holidays**, when are you taking yours?
  . . . ., when are you taking yours?

226 Participles

▶ Finder 121–12

Write a second sentence so that it has a similar meaning to the previous one. Use the wor in brackets in a participle construction.

▶ If you use it properly, this gadget is quite effective. (used)
  ...*Used properly, this gadget is quite effective.*...

1 She lay in bed and worried all night. (worrying)

  . . . .
2 We've been invited to the wedding, so we've decided to go. (having)

  . . . .
3 If the weather is all right, we might go out. (permitting)

  . . . .
4 I didn't have much money, so I couldn't buy a ticket. (having)

  . . . .
5 It would be nice to have a ride somewhere. (riding)

  . . . .

114   224 • The use of participle clauses

6 The team that wins will be awarded the trophy. (winning)

. . . .

7 I waited hours, and then I was told to come back the next day. (having)

. . . .

8 In view of what's happened, I think you've been proved right. (considering)

. . . .

9 Never use a mobile phone and drive a car at the same time. (while)

. . . .

10 The stereo was blasting out rock music, so conversation was impossible. (with)

. . . .

227 Introduction to nouns   ▶ Finder 130A

Read the story and then write each noun in the correct place.

A motorist kept parking illegally because of his love for a traffic warden. An engineer called Brian fell for Susan after she gave him a ticket for leaving his car on a main road. The experience impressed him so much that he couldn't stop trying to attract her attention. The two are now good friends, but they will not say if their friendship is likely to lead to marriage.

1 Concrete nouns: *traffic,* . . . .
2 Roles: *motorist,* . . . .
3 Abstract nouns: *love,* . . . .
4 Names: . . . .

228 The plural of nouns   ▶ Finder 131

Complete each sentence. Put in the singular or plural form of a noun.

▶ The book is over 500 . . *pages* . . long.

1 A man went into the newsagent's and then came out again five . . . . later.
2 The waiter poured two . . . . of wine.
3 We played football, and I scored a . . . .
4 The school was closed, and all the . . . . were sent home.
5 I can't drive anywhere because my . . . . has been stolen.
6 I'm always busy during the week, but I usually have some spare time at . . . .
7 You can't buy anything here because there are no . . . . in the village.
8 There was only one . . . . still free, so I went and sat there.
9 Now you've heard what I've had to say, are there any . . . . you'd like to ask?
10 The winner got a gold medal, and the two . . . . got silver ones.

229 The possessive form

▶ Finder 132

Rewrite the phrases using a possessive form.

▶ the bag that belongs to Sarah   . . *Sarah's bag* . .
1 the name of the man   . . . .
2 the flat where my friends live   . . . .
3 a cat that belongs to someone   . . . .
4 the team that the women have formed . . . .
5 problems that students have   . . . .
6 the son of my father's friend   . . . .

230 Possessive form or *of*?

▶ Finder 133

Complete each sentence with the words in brackets. Use the possessive form or *of*.

▶ The car damaged . . *the woman's bike* . . (the bike/the woman)
▶ We live at . . *the end of the street* . . (the end/the street)

1 Can you tell me . . . . ? (the cost/a visa)
2 I can't find . . . ., and he needs feeding. (the food/the dog)
3 In the middle of the lawn lay . . . . (the football/the boys)
4 The police took . . . .
  (the names/everyone attending the meeting)
5 . . . . was broken when he fell. (the arm/Robert)
6 Those are . . . . (the lunch boxes/the workmen)
7 You get a good view from . . . . (the top/the tower)
8 Is this . . . . ? (the correct spelling/the word)

231 Some other uses of the possessive

▶ Finder 134

These sentences are correct, but you could make them a little shorter. Rewrite them using the possessive form.

▶ The shop sells clothes for children.
  . . *The shop sells children's clothes.* . .
1 The behaviour of your friends was disgraceful.
  . . . .
2 We are very grateful for the generosity of our sponsor.
  . . . .
3 The selection of the player for the national team was inevitable.
  . . . .
4 There's a changing room for women along the corridor.
  . . . .

5 The resignation of the minister surprised everyone.

. . . .

6 I prefer milk from a cow to milk from a goat.

. . . .

7 The popularity of the star will guarantee the success of the film.

. . . .

232 *Today's weather, at Sophie's*, etc ▶ Finder 135–136

Rewrite the phrases in **bold** using a possessive form.

▶ Were you at **the annual dinner last year**? . . *last year's annual dinner* . . .
▶ We're all going to meet **where Matthew lives**. . . *at Matthew's* . . . .

1 We're all looking forward to **the game on Saturday**. . . . .
2 I always enjoy **a day spent fishing**. . . . .
3 Do you know **the code word for this month**? . . . .
4 The article was in *Time Magazine* **last week**. . . . .
5 Over there is **where the Wilsons live**. . . . .
6 To put things right will be **the work of a whole week**. . . . .
7 There was **a silence of a few seconds**. . . . .

233 Countable and uncountable nouns ▶ Finder 137

Put one of these words into each sentence: *car*, ~~*chair*~~, *food*, *health*, *idea*, *photo*, *problem*, *town*, *violence*. Choose the correct form, e.g. *chair*, *a chair*, or *chairs*.

▶ If everyone wants to sit down, we'll need about fifty . . *chairs.* . .

1 If you're going to the supermarket, take plenty of money. . . . . is really expensive here.

2 There's no bus service. I can't get to work without . . . .·

3 Nothing ever runs smoothly in my job. There are always . . . .·

4 I can't stand all this fighting. I hate . . . .·

5 I love looking at . . . . They always bring back memories, don't they?

6 Gateshead is . . . . in the north-east of England.

7 I'm lucky that I've never been seriously ill. . . . . is important, isn't it?

8 I've got . . . .· It came to me suddenly while I was lying in bed.

234 Countable and uncountable nouns

▶ Finder 137E

Decide which is correct.

▶ I didn't have a camera, so I couldn't take . . *any photos.* . . .
a) any photo   b) any photos   c) photo

1 We don't use so . . . . electricity in summer.
a) much   b) many   c) great an
2 I think there's . . . . in the fridge.
a) a butter   b) some butter   c) some butters
3 The guests ate . . . . food. There was none left over.
a) many   b) every   c) all the
4 You've bought a lot of . . . .
a) banana   b) egg   c) water
5 I'm out of work. I'm looking for . . . .
a) job   b) a job   c) some job
6 There aren't . . . . cars on the road today.
a) every   b) many   c) much

235 The of-structure expressing quantity

▶ Finder 138

Write phrases with *of*.

▶ . . *a bottle of water* . . .
▶ . . *two kilos of flour* . . .

1 . . . .   2 . . . .
3 . . . .   4 . . . .
5 . . . .   6 . . . .

236 *Information, news,* etc

▶ Finder 139

Choose the correct form.

▶ Could you give me some information/~~informations~~, please?

1 I've been busy today, but I don't seem to have done much work/many works.
2 People had left litter/litters everywhere.
3 I've seen lots of advertisement/advertisements for this product.
4 There's very few/little traffic here in winter.
5 My baggage has/baggages have all been sent to Chicago.
6 The ground's wet, so we must have had a rain/a shower.
7 They're going to install several new machine/machines.
8 Let's hope we get a/some nice weather.
9 A lot of very valuable jewel was/jewels were stolen.
10 If you're going to climb a mountain, you'll need the right equipment/equipments.
11 I need an/some advice on what to do.
12 Have you got permission/a permission to use this computer?
13 There's a/some lovely scenery around here.
14 Scientists are doing research/a research into the problem.
15 The oil spillage from the tanker is bound to cause a lot of pollution/pollutions.

237 Nouns that can be either countable or uncountable

▶ Finder 140

Put one of these words in each sentence: *conversation, egg, experience, glass, iron, light, shame, sport, success.* Decide if you need to use *a/an* or not.

▶ Have you ever drunk tea from . . *a glass* . .?

1 Everyone enjoyed the party, so it must have been . . . .

2 When I woke the room was filled with . . . .

3 I'm not very athletic, and I don't like . . . . at all.

4 What's in this sandwich? Is it . . . .?

5 I'm looking forward to the fireworks. It would be . . . . to miss them.

6 To travel round the world really would be . . . .

7 I met the principal, and we had . . . . about the course.

8 The Celts were an ancient people who used . . . . to make tools.

238 Nouns that can be either countable or uncountable

► Finder 140

Some of these sentences have a mistake in them. Find the mistakes and write the sentences correctly.

a) My father runs small electrical business.
b) Can I have two coffee, please?
c) It's a pleasure to do business with you.
d) My brother is doing a course in business.
e) I ought to wash my hairs tonight.
f) I haven't heard the news, so I might buy a paper.
g) I was woken by sudden noise.
h) There was interesting painting on the wall.
i) I had a lot of difficulty getting a ticket.
j) All the men were wearing an evening dress.

►   *a) My father runs a small electrical business.*
1 ....
2 ....
3 ....
4 ....
5 ....

239 Two nouns together

► Finder 141A

What can you see in the pictures? Use these words.

ball	door	handle	~~shirt~~
bed	fish	helmet	tank
box	~~football~~	hospital	telephone
church	golf	safety	tower

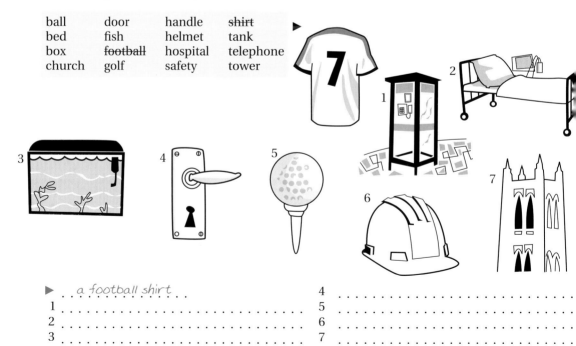

►   *a football shirt*   4 ....
1 ....   5 ....
2 ....   6 ....
3 ....   7 ....

▶ Finder 141–142

Write the phrase for each explanation.

▶ someone who plays tennis   *a tennis player* . . . .
▶ tea in the afternoon   *afternoon tea* . . . .

1 a door made of glass . . . .
2 a bill for electricity . . . .
3 a knife for cutting bread . . . .
4 the wall of a garden . . . .
5 shops in the centre of town . . . .
6 an exhibition of books . . . .
7 a machine that mixes concrete . . . .
8 a bottle for holding beer . . . .
9 an assistant in a shop . . . .
10 news about business . . . .
11 the figures relating to sales . . . .
12 a cooker that uses gas . . . .
13 a forecast of what the weather will be . . . .
14 a carton for holding yogurt . . . .
15 employees working in the steel industry . . . .

▶ Finder 143

Combine the information into one sentence. Use a phrase to modify a noun.

▶ That man is my boss. He's in the corner.
. . . *The man in the corner is my boss.* . . .

1 The restaurant is closing down. It's near our office.
. . . .

2 The discussion was very interesting. It was yesterday.
. . . .

3 A piece of rock fell down the cliff. It was the size of a football.
. . . .

4 Our holiday was wonderful. It was on the island of St Lucia.
. . . .

5 People will complain. Well, they will if they are aware of their rights.
. . . .

6 There's a photo. It's of the group. They were at a street market. The market was in France.
. . . .

7 My brother goes to a school. It's for young children. They have learning difficulties.
. . . .

Decide which answer is correct.

▶ I'm hoping to hear ..*some news*.. soon.
a) a new   b) a news   c) some new   d) some news

1 It's . . . . walk from here to the university.
a) hour   b) an hour   c) an hour's   d) an hours'
2 I need . . . . paper to write on.
a) a   b) a piece   c) piece of   d) a piece of
3 We climbed up the stairs to the . . . .
a) building's top   b) buildings' top   c) top of building   d) top of the building
4 I'm afraid I haven't got . . . .
a) much money   b) much moneys   c) many money   d) many moneys
5 A bookshelf is a . . . .
a) shelf full of books   b) shelf made of books   c) shelf for putting books on
d) book about shelves
6 Luckily there was . . . . in our hotel room
a) iron   b) an iron   c) some iron   d) some irons
7 Why shouldn't . . . . do as good a job as men do?
a) woman pilot   b) women pilot   c) woman pilots   d) women pilots
8 The horse has won lots of races. It's a champion . . . .
a) horserace   b) racehorse   c) horses race   d) races horse
9 The . . . . is his fighting spirit
a) player's strong   b) players' strong   c) player's strength   d) players' strength
10 Unfortunately we've made . . . .
a) little progress   b) little progresses   c) few progress   d) few progresses

243 Singular and plural subjects

Match the two parts of the sentence and join them together with *is* or *are*.

~~Art and music~~	... a wonderful city.
Two hours	... a play by Shakespeare.
Both my mother and my father	... now on the market.
Either blue or green	... going to be cut down.
Rome, my birthplace,	... quite tiring.
The trees next to the school	... the right colour for this room.
Walking up hills	... doctors.
The house, together with a piece of land,	... modern forms of communication.
Fax and e-mail	... ~~my favourite subjects~~.
Antony and Cleopatra	... a long time to have to wait.

▶ . .Art and music are my favourite subjects. . .

1 . . . .

2 . . . .

3 . . . .

4 . . . .

5 . . . .

6 . . . .

7 . . . .

8 . . . .

9 . . . .

244 *One of, a number of, every,* etc

▶ Finder 146

Choose the correct form.

▶ A lot of tourists ~~visits~~/visit Orlando.

1 Every new product has/have to be advertised.
2 Huge amounts of cocaine was/were found in the containers.
3 One of my sisters lives/live in Australia.
4 There was/were an explosion at the factory.
5 All the pictures is/are for sale.
6 Which countries uses/use the euro as their currency?
7 A number of computers has/have been stolen.
8 Everybody was/were asking me questions.
9 The number of violent crimes has/have gone up dramatically.
10 No message has/have been received.
11 Two thirds of my time goes/go on visiting customers.
12 Who thinks/think they know the answer?

243 • Singular and plural subjects   123

245 Nouns with and without -s

► Finder 147A

Write a sentence with a similar meaning. Use the word in brackets and decide if you need the -s ending or not.

► What is left of the old church is today a major tourist attraction. (remain/s)
   The remains of the old church are today a major tourist attraction.

1 What I was wearing wasn't right for the occasion. (clothe/s)

   . . . .

2 What the bump did to my car is going to cost £1,000 to repair. (damage/s)

   . . . .

3 What's in the parcel has to be listed on the form. (content/s of)

   . . . .

4 The things that belonged to me were stored in the cellar. (belonging/s)

   . . . .

5 What the article says is nothing new. (content/s of)

   . . . .

6 All the money I've saved is in the bank. (saving/s)

   . . . .

7 The flat is nice, but the area around it isn't very beautiful. (surrounding/s)

   . . . .

246 Nouns with a plural form

► Finder 147

Rewrite the sentences without *can, could, may*, or *might* and so make them more certain. The verb must agree with the subject.

► Physics could be really interesting.
   Physics is really interesting.
► Average earnings may be rising sharply.
   Average earnings are rising sharply.

1 Measles can be a serious illness.

   . . . .

2 The premises might be locked on a Sunday.

   . . . .

3 All means of transport can have disadvantages.

   . . . .

4 Statistics might be a useful subject.

   . . . .

5 The goods may already be on their way.

   . . . .

6 A new TV wildlife series may be coming soon.

   . . . .

7 Billiards might not be as much fun as snooker.

   . . . .

8 The statistics could be showing an increase in inflation.

   . . . .

9 The odds on our winning may not be very high.

   . . . .

247 Pair nouns

Complete the conversation. Put one word in each space.

Lisa: I must get a pair (►) . *of* . tights here. They've got my size.
Emily: You can't buy just one (1) . . . . There are three in a pack.
Lisa: Well, three (2) . . . . then. And I need (3) . . . . sunglasses.
Emily: Sunglasses (4) . . . . over there, look.
Lisa: OK, let's go and have a look.
Emily: Oh, there quite a few. What about (5) . . . .?
Lisa: Yes, I like (6) . . . . Thanks. And (7) . . . . fit all right. But I might
        get (8) . . . . cheaper pair somewhere else.
Emily: OK, but just a minute. I'm too hot in these trousers. I want to look for some
        (9) . . . . ·

248 Group nouns

Match the two sentence parts and complete the sentence with *is, are, has,* or *have*.
Sometimes there can be either a singular or a plural verb.

The navy	. . . arguing about how to cut the company's costs.
The management	. . . decided that the man is innocent.
The company's staff	. . . taking it in turns to go on shore.
The jury	. . . the most famous ever to play in this concert hall.
The team who won	. . . demanding more money to maintain its fleet.
The population	. . . taking their seats in the theatre.
The BBC	. . . all amateur players.
The crew of the ship	. . . worried about losing their jobs.
The orchestra	. . . showing the programme later this year.
The audience	. . . ninety per cent white.

► . . *The navy is demanding more money to maintain its fleet.* . . .
► . . *The management are arguing about how to cut the company's costs.* . .

1 . . . .

2 . . . .

3 . . . .

4 . . . .

5 . . . .

6 . . . .

7 . . . .

8 . . . .

249 Agreement

▶ Finder 144–14

Choose the correct form.

▶ 'The Red and the Green' is/are a novel by Iris Murdoch.

1 Who knows/know what might happen next?
2 The new boy band wants/want to make a name for themselves.
3 Someone was/were shouting and screaming.
4 A lot of TV programmes is/are complete rubbish.
5 I'll take a binocular/some binoculars with me.
6 Billiards doesn't/don't look a very exciting game.
7 My trousers looks/look absolutely filthy.
8 The police is/are investigating the incident.
9 The Prime Minister and his wife is/are in Paris.
10 Each setback just makes/make us even more determined to succeed.
11 The party which won the election intends/intend to increase welfare benefits.
12 I think congratulations is/are called for. Well done!

250 Agreement

▶ Finder 144–14

Some of these sentences have a mistake. Find the mistakes and write the sentences correctly

a) This coat need cleaning.
b) Maths is my favourite subject.
c) One of our students have gone missing.
d) I'm looking for a scissor.
e) A number of problems have arisen.
f) The roads were very busy.
g) The outskirts of the town is very dreary.
h) Everything seem to be OK.
i) The dog and the cat gets on well together.
j) The public are fed up with politicians.
k) The crossroads by the hospital is quite dangerou
l) 'War and Peace' are a very long book.

▶ _a) This coat needs cleaning._

1 ....
2 ....
3 ....
4 ....
5 ....
6 ....

251 The form of the articles

▶ Finder 15

These sentences are about new novels. Complete each sentence by putting in _a_ or _an_.

▶ _Home_ is about _an_ American Indian tribe driven off their land by _a_ mining company
1 _Black and White_ is about . . . . . artist who makes . . . . . complete mess of his life.
2 The novel _Moments of Danger_ is about . . . . . US president who disappears for . . . . . hou
3 _Big Money_ is about . . . . . business executive who makes . . . . . expensive mistake.
4 _House Party_ is a novel about . . . . . affair between . . . . . MP and his secretary.
5 The book _Two Lives_ is about . . . . . BBC reporter who becomes . . . . . secret agent.
6 _One Summer_ tells the story of . . . . . holiday which has . . . . . unusual ending.
7 _Ice_ is a novel about . . . . . SAS man who gets lost on . . . . . expedition to the South Pole
8 _Lesson in Death_ is about . . . . . university professor who murders . . . . . student.
9 _There and Back_ is about . . . . . old woman who goes on . . . . . one-year world trip.

Read each paragraph and write down the part that illustrates the rule.

▶ Richard was lying on a beach somewhere, far away from the crowds. The sun was beating down. He was completely relaxed. It was the most wonderful holiday he'd had for a long time.

We use *the* when there is only one in the context,
e.g. *The world was at war* or . . *The sun was beating down.* . . .

1 I went to the supermarket to get a pizza. I was only in there a few moments. When I got to the check-out, I discovered that my wallet was missing. It was an awful shock. I was sure I'd brought it with me.

We use *a/an* to describe something,
e.g. *It's a lovely day* or . . . .

2 I love books. My flat is full of books. They're everywhere. I spend hours reading them. I'd much rather read than watch television.

We can use a plural noun in a generalization, when we talk about things in general,
e.g. *Dogs make good pets* or . . . .

3 The town isn't as busy as it once was. The High Street looks sad and forgotten. The chemist's in Station Road has closed down. People don't come here to shop any more.

We use *the* before a noun when a phrase after the noun makes clear which one is meant,
e.g. *the car outside our house* or . . . .

4 The police advised Debbie to get a burglar alarm. So she rang a security company, and a man came and fixed the alarm. But a burglar alarm doesn't always behave as it should. Debbie's alarm started ringing for no reason. It was a real nuisance.

We can use *a/an* in a generalization, e.g. *A dog makes a good pet*
or . . . .

5 I stayed in a hotel not long ago. It was a very old building, deep in the English countryside. The weather was awful. But the hotel was really nice. And it had a ghost. The manager told me about it. I didn't believe her of course. But I saw the ghost. I really did. It was Lady Helen Graves, who died there three hundred years ago.

We use *a/an* when we first mention something, e.g. *I went to a concert last night*
or . . . .
or . . . .

We use *the* when we mention it again, e.g. *The concert was good*
or . . . .
or . . . .

253 The main uses of the articles

► Finder 152

Complete this story. Put in *a, an,* or *the*.

This is (►) _a_ true story. It's about (1) . . . . . politician. He was (2) . . . . . Member of Parliament (MP) in Britain. (3) . . . . . story happened back in the 1980s, and (4) . . . . . MP was called Richard Alexander. At that time, (5) . . . . . Irish Republican Army was conducting (6) . . . . . bombing campaign in Britain. A few days earlier, (7) . . . . . parcel bomb had been sent to (8) . . . . . government minister. So politicians were warned to be extra careful about opening parcels.

One day (9) . . . . . parcel was delivered to Mr Alexander's office at Retford, in (10) . . . . . English Midlands. (11) . . . . . MP thought he heard (12) . . . . . sound of (13) . . . . . ticking clock inside (14) . . . . . parcel, so thinking it might be (15) . . . . . bomb, he rang (16) . . . . local police station. Soon (17) . . . . . squad of army bomb specialists arrived at (18) . . . . . office and X-rayed (19) . . . . . parcel. They saw that what Mr Alexander could hear was indeed (20) . . . . . timing mechanism. Obviously, (21) . . . . . only safe thing to do was to blow it up, which they did. (22) . . . . . squad then pieced together (23) . . . . . contents of (24) . . . . . parcel. It had contained some pyjamas, (25) . . . . . toothbrush and (26) . . . . . small alarm clock. (27) . . . . . MP had recently stayed at (28) . . . . . hotel after making (29) . . . . . speech one evening, and (30) . . . . . hotel had kindly sent on his belongings after he had accidentally left them there. (31) . . . . . clock had been (32) . . . . . present from his wife.

254 The articles in generalizations

► Finder 153

Read this paragraph about holidays. Then look at each phrase in **bold type** and decide whether the meaning is general (e.g. about all holidays or a type of holiday) or specific (e.g. about one holiday or a number of holidays).

(1) **Holidays** are bad for you. I had (2) **a holiday** once. It was (3) **a self-catering holiday**. Perhaps that was (4) **a mistake**. Buying food and cooking on holiday is much more difficult than at home. And I had to live in (5) **a very small flat**. (6) **A self-catering holiday** isn't really a holiday at all. Everyone knows that when you get home from (7) **a holiday**, you need a few days off to recover from it. And (8) **the place** I went to wasn't as nice as it looked in (9) **the brochure**. That's another problem. You have to deal with that strange person, (10) **the travel agent**. And (11) **travel agents** don't speak the same language as the rest of us. I made (12) **the mistake** of believing what (13) **the travel agent** told me. I'm afraid the idea of (14) **a holiday** fills me with horror.

General meaning: (1) Holidays, ...
. . . .
Specific meaning: (2) a holiday, ...
. . . .
. . . .

255 The articles in generalizations

▶ Finder 153

Match the two parts of the sentence and write the noun with *a/an* or *the* or without an article.

▶ (Canoe) is	too much for food.
(Bad workman) blames	is called (saw).
Galileo invented	~~a kind of boat.~~
(Whale) are	(telescope).
(Mobile phone) has made	his tools.
A thing you cut wood with	life easier for many people.
(Consumer) is paying	huge animals.

▶ . *A canoe is a kind of boat.* . . .

1 . . . .
2 . . . .
3 . . . .
4 . . . .
5 . . . .
6 . . . .

256 The articles: some special uses

▶ Finder 154

Choose the correct form.

▶ How about a trip to ~~seaside~~/the seaside?

1 I usually go home on train/on the train.

2 Policeman/A policeman was knocking at the door.

3 My uncle plays violin/the violin in an orchestra.

4 Television/The television is a powerful medium.

5 I like cities. I'd hate to live in country/in the country.

6 There's something on radio/on the radio I want to listen to.

7 We've got television/a television, but it doesn't work.

8 Have you ever played billiards/the billiards?

9 I love going to theatre/the theatre.

10 I think we should phone police/the police.

Look at these pictures. They tell the story of Mike and Elaine and their new car.

1

2  3  4

5  6  7

Complete the story. The missing words may be *a, an, the,* or a noun.

1 One summer Mike and Elaine bought . . *a* . . new . . *car.* . . It was . . . .
   nicest . . . . they had ever had. They decided to go out in it for the day. They wanted
   to go to . . . . seaside. . . . . nice sunny day isn't something you should
   waste, they thought.

2 So they jumped in, and Elaine drove away. . . . . was shining, ... was
   blue, and . . . . countryside was beautiful. They looked at . . . . countryside
   and listened to . . . . radio.

3 Soon it was Mike's turn to drive. They decided to go to Seathorpe, which is . . . . nice
   little seaside town. When they got there, they found . . . . town busy with traffic. '
   hope there's . . . . here,' said Mike. But when they got to . . . .'
   it was full. So they decided to go somewhere else. '. . . . . are wonderfully convenient
   until you need to park them,' said Mike.

4 . . . . road they took out of Seathorpe went up . . . . steep hill. When they
   noticed . . . . sign saying 'Cliff-top car park', they parked near . . . . edge
   of . . . . cliff.

5 There was . . . . lovely view over . . . . English Channel. They stood and
   looked at . . . .

6 Suddenly . . . . started rolling towards . . . . edge of . . . . cliff
   Mike and Elaine watched in horror as it rolled over . . . . and onto . . . .
   rocks below. It was . . . . terrible moment.

7 They stood at . . . . top of . . . . and looked down at . . . .
   wreck below. Elaine spoke first.'Didn't you put . . . . on?' she asked.
   Soon . . . . police arrived and later they had to go home on . . . . bus.

258 *Twice a day*, etc

▶ Finder 155A

Alan Power is a top racing driver. Rewrite the sentences about him using a phrase with *a* or *an*.

▶ Alan is a Formula One driver. Every year he drives in sixteen Grand Prix races.

  He drives in sixteen Grand Prix races a year.

1 He's very rich. In a week he earns many thousands of pounds.

  . . . .

2 When he is overtaking, his heart beats very fast. In one minute it beats 150 times.

  . . . .

3 He has to be fit. Every week he trains five or six days.

  . . . .

4 He doesn't go to night clubs. Every night he sleeps eight hours.

  . . . .

5 He eats lots of pasta. Every day he has three good meals.

  . . . .

6 He talks to the media a lot. Every month he is interviewed several times.

  . . . .

259 *A* or *one*?

▶ Finder 156

Put in *a* or *one*.

▶ I can't pay in cash, but I can write . . *a* . . cheque.

▶ There's only . . *one* . . cheque left in the book.

1 You can take . . . . . small bag on the plane but not two.

2 In my left hand I was carrying . . . . . small bag with things I would need on the journey.

3 . . . . . or two of our house plants had died, but most of them looked OK.

4 You must come and see us . . . . . day.

5 There are seven of us. We'll need more than . . . . . car. Can you bring yours as well?

6 There's no public transport. You can't get there without . . . . . car.

7 Someone knocked . . . . . of the glasses off the table, and it broke.

8 . . . . . player in the team had blue shorts, but the others had white.

9 I saw Martin in town . . . . . afternoon last week.

10 At . . . . . time I was out of work for a whole year.

260 *A/an*, *some*, and a noun on its own ▶ Finder 157E

Some of these sentences have a mistake in them. Find the mistakes and write the sentences correctly.

a) Some strawberries are my favourite fruit.
b) Are these plates or saucers?
c) A mouse can bite through electrical wires.
d) These are some lovely photos, aren't they?
e) That animal is tiger not lion.

f) There's some coffee in this flask.
g) Chocolate is bad for a dog.
h) Is this some salt in here, or is it some pepp▸
i) This is horrible coffee.

▶ . *(a) Strawberries are my favourite fruit.* .

1 . . . .
2 . . . .
3 . . . .

261 *Sugar* or *the sugar*, *oil* or *the oil*, etc ▶ Finder 158A

Complete the conversations using the nouns in brackets. They are all plural or uncountable nouns. Decide if you need *the* before the noun.

▶ Adam: Hi, Leanne. How's *life* . (life)?
Leanne: Fine, thanks. Enjoying the party?
Adam: Yes. I've just been talking to a very strange woman. She was telling me about . *the life* . (life) she led in an earlier existence.

1 Mark: . . . . (computers) are wonderful things, aren't they?
Simon: Well, sometimes. . . . . (computers) that we have at work keep breaking down.

2 Kate: I need to put some oil in the car. They sell . . . . (oil) at the garage don't they?
Tim: Yes, but can't you use . . . . (oil) you bought at the weekend?
Kate: No, I didn't buy any in the end.

3 Gemma: . . . . (furniture) in your flat all looks so nice. . . . . (chairs) you've just got are lovely.
Sarah: Oh, thank you. But I can never find exactly what I want. I always hate buying . . . . (furniture).

4 Peter: I think . . . . (golf) is a boring game. . . . . (tennis) is much more exciting.
Kirsty: Oh, I don't know. . . . . (golf) I saw on television yesterday afternoon was quite exciting.

5 Robert: We could look round an art gallery. Do you like . . . . (art)?
Lucy: Yes, let's do that. I love looking at . . . . (pictures). I liked . . . . (pictures) you were showing me earlier.

6 Nicola: I expect you've heard . . . . (dogs) in the next house. They often bark all day. . . . . (noise) drives me mad sometimes.
Lauren: . . . . (dogs) can be a nuisance sometimes, can't they? I prefer . . . . (cats) in general.

262 Review of article uses

▶ Finder 152, 157, 158

Complete the story. Choose the correct words.

Not long ago I was staying in (▶) a/~~the~~ hotel in Toronto. It was (1) a/the big modern place. I don't normally like (2) big hotels/some big hotels, but I didn't know where else to stay. I was there for (3) a/the business meeting. On (4) a/the first evening after my flight from London, I sat in my room reading. I went to bed at about midnight. I could hear (5) some/the music coming from (6) a/the next room. I think it was (7) reggae music/the reggae music. It was quite loud, but I managed to go to sleep. (8) Noise/The noise usually keeps me awake, but I suppose I was tired after (9) a/the flight. Anyway, I slept. I woke up suddenly at ten to three, and (10) some/the music seemed louder than ever. It was becoming (11) a/the real problem. Should I bang on (12) a/the wall by my bed, or should I go to (13) a/the next room and ask (14) a/the person in there to turn (15) some/the music down? In the end I called reception, and soon (16) a/the man in uniform arrived. I explained (17) a/the problem. He walked to my bedside table and pressed (18) a/the button. There was silence. (19) Some/The music had been coming from my own radio, which must have been playing the whole time I had been in (20) a/the room.

263 A singular noun on its own

▶ Finder 159

Here are some rules about where we can use a singular noun on its own, without *a/an* or *the*.

  a before an institution: *go to **school***
  b in some phrases of time: *in **October***
  c where we repeat a noun, or where two nouns are in contrast: *set **side** by **side**, search from **top** to **bottom***
  d with *by* + means: *by **bus***
  e in many idioms: *for **sale***
  f when we talk about a job which is for one person only: *he was made **captain***
  g names of people: *Oh look, here's **Andrew**.*
  h to avoid repeating *a/an* or *the*: *a cup and **saucer**, the pen and **pencil***
  j in a written instruction: *Place **cup** here and press **button**.*

Look at each of these sentences and say which rule it illustrates.

  ▶ We crossed the river by **ferry**. . . *d* . .
  1 I hope you get there in **time**. . . . . .
  2 I'll see you on **Monday** then. . . . . .
  3 You'd better wear a shirt and **tie**. . . . . .
  4 The man spent a year in **prison**. . . . . .
  5 We travelled across America from **coast** to **coast**. . . . . .
  6 Car park: all cars stop here and take **ticket**. . . . . .
  7 I've invited **Jemima** to the party. . . . . .
  8 Your sister was elected **spokesperson**. . . . . .

264 A singular noun on its own

▶ Finder 160–162

Decide if you need *the* with the words in brackets.

▶ We have a cooked meal in .. *the evening* .. (evening).
▶ The leader of the gang went to .. *prison* .. (prison).

1 We live near . . . . (church) in the centre of the village.
2 It rained heavily during . . . . (night).
3 We moved here in . . . . (1995).
4 It's late. I'm going to . . . . (bed).
5 The phone rang at . . . . (midnight).
6 I met . . . . (Alex) in the park yesterday.
7 I usually get to . . . . (work) at ten to nine.
8 I spent all day in . . . . (office).
9 We went to Greece . . . . (last year).
10 . . . . (David) I'm talking about works at the supermarket.
11 There's usually a family reunion at . . . . (Easter).
12 I remember that . . . . (year) 2000 was an important one for us.
13 Tom had made all the arrangements . . . . (previous week).
14 Our children go to . . . . (new school).
15 We went on holiday with our friends, ... (Mitchells).
16 Jane was sitting on . . . . (bed) reading.
17 You can't possibly read in . . . . (dark).
18 We're going away for a few days in . . . . (September).
19 Are you religious? Do you go to . . . . (church)?
20 I've been to see . . . . (Doctor) Simpson.
21 We have . . . . (lunch) at one o'clock most days.
22 We haven't been here since . . . . (Christmas) just after we first met

265 Place names and *the*

▶ Finder 162A, 163

Paul has been to New York City, and Maria has been to London. What did they see?

Statue of Liberty – Brooklyn Bridge –
Ellis Island – Chinatown –
Rockefeller Centre – Macy's –
Fifth Avenue – Empire State Building –
Central Park

Westminster Abbey –
Houses of Parliament –
Buckingham Palace – Oxford Street –
Piccadilly Circus – British Museum –
River Thames – Kew Gardens –
Tower of London

1 Carl saw *the Statue of Liberty,* . . . .
. . . .
. . . .

2 Maria saw *Westminster Abbey,* . . . .
. . . .
. . . .

266 Review of the articles

▶ Finder 150–163

Choose the correct answer.

▶ I was listening to . . *the radio.* . . .
  a) radio   b) the radio

1 Everyone was coming home from . . . .·
  a) work   b) a work   c) the work

2 The man was arrested by . . . . FBI officer.
  a) a   b) an

3 We saw Liverpool play Arsenal. It was . . . . ·
  a) great game   b) a great game   c) the great game

4 When did you last go to . . . .?
  a) cinema   b) the cinema

5 . . . . Theatre isn't far from Waterloo Station.
  a) National   b) The National

6 A boy and a girl came into the room. . . . . had long hair.
  a) Boy   b) A boy   c) The boy

7 They say that . . . . is a man's best friend.
  a) a dog   b) all dog   c) dog

8 The rent is £200 . . . .·
  a) a week   b) the week   c) week

9 What are these things here? ~ They're . . . . ·
  a) computer disks   b) some computer disks

10 It was a photo of a house with a woman standing at . . . . front door.
  a) a   b) the

11 I usually leave the house straight after . . . . ·
  a) a breakfast   b) breakfast   c) the breakfast

12 . . . . makes the world go around.
  a) Love   b) The love

13 If you want, you can use . . . . . calculator in the exam.
  a) a   b) one

14 They searched the whole house . . . . by . . . .·
  a) a room   b) room   c) rooms   d) the room

267 Review of the articles

Complete the conversation. Use *a, an* or *the* with the words in brackets, or use the words on their own.

Louise:	Are you going back to (►) . . *the office* . .(office) now? Could you give me a lift, please?
Tom:	Sure, no problem.
Louise:	I'm afraid I've been disqualified from driving. It's (1) . . . . (terrible nuisance).
Tom:	Oh, what happened?
Louise:	I was caught speeding. It was in (2) . . . . (August) on (3) . . . . (M6) motorway near (4) . . . . (Birmingham). I was in (5) . . . . (hurry). I was late for (6) . . . .(work).
Tom:	Didn't that happen to you once before?
Louise:	Yes, it was (7) . . . . (same place) as before.
Tom:	Did (8) . . . . (police) stop you?
Louise:	No, there was (9) . . . . (speed camera). I didn't realize it at the time. But (10) . . . . (camera) took a photo of me. I got (11) . . . . (letter) (12) . . . . (following week). It said I'd been driving at 95 miles (13) . . . . (hour).
Tom:	So did you have to appear in (14) . . . . (court)?
Louise:	No, I didn't. There was nothing I could say, really. But I can't drive now. I have to travel by (15) . . . . (bus). (16) . . . . (bus) I got this morning was twenty minutes late. And I can't drive again until (17) . . . . (next year). That's (18) . . . . (life), I guess.

268 Possessive adjectives

► Finder 164A–B

Complete these paragraphs from Louise's letter to her friend Sophie. Put in the possessive adjectives.

Last week we had a visit from Jeremy's sister Debbie and (►) . . *her* . . husband Mike and the children Katie and Connor. Our son Joseph was pleased to see (1) . . . . cousins, and they all seemed to be having the best time of (2) . . . . lives together.

More excitement yesterday. One of the school buildings had part of (3) . . . . roof blown off in the storm. So Joseph is at home. I had to ring (4) . . . . boss and arrange to work at home.

What are (5) . . . . plans for the summer? Would you like to come and visit us and see (6) . . . . new house? We'd love to see you.

269 Possessive pronouns
► Finder 164A–B

Complete the conversation. Put in a possessive pronoun instead of the phrase in brackets.

Oliver: I think I need a new computer.
Linda: Really? But you haven't had (►) . . <u>yours</u> . . (your computer) as long as I've had
          (1) . . . . (my computer). What's wrong with it, anyway?
Oliver: Nothing really. I just like to have the latest model. Simon has just bought a new one,
          and I don't want one that's older than (2) . . . . (his computer).
Linda: What we need is a new car. I think (3) . . . . (our car) is the oldest on the
          street.
Oliver: OK, we'll get a car first if you like. Actually we really need one each.
Linda: Paul and Sarah's new car looks very sporty. I don't know what make it is, but I'd quite
          like one like (4) . . . . (their car).
Oliver: You want a sports car? What on earth for?
Linda: I just want one like Paul and Sarah's. It looks good. Maybe I'd like an understanding
          partner like (5) . . . . (her partner) too.

270 Possessives
► Finder 164

Choose the correct form.

►   Our team colours are red and ~~their~~/theirs are blue.

1 Those people over there are friends of <u>ours</u>/<u>us</u>.
2 One soldier was wounded in <u>his</u>/<u>the</u> leg.
3 Your camera is a much better one than <u>mine</u>/<u>my</u>.
4 David wants to do a project <u>his own</u>/<u>for his own</u>/<u>of his own</u>.
5 The girl had a red ribbon in <u>her</u>/<u>the</u> hair.
6 Is this <u>your</u>/<u>yours</u>/<u>your's</u> coat?
7 All the victims were shot in <u>the</u>/<u>their</u> back.
8 My brother is always interfering in things that are no business of <u>him</u>/<u>his</u>.
9 I saw the whole thing happen with <u>mine own</u>/<u>my own</u>/<u>the own</u> eyes.

271 Demonstratives
► Finder 165A

Write the sentences. Choose the right words from the box below and add a phrase with
this, that, these, or *those.*

… don't look very comfortable.
Did you take …?
… is complete rubbish.
~~I wonder what's on the other side of~~ …
Who's left … there?

►   . . <u>I wonder what's on the other side of those gates.</u> . .

1 . . . .
2 . . . .
3 . . . .
4 . . . .

272 Demonstratives

▶ Finder 16!

Put in *this*, *that*, *these*, or *those*.

▶ I like . . *this* . . picture here. ~ Yes, it's good, but . . *that* . . one over there is my favourite

1 . . . . sunshine is a nice change, isn't it?
   ~ Yes, but I don't like the look of . . . . dark clouds over there.

2 I've just realized that . . . . socks I'm wearing don't match.
   ~ Oh, ... doesn't matter. No one will notice.

3 I'm free today, so how about a game of tennis . . . . afternoon?
   ~ Sorry, I can't. I'm very busy . . . . week. I might be OK for the weekend.

4 Do you remember . . . . very strange girlfriend Steve had at one time?
   ~ Yes, I do. And . . . . very colourful clothes she wore.

5 Oh, here's something interesting. Listen to . . . . There's going to be a Robbie
   Williams concert on the eighteenth of next month.
   ~ Oh, I think . . . . might be the weekend I'm away.

6 My grandmother is always talking about the good old days. Her favourite saying is
   ' . . . . were the days.'
   ~ And I suppose nothing is any good . . . . days.

7 . . . . is a nice place. I like it here.
   ~ It says in the guidebook that the landscape is similar to . . . . of the Alps.
   ~ Well, I suppose it is.

8 Hello. . . . . is Alice. Can I speak to Marcus, please?
   ~ Sorry, he's out. He'll be back later . . . . evening.

9 Look what I've got here. Robert has just brought me . . . .
   ~ Oh, what lovely flowers.
   ~ Yes, aren't they? I'll put them in . . . . new vase we bought last week. I think it'
   in the dining-room.

10 I think we should reward companies which obey the law and punish . . . . whicl
   cause a lot of pollution.
   ~ Well, no one could argue with . . . .

273 Large and small quantities

▶ Finder 166

Decide which answer is correct.

▶ I can't go out tonight. I have . . *some* . . work to do.
  a) any   b) bit   c) several   d) some

1 I know this place. I've been here a . . . . times before.
  a) bit   b) few   c) little   d) several
2 There are . . . . casinos in Las Vegas. They're everywhere you look.
  a) lots   b) much   c) numerous   d) several
3 Planes are big polluters. They cause a . . . . of pollution.
  a) considerable lot   b) great deal   c) large deal   d) small amount
4 There's been a . . . . of rain but not very much.
  a) bit   b) few   c) little   d) lot
5 It's very peaceful on the island because there are . . . . cars.
  a) any   b) many   c) much   d) no
6 It'll cost us a certain . . . . of money, but it won't be a lot.
  a) amount   b) deal   c) few   d) number
7 There are a . . . . of bugs in the program. I'm surprised there are so many.
  a) big deal   b) large amount   c) large number   d) little bit

274 *A lot of, many, much, a few, a little, and a bit of*

▶ Finder 167

Write a second sentence so that it has a similar meaning to the previous one. Use the word in brackets.

▶ We had very little time to prepare. (much)
  . . *We didn't have very much time to prepare.* . . .

1 I drank a little tea. (bit)
  . . . .
2 Many families have only got one car. (lot)
  . . . .
3 There are few unspoilt areas left. (many)
  . . . .
4 There's hardly any time to relax. (little)
  . . . .
5 I bought several things in town. (few)
  . . . .
6 There are such a lot of things to do. (so)
  . . . .
7 There hasn't been much interest in the scheme. (little)
  . . . .
8 We eat more sugar than we should. (too)
  . . . .

275 *A lot of, many, much, a few, a little,* and *a bit of*

► Finder 16

Put the words in the right order to form a sensible statement.

► Oh, not another commercial break. (are/commercials/many/there/too)
There are too many commercials.

1 The place is just a short drive away. (a/few/it's/miles/only)

. . . .

2 James is very popular. (a/friends/has/he/lot/of)

. . . .

3 You're too generous, you know. (faults/few/it's/of/one/your)

. . . .

4 It's a very complicated soap opera. (a/are/characters/great/many/there)

. . . .

5 The new machines are fine. (few/had/problems/them/very/we've/with)

. . . .

6 Come on, don't spoil the party. (a/bit/could/enthusiasm/little/of/show/you)

. . . .

276 Whole and part quantities

► Finder 16

Read the sentences and answer the questions about them.

► 'There are curtains at every window.'
How many windows are without curtains: none, several, or all of them?
. . *None.* . . .

1 'Not many of my friends are interested in football.'
How many football fans are there among my friends: none, a few, or a lot?

. . . .

2 'We haven't painted the whole flat, but we've done most of it.'
How much of the flat have they painted: less than half, more than half, or all of it?

. . . .

3 'Part of the wall was damaged when a car crashed into it.'
How much of the wall has to be rebuilt: some of it, most of it, or all of it?

. . . .

4 Sam tells us a lot of stories - amusing things that have happened to him and his friends.
~ Yes, but a lot of the stories he tells aren't true. He just makes them up.
Which quantity is greater here: a lot of stories, or a lot of the stories?

. . . .

277 *All*, *most*, *half*, *none*, and *whole*

▶ Finder 169

Some of these sentences are correct, and some have a word which should not be there. If a sentence is correct, put a tick (✓). If it is incorrect, cross the unnecessary word out of the sentence and write it in the space.

▶ Most of my clothes are out of fashion.   . . ✓ . .

▶ These plates are all ~~of~~ dirty.   . . *of* . .

1 I'll have to spend the whole of day on revision.   . . . .
2 None of our maps showed the new motorway.   . . . .
3 All of matter is made of atoms.   . . . .
4 The most people would agree with you.   . . . .
5 He fired four shots and all of them missed.   . . . .
6 Most the villages have a pub.   . . . .
7 More than half of the houses in the street are for sale.   . . . .
8 I've been playing golf all of afternoon.   . . . .
9 I baked a cake, but we've eaten it of all.   . . . .

278 *All*, *most*, *none*, *both*, *either*, and *neither*

▶ Finder 169–170

Read the text and then complete the sentences below using phrases like *all of them, most of them*, etc.

WHERE TO STAY IN MIDCASTER

It is not difficult to find accommodation in Midcaster. The town has about a dozen hotels, the majority of which are in the centre of town. The two best known are in Castle Street. They are the 16th century Bridge Hotel and the 17th century Crossways Hotel. Both of them are fairly small and lack a car park, and in summer they are completely taken over by visitors from the US, so it is unlikely you will find a room available. But Midcaster also has a number of bed and breakfast establishments, which are without exception clean and comfortable and reasonably priced. These guest houses are mostly located in the outlying parts of the town.

▶ Midcaster has a number of hotels. . . *Most of them* . . are located in the town centre.

1 The Bridge Hotel and the Crossways Hotel are in Castle Street. . . . . are centuries old.
2 The two hotels are both famous, but . . . . is very big.
3 Both hotels are in the centre of Midcaster, and . . . . has a car park.
4 The two famous old hotels attract a lot of tourists. . . . . are popular with Americans.
5 Both hotels will be fully booked for the summer, so you probably won't be able to get a room in . . . .
6 There are also bed and breakfast places in Midcaster. . . . . are clean and comfortable.
7 There is a wide choice of bed and breakfast establishments, and . . . . are very expensive.
8 A guest house may not be convenient because . . . . are outside the centre.

279 *Both, either,* and *neither*

▶ Finder 170

What might you say in these situations? Begin each sentence with *both, either,* or *neither*

▶ After a long walk you had blisters on your foot. The other foot was just as bad.
. . *Both my feet had blisters on them.* . . .

1 You have two cameras, but they don't work.

. . . .

2 There are two candidates for a job. The first candidate would be an excellent choice, and so would the second.

. . . .

3 A car with two passengers in it was involved in an accident. The driver escaped without injury, but the other two people were injured.

. . . .

4 You have two brothers. Peter hasn't sent you a birthday card, and nor has Steve.

. . . .

5 You have just seen a game of football. The result was a draw. United were happy with the result, and so were the other team.

. . . .

6 You and your friend have to choose between two empty tables in a café. One would be OK but then so would the other.

. . . .

280 *Every* and *each*

▶ Finder 171

Some of these sentences have a mistake in them. Find the mistakes and write the sentences correctly.

a) The witnesses every gave their evidence.
b) Almost every student passed the exam.
c) At the airport every passenger are searched.
d) I enjoyed every single minute of the holiday.
e) Every of the pages has a number.
f) The Olympics are each four years.
g) Each house is different from the others
h) Each of the states has its own governor.
i) I ring my girlfriend almost each day.
j) There was a path on every side of the canal.
k) There's a train every hour in each direction.
l) Each of the photos hasn't come out properly.

▶ . . *a) The witnesses each gave their evidence.* . . .

1 . . . .
2 . . . .
3 . . . .
4 . . . .
5 . . . .
6 . . . .

281 Some, any, and no

▶ Finder 172

Complete the conversation. Put in *some, any,* or *no.*

Anita: I need to get the bus, and I haven't got (▶) . . *any* . . money.
Oliver: I can lend you (1) . . . . money. Here's a tenner.
Anita: I can't keep borrowing money from you.
Oliver: It's (2) . . . . problem. Don't worry.
Anita: I'll pay you back (3) . . . . time.
Oliver: (4) . . . . time will do. There's (5) . . . . hurry.
Anita: You lent me twenty pounds last week, so that's thirty I owe you. Look, I'll try to pay
         (6) . . . . of it back by the weekend.
Oliver: That's fine.
Anita: Thanks very much, Oliver. I never seem to have (7) . . . . money when I
         need it.
Oliver: Don't worry about it.
Anita: Well, I'd better go. The bus will be coming (8) . . . . minute.

282 Some, any, and no

▶ Finder 172

Choose the correct answer.

▶ Let's go in this shop and buy some/~~any~~ postcards.
1 The bookshop will order some/any book that's in print.
2 It was very quiet. There were hardly some/any/no people on the streets.
3 I was asleep. I didn't hear something/anything.
4 I've heard of Iris Murdoch, but I haven't read some/any of her books.
5 I want to sit somewhere quiet where there's any/no music.
6 I'm afraid we haven't got some/any milk.
7 Please keep this area tidy. Leave any/no litter.
8 When I opened the box, I found that some/any of the eggs were broken.
9 It's perfectly simple. Someone/Anyone could understand it.
10 Would you like some/any chocolate? Go on, it really is delicious.
11 I can't remember when it was, but we met before at some/any party or other.
12 We trust you will be satisfied with the service you receive from us, but some/any complaints
   should be made in writing to our head office.

283 Enough, plenty of, and too many/much

▶ Finder 173A–B

Write a sentence about each situation. Use *enough, plenty of, too many,* or *too much.*

▶ The team needs 45 points to qualify, and it has 47.
  The team has enough points to qualify.
  . . . .

1 I took two bags on to the plane, and you're only supposed to take one.

. . . .
2 There are twenty-five people here, and we've got exactly twenty-five chairs.

. . . .

3 We bought enough food for twenty people, and only nine people came.

. . . .

4 I only needed twelve votes, and I got twenty-two.

. . . .

5 It takes half an hour to walk to the cinema, and the film starts in twenty-five minutes.

. . . .

284 *Another, some more*, etc ▶ Finder 173C–E

Put in *another, other, others, some more,* or *any more*.

▶ That was great. Let's have . . *another* . . game, shall we?
1 We took a bus into town, and there were only two . . . . people on the bus.
2 My sides are aching. I just don't want to hear . . . . jokes.
3 I've been in this country a year, and I'm allowed to stay for . . . . six months.
4 Two people were taken to hospital, and the . . . . were treated at the scene of the accident.
5 I'll get . . . . sweets. We've eaten nearly all these.
6 OK, I'll be quiet. I won't say . . . . word.
7 I want to see the world, but my parents have . . . . plans for me.
8 I'll move my seat forward and give you . . . . room in the back there.
9 Only half the players were training. The . . . . were resting.

285 Quantifiers without a noun ▶ Finder 174

Split each sentence into two shorter ones. Begin the second sentence with a quantifier on its own.

▶ Some of the ten car parks in the town are free.
The town has . . *ten car parks. Some are free.* . .

1 Three of the five men arrested were later released.
The police arrested . . . .
2 None of the twelve new hi-fi systems we tested was completely satisfactory.
We tested . . . .
3 Few of the hundreds of job adverts I've looked at seem promising.
I've looked at . . . .
4 Plenty of the dozens of cafés we looked into had free tables.
We looked into . . . .
5 Each of the several phone boxes we passed had been vandalized.
We passed . . . .
6 Many of the fans disappointed by the result were actually crying.
The fans felt . . . .
7 Lots of the tickets have been sold already, and they have only recently been available.
Tickets have only recently . . . .
8 Most computer manuals are incomprehensible to me, which is why I never read them.
I never read . . . .

286 Quantifiers

▶ Finder 166–174

Put each word in brackets in the correct place.

▶ We need *some* more memory for the computer. (some)

1 The story was an invention from start to finish. (whole)

2 More than half the pupils were ill. (of)

3 I've got a lot of work at the moment. (quite)

4 We had our photo taken. (each)

5 I might sell this car and buy another. (one)

6 We fell ill not long after the meal. (both)

7 We've had a deal of trouble with these products. (great)

8 Rick lives in a beautiful flat, and he owns two flats. (other)

287 Quantifiers

▶ Finder 166–174

Contradict what is said by using a different quantifier.

▶ We haven't got much time.
  Yes, we have. *We've got lots of time.*

1 We need some help.
  We're OK. . . . .
2 All these sweaters are nice.
  No, they aren't. . . . .
3 A lot of the information is new.
  I think you'll find . . . .
4 I haven't got many videos.
  What do you mean? . . . .
5 You're hiding something.
  What do you mean? . . . .
6 Each one of these four signatures is genuine.
  I'm afraid you're wrong. . . . .
7 Both the sisters studied art.
  I don't think so. . . . .
8 I've bought too much paint.
  Just the two cans? . . . .

288 Quantifiers

Write a second sentence so that it has a similar meaning. Use the word in brackets.

▶ Much discussion has taken place. (deal)
   A great deal of discussion has taken place.

1 More than half of the island is forest. (most)

. . . .

2 We're staying in, but the rest of the people are going clubbing. (others)

. . . .

3 I had to make a few phone calls. (small)

. . . .

4 There's very little food in the house. (hardly)

. . . .

5 We don't watch very much television. (little)

. . . .

6 Some garages stay open late, but many don't. (lot)

. . . .

7 Those two boxes are damaged. (both)

. . . .

8 I write my diary every day without fail. (single)

. . . .

9 Not everyone likes heavy metal. (some)

. . . .

10 It doesn't matter which day next week – it'll be OK by me. (any)

. . . .

289 Personal pronouns

Put in the personal pronouns.

Are (▶) . *you* . in control of your mobile phone? Is (1) . . . . your friend or your enemy? Mobile phones were supposed to make our lives easier. But maybe (2) . . . . have just made (3) . . . . more complicated and stressful. When 26-year-old Andy Barton was interrupted by his mobile phone for the fourth time in fifteen minutes, a sudden rage came over (4) . . . . , and (5) . . . . threw (6) . . . . against a wall. 'The phone broke and (7) . . . . felt really happy,' (8) . . . . said. 'The thing was becoming a nuisance to (9) . . . . My wife has thrown her phone away too, and (10) . . . . thinks life is much nicer without (11) . . . . Our phone bills are lower because (12) . . . . make fewer calls. Mobile phones had made slaves of (13) . . . . It sounds crazy, but I can assure (14) . . . . it's true.'

290 Personal pronouns

▶ Finder 175–176

Say what each pronoun means.

Gemma: Do **you** think Karen fancies Simon?
Anita: I don't know. What makes **you** think that?
Gemma: Just the way **she** looks at **him** sometimes.
Anita: But **he**'s such an idiot.
Gemma: I saw **them** together at lunch time yesterday.
Anita: Well, **you** never know. Maybe **you**'re right. **They** say love is blind, don't they?
Gemma: I don't know why **we**'re still sitting here gossiping. **It**'s two o'clock.

▶ you = *Anita* . . . .
1 I = ...
2 you = ...
3 she = ...
4 him = ...
5 he = ...
6 them = ...

7 you = ...
8 you = ...
9 they = ...
10 I = ...
11 we = ...
12 it = ...

291 Personal pronouns

▶ Finder 175–176

Put in the pronouns.

▶ Have . . *you* . . seen Paul recently? ~ Yes, I saw . . *him* . . yesterday at the club.

1 Who's taken the glasses that were on the table. ~ . . . . I put . . . . in the kitchen.
2 . . . .'s very difficult to cross this road. ~ Yes, ...'re right. . . . . think . . . . should put a crossing here. That's my opinion. anyway.
3 Are these bottles really worth recycling? ~ Yes, of course . . . . are. . . . .'re all responsible for the state of the planet, don't forget.
4 . . . .'s one o'clock in the morning. And . . . . have to get up at six. ~ Well, no wonder you're tired. Remember what . . . . say: . . . . can't burn the candle at both ends.
5 Has Mrs Wilson decided who the new supervisor is going to be? And will . . . . be a man or a woman? ~ No, ... hasn't decided yet. But whoever the successful applicant is, ... will be starting on Monday.

292 Noun or pronoun?

▶ Finder 175E

Look at each phrase in italics and decide if it should be replaced with a pronoun. If so, cross it out and write the pronoun. If not, put a tick. (This is a matter of good style rather than correct grammar. Sometimes it is possible to use either a noun or a pronoun.)

Back in the 1970s Bill Gates and Paul Allen were at high school in Seattle. (▶) *Bill and Paul* . . ✓ . . were great friends, and (▶) *Bill and Paul* . . *they* . . were both interested in computers and in writing programs for (1) *computers* . . . . In 1975 the first personal computer came on the market, a very primitive machine by today's standards. At this time

(2) *Bill* . . . . was at Harvard, and (3) *Paul* . . . . had a job. (4) *Bill and Paul* . . . . immediately decided that (5) *Bill and Paul* . . . . would write software for the computer. The owner of the computer company was a man called Ed Roberts. (6) *Paul* . . . . phoned (7) *Ed* . . . . and told (8) *Ed* . . . . that (9) *Bill and Paul* . . . . could offer (10) *Ed* . . . . some software. (11) *Bill and Paul* . . . . then wrote the program in a big hurry. (12) *Ed* . . . . invited (13) *Bill and Paul* . . . . to visit his company in Albuquerque, New Mexico. But (14) *Bill and Paul* . . . . didn't have enough money for two plane tickets, so (15) *Paul* . . . . flew there on his own and met (16) *Ed* . . . . When (17) *Paul* . . . . loaded the software into the computer, it worked. (18) *Ed* . . . . was impressed. (19) *Ed* . . . . immediately agreed that the two men should work on software for the computer, and (20) *Bill* . . . . flew to New Mexico to join (21) *Paul* . . . . Soon (22) *Bill* . . . . gave up college and (23) *Paul* . . . . gave up his job, and (24) *Bill and Paul* . . . . started their own software company. Later (25) *the software company* . . . . became the most famous software company in the world.

293 Reflexive and emphatic pronouns ▶ Finder 177A–B, E–F

Put in the reflexive or emphatic pronouns. Then write 'R' for 'reflexive' or 'E' for 'emphatic' in the brackets.

▶ Sit down, Lisa. Make . . *yourself* . . at home. (. . R . .)

1 Laura couldn't stop . . . . from bursting out laughing. (. . . . .)

2 The candidates . . . . are allowed to vote in the election. (. . . . .)

3 The company has given . . . . a new name. (. . . . .)

4 My father once met President Reagan . . . . (. . . . .)

5 I don't eat meat, ... (. . . . .)

6 We now find . . . . in a rather difficult situation. (. . . . .)

7 I'm depressed, but I'm not going to throw . . . . off a bridge. (. . . . .)

8 Could you all arrange . . . . in a circle, please? (. . . . .)

9 Lucy designed the website . . . . (. . . . .)

10 The new pupils will have to familiarize . . . . with the school routine. (. . . . .)

11 My friend Tom regards . . . . as God's gift to women. (. . . . .)

12 The pop festival is five miles away and not actually in Glastonbury . . . . (. . . . .)

Write a second sentence so that it has a similar meaning. Use the word or words in brackets. Sometimes you also need to use a reflexive pronoun.

▶ I can't bring to mind the man's name. (remember)
   I can't remember the man's name.
▶ The men ought to be able to get their own meals ready. (cook/for)
   The men ought to be able to cook for themselves.

1 Have a good time, all of you. (enjoy)
   . . . .
2 Tim will never trust Oliver again, and Oliver will never trust Tim again. (other)
   . . . .
3 You've got water all over you, Emma. (made/wet)
   . . . .
4 Why don't you just sit down and have a rest? (relax)
   . . . .
5 Sam was getting on Joanna's nerves, and she was getting on his. (each)
   . . . .
6 I hope my brother is going to act sensibly. (behave)
   . . . .
7 Families cross the border to visit other families. (another)
   . . . .
8 The students ought to produce their own ideas. (think/for)
   . . . .
9 I often ask myself where I'll be in ten years' time. (wonder)
   . . . .
10 It's dangerous for a woman to travel alone in some areas. (by)
   . . . .
11 All the atoms interact one with another. (each)
   . . . .
12 I haven't got enough money for a holiday. (afford)
   . . . .

295 Preposition + pronoun ▶ Finder 177C

Put in the correct personal or reflexive pronoun, e.g. *me* or *myself*. The pronoun refers back to the subject.

▶ Unfortunately Leanne didn't have any money on . *her.* .

1 Why are you looking so pleased with . . . . ?
2 I always carry my identity card with . . . .
3 While we were having lunch, a famous TV presenter came and sat near . . . .
4 Before the police could arrest him, the gunman turned the gun on . . . .
5 Peter has a very responsible job. There are sixty people working under . . . .
6 If we're honest with . . . . , we must admit we've made a big mistake.

296 Personal pronouns, possessives, and reflexives

► Finder 178

Put in the missing words. Use *we, you, his, ours, themselves,* etc.

Dear Debbie,

How are (►) . *you* . ? Lisa and (1) . . . . are having a marvellous holiday.
(2) . . . .'re really enjoying (3) . . . . The beach is great. We've also been on
several trips and enjoyed (4) . . . . all. Already (5) . . . .'s only a week before
(6) . . . . flight back home.

There's been one problem. Lisa lost (7) . . . . purse. She was very worried and annoyed
with (8) . . . . for not being more careful. Luckily one of the waiters found
(9) . . . . in the restaurant and gave (10) . . . . back to (11) . . . .
Lisa was lucky. (12) . . . . could easily have kept the purse for (13) . . . . So
(14) . . . . gave (15) . . . . a big tip. Now she's promised to take more care of
(16) . . . . things. I'm keeping a careful eye on (17) . . . ., too, because I can't
afford to lose it.

I hope you and Andrew enjoy (18) . . . . next week and that (19) . . . .
holiday is as good as (20) . . . .

Love, Karen

297 *One* and *ones*

► Finder 179A, C

Answer each question using *one* or *ones*.

► Two bags are both the same size. One is full of cardboard and the other is full of coins. Which one is heavier?
. . *The one full of coins.* . . .

1 A fair-haired man is six feet tall. He is talking to a dark-haired man who is 1.8 metres. Which man is taller?

. . . .

2 In England a woman in a tracksuit is doing the high jump. On the moon a woman in a spacesuit is also doing the high jump. They are both equally fit. Which of them can jump higher?

. . . .

3 A lorry has four small tyres at the front and four large tyres at the back. If all eight tyres are the same quality, which will wear out first?

. . . .

4 You're holding two balloons. One is full of air, and the other is full of helium. If you let them go, which will rise the quickest.

. . . .

One, ones, some, it, and *them*   ► Finder 179

Decide if the sentences are correct or not. If they are correct, put a tick (✓). Sometimes there is a word missing from the second sentence. If so, put a cross (X). Rewrite the sentence putting in *one, ones, some, it,* or *them.*

► There are lots of parks in London. Hyde Park is perhaps the most famous. . .✓. .
► I need an umbrella. I know I've got somewhere. . .X. .
1 I'd love to buy a yacht. I'm thinking of buying. . . . . .
2 We haven't got any water. I ought to have brought. . . . . .
3 Snowflakes have beautiful patterns. Each is slightly different from the others. . . . . .
4 These shoes are all nice. I can't decide which to buy. . . . . .
5 I've lost my bag. I left on the train. . . . . .
6 This bus is going to Bristol. The to Cardiff has already left. . . . . .
7 I like all these posters. But this is the best. . . . . .
8 I wrote several letters yesterday. I haven't posted yet. . . . . .
9 These biscuits are nice. Could I have another, please? . . . . .
10 Yes, we do sell radios. There are over there. . . . . .
11 I've got lots of blue shirts. I think every is in the wash at the moment. . . . . .
12 I'm working on several different projects at the moment. There are some quite interesting. . . . . .

(►) I know I've got one somewhere. . . . .

. . . .
. . . .
. . . .
. . . .
. . . .
. . . .
. . . .
. . . .
. . . .

Everyone, something, etc   ► Finder 180A–E

Put in a word like *everyone, something,* etc.

James: Is (►) . . *everyone* . . here? Are we all ready?
Louise: There are only fourteen people here, not fifteen, so (1) . . . . is missing.
Nicola: It's Gary. Has (2) . . . . seen Gary?
Rick: I've already asked. (3) . . . . has seen him
           (4) . . . . I'm afraid he's (5) . . . . to be found.
Nicola: Well, he must be (6) . . . .
Adam: It's OK. He's just rung me on his mobile. He'll be here in ten minutes. He just had
           (7) . . . . to do first.
James: OK, let's get (8) . . . . loaded into the trailer, and then we'll
           be ready. And make sure all your stuff goes in. We don't want to leave
           (9) . . . . behind.

300 *Everyone, something*, etc

▶ Finder 180

Rewrite the sentences replacing the phrase in italics. Use a *everyone, something*, etc.

▶ New supermarkets are sometimes opened by *a famous person*.
.. *New supermarkets are sometimes opened by someone famous.* ..

1 The doctors are doing *all things* possible for your friend.

. . . .

2 There's *another thing* I wanted to tell you.

. . . .

3 Let's find *a place which is quiet*.

. . . .

4 During the World Cup we saw hardly *any people* on the streets.

. . . .

5 *One person's* mobile phone rang during the performance.

. . . .

6 *No unusual event* has happened during the last week.

. . . .

7 I wouldn't do a favour like this for *any other person*.

. . . .

8 I've looked *in all the places* I can think of for that computer disk.

. . . .

9 *The luggage of all the people* had to be weighed.

. . . .

301 Pronouns

▶ Finder 175–180

Decide which answer is correct.

▶ These shoes are no good. .. *They* .. let in water.
a) He   b) It   c) Them   d) They

1 We had an unexpected guest. . . . . Susan.
a) It was   b) She was   c) They were

2 We're the same size. We can wear . . . . clothes.
a) each other's   b) one other's   c) ourselves   d) the other's

3 . . . . happened to our friend.
a) Awful something has   b) Something awful has   c) Something awful have

4 Do you need thick paper or . . . .?
a) the thin one   b) thin   c) thin one   d) thin ones

5 Is this a portrait of your sister? It doesn't look much like . . . .
a) her   b) hers   c) herself   d) she

6 You know what . . . . A job begun is a job half done.
a) it says   b) one says   c) they say   d) you say

7 We simply intend to . . . . and do nothing.
a) relax   b) relax ourselves   c) relax us

8 This hotel is much better than . . . . we stayed in last year.
  a) a one   b) one   c) the   d) the one

9 I thought I recognized the man standing next to . . . .
  a) I   b) me   c) my   d) myself

10 It doesn't matter if someone is male or female, ... should be accepted as a member.
  a) he   b) it   c) she   d) they

302 Introduction to adjectives

▶ Finder 181

Read this short article.

HEDGEHOGS

The hedgehog is a wonderful creature. It has spines on its back and coarse hair underneath. The spines are quite sharp, but you can pick a hedgehog up if you're careful. The animal has short legs and small eyes and ears. The hedgehog is a nocturnal animal. It hides during the day and hunts for food at night, using its powerful sense of smell and hearing. It is busiest at nightfall and at daybreak. It will eat a wide variety of insects, worms, birds' eggs, and even rats or mice.

Hedgehogs build their nests of grass in a hedge or perhaps an old rabbit hole. When young hedgehogs are born, they are blind and have soft hair which soon grows into spines. The animals sleep through the winter. Their main natural enemies are foxes and badgers. Many hedgehogs are killed by cars because their traditional defence – rolling up into a ball – is completely useless in such a situation.

1 Underline all the adjectives you can find in the article. There are eighteen.
2 Which adjective expresses the writer's opinion about hedgehogs?

. . . .
3 Which adjective classifies the hedgehog as an animal that is active at night?

. . . .
4 Find two adjectives together and write down the noun phrase which contains them.

. . . .
5 Find two adjectives which each have an adverb of degree in front of them. Write down each adverb + adjective combination.

. . . .
. . . .
6 Which adjective has a superlative ending?

. . . .
7 There are seven other words which have endings showing that they are adjectives. Write down the seven words.

. . . .
. . . .

303 The position of adjectives

▶ Finder 18?

Find the right place for the word in brackets.

▶ We all had a *marvellous* ⋏ time. (marvellous)

1 On the whole I thought Gulftown was a place. (nice)

2 Our apartment by the water was really. (big)

3 The weather was much better than. (usual)

4 We were only a distance from the beach. (short)

5 The view from our balcony was absolutely. (magnificent)

6 If I'd like to go there again some time. (possible)

7 People could swim in the sea because it was so. (warm)

8 Although, the holiday was definitely worth it. (expensive)

304 Adjectives used in one position only

▶ Finder 18?

Choose the correct word.

▶ The Sales Manager is a ~~glad~~/happy/~~pleased~~ man today.

1 Our headquarters are very central/inner.
2 There are two very alike/similar products in competition.
3 The receptionist gave us an ashamed/embarrassed smile.
4 The question of cost is chief/primary/principal.
5 It's obvious that fine/healthy/well employees work better than sick ones.
6 Every business needs content/pleased/satisfied customers.
7 Our control of the market is mere/sole/total.
8 The boss is a live/a living/an alive legend in the business world.
9 The financier's disgrace was complete/sheer/utter.

305 Adjectives after nouns

▶ Finder 184A

Express the meaning more briefly by putting the adjective after the first noun.

▶ People can win a lot of money if they're good at quizzes.
. . *People good at quizzes can earn a lot of money.* . .

1 A bus came down the hill. It was full of passengers.
. . . .

2 The men have been sent to prison. They are guilty of robbery.
. . . .

3 People shouldn't climb the tower if they're nervous of heights.

. . . .

4 Some visitors were in the café. They were tired of looking round the museum.

. . . .

5 Substances should be banned from food if they are harmful to our health.

. . . .

306 Adjectives after nouns and pronouns ▶ Finder 184C–D

Put in the two words in brackets in the correct order.

▶ I think you've made a .. *responsible decision.* .. (decision, responsible)

1 There is no news at the . . . . (time, present)
2 I've never met . . . . (anyone, famous)
3 You have to read some . . . . before you can run the program. (instructions, involved)
4 There was a plan to build a leisure centre, but the . . . . has gone bankrupt. (company, concerned)
5 There were only a handful of . . . . at the reception. (people, present)
6 Let's do . . . . for a change. (something, different)
7 The police will find the . . . . for these crimes. (man, responsible)
8 They have interviewed all the . . . . in the affair. (people, involved)

307 The order of adjectives ▶ Finder 185A–D

Look at the information and write a brief description of each product.

▶ It's a towel, you use it after a bath, it's green, and it's large.
.. *It's a large green bath towel.* ..

1 It's an alarm, it's inexpensive, and it detects smoke.

. . . .

2 It's a chair, it's aluminium, it's for the garden, and it's stylish.

. . . .

3 It's a mirror, it's circular, it's small, and it goes on the wall.

. . . .

4 It's a kind of bag, it's blue, it's made of polyester, and it's for sleeping in.

. . . .

5 It's a cupboard, it's large, it's for storage, and it's wood-effect.

. . . .

6 It's a hat, it's American, it's for a cowboy, and it's traditional.

. . . .

7 It's a radiator, it's electric, it's oil-filled, and it's two-kilowatt.

. . . .

8 It's a bed, it's folding, it's for a guest, and it's useful.

. . . .

9 It's a workstation, it's for a computer, it's light grey, and it's new.

. . . .

308 Two adjectives together

▶ Finder 185E–

Decide if each sentence is correct or not. Put a tick or a cross.

▶ an awkward, clumsy boy (. . ✓ . .)
▶ a blue, yellow bird (. . X . .)
1 a longer but quicker route (. . . . .)
2 an important and industrial area (. . . . .)
3 red, white shirts (. . . . .)
4 a troublesome, unpopular person (. . . . .)
5 an unpopular, troublesome person (. . . . .)
6 a troublesome and unpopular person (. . . . .)
7 a troublesome but unpopular person (. . . . .)

309 Gradable and ungradable adjectives

▶ Finder 18

Choose the correct word.

▶ The tour was ~~absolutely~~/very interesting.
▶ These instructions are totally/~~very~~ incomprehensible.

1 The meal was totally/very nice.
2 It's absolutely/very essential we don't tell anyone.
3 These scissors are extremely/totally useless.
4 The news was a bit/absolutely surprising.
5 Julie wore a completely/very silly costume.
6 The rumour was completely/very false.
7 It was an absolutely/a very dreadful game.
8 Your writing is a bit/completely difficult to read.

310 *Amusing* and *amused*, *interesting* and *interested*

▶ Finder 18

Complete the conversation. Write a word ending in *-ing* or *-ed* in each space.

Mark: So how did you and Emma get on in New Zealand?
Laura: It was great. We were(▶) . . amazed . . (amaze) how much sport you can do there
          There are lots of extreme sports.
Mark: What was the most (▶) . . exciting . . (excite) thing you did?
Laura: Skydiving. We were (1) . . . . (thrill) to do that. It was
          (2) . . . . (amaze).
Mark: Weren't you nervous?
Laura: Yes, of course. We were quite (3) . . . . (frighten). In fact w
          were (4) . . . . (terrify). But when you're doing it, it's just
          great. Actually, bungee jumping is more (5) . . . . (frighter
          than skydiving.
Mark: You did bungee jumping, too?
Laura: Yes, just once. But it was a bit (6) . . . . (disappoint). It's
          over so quickly.

Mark: And did you travel around the country?

Laura: Yes, we went to both islands. We did lots of (7) . . . . (interest) walks.

Mark: And are you (8) . . . . (please) to be back?

Laura: No, not really. I'm (9) . . . . (depress) about going back to work. Life suddenly seems so (10) . . . . (bore).

311 *The poor, the disabled*, etc

▶ Finder 188

Rewrite the phrases in italics. Begin with *the, a,* or *some* and decide if you need a word like *people, man, woman,* or *thing*. Make sure your phrase would fit the context.

▶ There are special TV programmes for *people who can't hear.*
. . *the deaf* . .

▶ *A man with no home* was sitting on the pavement begging.
. . *a homeless man* . .

1 *Those out of work* receive welfare benefits from the state.

. . . .

2 A good rule in life is always to expect *what you don't expect.*

. . . .

3 *The woman who died* has not yet been identified.

. . . .

4 *Disabled people in general* are becoming more militant and demanding their rights.

. . . .

5 *What was good* about the situation was that the airline paid us £100 to go on a later flight.

. . . .

6 *A group of people who are disabled* attended the meeting yesterday.

. . . .

7 *People who are old* are greatly respected in many parts of the world.

. . . .

8 I can do lots of things, but I can't do *what isn't possible.*

. . . .

9 *A man of advanced years* was knocked down while crossing the road.

. . . .

10 Why are you so interested in *things that can't be explained*?

. . . .

11 Are there special colleges for *people who can't see*?

. . . .

12 *What was really strange* was that the place seemed familiar even though I'd never been there before.

. . . .

13 What can be done for *people who have nowhere to live*?

. . . .

14 *Rich people* are often less generous with their money than *poor people.*

. . . .

312 Review of adjectives

▶ Finder 181–18

Some of these sentences have a mistake in them. Find the mistakes and write the sentences correctly.

a) The work we do is very tired
b) I couldn't find anything of nice in the shops.
c) Those stories are mere fantasy.
d) The nights are very colds.
e) The strong has a duty to care for the weak.
f) I had the same as usual for lunch.
g) The view was very magnificent.
h) I was shocked to see how ill my father looked.
i) I've got a good at tennis brother.
j) The child leads a rather alone existence.
k) It was a Japanese digital expensive camera.
l) The tower was tall and imposing.
m) The good is that we all get on well together.

▶   *a) The work we do is very tiring.*

1 ....
2 ....
3 ....
4 ....
5 ....
6 ....
7 ....
8 ....

313 Introduction to adverbials

▶ Finder 189A–

Read each sentence and write down the adverbial. Say if it is an adverb, a prepositiona phrase, or a noun phrase.

▶ You deliberately failed the test, didn't you?   *deliberately, adverb*

1 Suddenly I felt very tired. ....
2 I haven't worked for six months. ....
3 I'll be on holiday next week. ....
4 I removed the wrapping paper carefully. ....
5 Everyone put their coats on the bed. ....
6 The patient will soon recover. ....
7 You've been playing computer games all afternoon. ....

Write down the sentence where the adverbial cannot be left out.

8 ....

314 Mid position

▶ Finder 190C–E

Write the sentence and include the adverb. It should come in mid position or, if necessary, after the subject.

▶ I'm making progress. (slowly)
  I'm slowly making progress.

▶ Tom hasn't got any money. (probably)
  Tom probably hasn't got any money.

1 I watch quiz shows. (never)

. . . .

2 Someone has been telling me the news. (just)

. . . .

3 I have to work late. (usually)

. . . .

4 I don't get up so early. (always)

. . . .

5 We have moved house. (recently)

. . . .

6 You'll definitely pass the exam, but I won't. (probably)

. . . .

7 The bus is a few minutes late. (usually)

. . . .

8 But I do have a day off. (seldom)

. . . .

9 We're getting ready to go out. (just)

. . . .

10 I've been checking all these figures. (carefully)

. . . .

315 Adverbials and the object

▶ Finder 190F

Decide if each sentence is correct or not. If it is correct, put a tick (✓). If the word order is wrong, put a cross (✗) and write the sentence correctly below.

▶ You didn't shut down the computer properly. ✓
▶ The reporter asked a number of very searching questions politely. ✗

1 We're going to buy soon a new car.
2 The instruments could measure accurately the exact position of the ship.
3 You've been reading that book for ages.
4 I'll have finished in a week my course.
5 As a child I watched eagerly every single episode of that long-running soap opera.
6 I was studying all the sources of information I had found closely.
7 I enjoyed the party very much.
8 Joanna fastened securely the rope.

  (▶) *The reporter asked politely a number of very searching questions.*

. . . .

. . . .

. . . .

. . . .

. . . .

316 Order of adverbials in end position

Complete the sentences. Put the words and phrases in the correct order.

▶ We did it .. *easily at the second attempt.* .. (at the second attempt, easily)

1 Your brother played . . . . (in yesterday's game, well
2 I get to work . . . . (early, most days
3 I hope you'll visit us . . . . (here, soon
4 We're going . . . . (to a barbecue, tomorrow
5 I've just stopped . . . . (actually, at a café
6 My sister slept . . . . (soundly, the whole time
7 Mark does tend to act . . . . (sometimes, thoughtlessly
8 The bus leaves . . . . (most days, on time, surprisingly

317 Adverb forms
▶ Finder 192A–C

Look at each adjective (in **bold type**) and put in an adverb.

▶ There was a **steep** hill. I remember that the road climbed very .. *steeply.* ..

1 The fans were **happy**.
~ They were certainly smiling . . . .
2 They say snow is **likely**.
~ That's right. It'll . . . . snow tomorrow morning.
3 This isn't going to be a **long** visit. I won't stay . . . .
4 The rise in crime has been **dramatic**. Violent crime especially is
rising . . . .
5 Jeans aren't **suitable** for a wedding.
~ Well, I suppose I'll have to be . . . . dressed.
6 The balloon was **high** in the sky. It floated . . . . above
the countryside.
7 There are some **lovely** singers in the choir.
~ Yes, they sing absolutely . . . . , don't they?

318 Adverb forms
▶ Finder 192E–C

Complete this newspaper article. Choose the correct form.

Five years ago, Julia Pitman had a good job with the Ensure finance company. Today she is trying
(▶) hard/~~hardly~~ to build a new life after a long battle in the courts with her former employers
When Julia realised that Ensure was cheating its customers, she reported it to the authorities and
to a (1) day/daily newspaper. She was sacked from her job, and she took the company to court
The result was a financial scandal which was (2) high/highly embarrassing for Ensure. Now that
Julia has won her case, she can at last talk (3) free/freely about the company and about her
experience of the world of finance.

Julia is still the (4) good-looking/well-looking, (5) good-dressed/well-dressed young woman that
she was five years ago, but things have not been easy for her. Just (6) late/lately she hasn't been
(7) good/well, and she looks tired. 'It was a struggle,' she told me. 'Sometimes it (8) hard/hardl

seemed worth going on because everyone was against me. Several times I (9) near/nearly gave up. What angered me (10) most/mostly of all was that the authorities weren't interested in what I was telling them, even though I was uncovering criminal behaviour.'

You can read the first part of Julia's story in the *Sunday Informer* next week.

319 Adjectives and adverbs

▶ Finder 193A

Sarah and Lisa are in the park when Sarah says she feels unwell. Complete their conversation. Put in an adjective or an adverb form.

Sarah: I must sit down on this seat for a minute.
Lisa: Are you OK, Sarah? You look rather (▶) _pale_ (pale).
Sarah: I think I'm OK. I (▶) _suddenly_ (sudden) had this (1) . . . . (strange) feeling. It happened so (2) . . . . (quick). One moment I was (3) . . . . (fine), and then I felt (4) . . . . (dizzy).
Lisa: You seem to be breathing quite (5) . . . . (heavy). I think you'd better sit (6) . . . . (quiet) for a few minutes. And maybe I should ring for an ambulance.
Sarah: Oh no. It's very (7) . . . . (thoughtful) of you, Lisa, but I'm OK.
Lisa: Well, I think you should see a doctor (8) . . . . (immediate).
Sarah: No, let's just walk (9) . . . . (slow) back to the main road, and I'll get a taxi.
Lisa: Well, if you're sure.

320 Adverbials of manner

▶ Finder 193B–C

Complete each sentence so that it has the same meaning as the previous one.

▶ We hurriedly packed our suitcases.
  We packed our suitcases _in a_ hurry.

1 The business is not being run efficiently.
  The business is not being run . . . . manner.

2 I followed the instructions very carefully.
  I followed the instructions . . . . care.

3 I think we should organize things differently.
  I think we should organize things . . . . way.

4 The students worked silently.
  The students worked . . . . silence.

5 The woman greeted us unsmilingly.
  The woman greeted us . . . . smile.

321 Adverbials of time

Write the second part of each sentence with one of these adverbs in mid position: *finally*, *immediately*, *just*, *now*, *soon*, ~~*then*~~.

▶ The customer put the goods in her bag, and she walked out of the store.
. . . . .*She then walked out of the store.*. . . .

1 I'm feeling overworked, but I'll be on holiday.

. . . .

2 The photos must be here somewhere because I've been looking at them.

. . . .

3 I've been thinking about the offer for a long time, and I've made up my mind.

. . . .

4 My sister used to play tennis, but she spends all her time on the golf course.

. . . .

5 I saw smoke coming from the building, so I rang the fire brigade.

. . . .

322 Adverbials of time

Put in these words: *after*, *afterwards*, *already*, *any longer*, *far*, *long*, *no longer*, *still*, *yet*. Some of the words have to be used more than once.

▶ Richard: I've been here an hour, and I'm . . *still* . . waiting to see the doctor.
  Adam: Well, you haven't been waiting as . . *long* . . as some of the other patients.

1 Emma: Have you bought your ticket for the concert . . . .?
  Alice: No, not . . . .
  Emma: Well, don't leave it too . . . . They're going pretty fast. Most of them have . . . . been sold.

2 Mark: That nightclub we went to last year . . . . exists. In fact the building has been knocked down.
  Phil: It's only a few hours since I've been back, but I've . . . . noticed quite a few changes . . . . only a year away.

3 Leanne: I just can't live in that awful place . . . . It really gets on my nerves.
  Paul: So you . . . . haven't solved all the problems with your flatmates.
  Leanne: Not really. It's OK having meals together. We've done that right from the start. But we're . . . . having regular arguments about who washes up . . . . And anyway, I don't like living so . . . . from the city centre.

323 Adverbials of frequency

▶ Finder 195A–C

Put in an adverb which expresses the frequency. The adverb should go in mid position (or after the subject if necessary).

▶ Medium frequency: The postman leaves a parcel on the doorstep.
   The postman sometimes leaves a parcel on the doorstep.

1 Low frequency: The old man goes out of the house.
....

2 Full frequency: I'm pleased to see you.
....

3 Almost full frequency: We go into town on the bus.
....

4 Medium frequency: You can get nice things really cheap in the market.
....

5 High frequency: I've stayed late at the office.
....

6 Zero frequency: The work I do is boring.
....

7 Low frequency: We see policemen on the streets.
....

8 Medium frequency: The program doesn't work properly.
....

324 Adverbials of frequency

▶ Finder 195B–F

Combine the information in one sentence. Decide if the adverbial goes in mid position or end position.

▶ Steve: I lock the car. Always.
   Steve *always locks the car.*
▶ Debbie: I go to the gym. Twice a week I go there.
   Debbie *goes to the gym twice a week.*

1 Lucy: I buy a newspaper. Every day I get one.
   Lucy ....

2 Mark: I don't go to the theatre. Well, I seldom go.
   Mark ....

3 Adam: I've thought about emigrating. Often.
   Adam ....

4 Kate: In the evening I cook a meal. Well, most evenings I do.
   Kate ....

5 Alice: I won't get married. That'll never happen.
   Alice ....

325 Adverbs of degree

▶ Finder 196A–[

Put one of the adverbs in brackets into the second sentence.

▶ The flat has one disadvantage. Our neighbours are noisy. (much/very)
  Our neighbours are very noisy.

1 The two photos aren't identical. But they're similar. (fairly/hardly)
  . . . .

2 This is important to me. It matters. (a lot/extremely)
  . . . .

3 I don't like the other posters at all. This one is the best. (completely/easily)
  . . . .

4 Oliver shouted and swore at everyone. He behaved impolitely. (a bit/extremely)
  . . . .

5 I'm not quite sure if you're right. I'm convinced by your arguments. (completely/half)
  . . . .

6 Is the story true? Are you running a dating agency? (quite/really)
  . . . .

7 Our teacher is quite young. He isn't old. (slightly/very)
  . . . .

8 My new job is great. I feel happier now. (much/very)
  . . . .

9 The party was great. We enjoyed it. (nearly/very much)
  . . . .

10 I feel quite warm. I'm not cold. (at all/fairly)
  . . . .

11 I'm glad I met your friend. She's nice. (rather/slightly)
  . . . .

12 What's so good about this new version? Is it better than the old one? (any/some)
  . . . .

326 Modifying a quantifier

▶ Finder 196F

Write a sentence with the same meaning. Use the word in brackets.

▶ I saw a very small number of people. (few)
  I saw very few people.

1 I've spent a rather large amount of money. (lot)
  . . . .

2 I'll need considerably more information. (lot)
  . . . .

3 There's very little time left. (hardly)
  . . . .

4 You've eaten all the sweets except one or two. (almost)
  . . . .

5 You've made too great a number of mistakes. (many)
  . . . .

6 I wish those people wouldn't make quite so much noise. (little)
  . . . .

327 *Too* and *enough*

▶ Finder 196G

Comment on each situation using *too* or *enough* and the word in brackets.

▶ The project will never get off the ground because of the very high cost. (expensive)
  . . . *The project is too expensive.* . . .
▶ We can't hold the meeting in this room. We wouldn't all fit in here. (big)
  . . *The room isn't big enough.* . .

1 Gemma can't go to university because of her poor exam results. (good)
  . . . .
2 The software won't run on this computer. It hasn't got the necessary power. (powerful)
  . . . .
3 The bus drivers are on strike because their wages are below a reasonable level. (low)
  . . . .
4 No one plays the game because no one can understand the rules. (complicated)
  . . . .
5 I can't read Paul's note. His writing is illegible. (clearly)
  . . . .
6 The car was involved in an accident because its speed was excessive. (fast)
  . . . .

328 Adverbs of degree and *a/an*

▶ Finder 196H

Put the words into the correct order and form a statement.

▶ The holiday was OK. (a / good / quite / time / we had)
  . . *We had quite a good time.* . . .
▶ I feel terrible. (a / I've had / rather / shock)
  . . *I've had rather a shock.* . .
1 Mark and I didn't agree. (an / argument / I had / quite / with him)
  . . . .
2 I like Judy very much. (a / nice / personality / she's got / such)
  . . . .
3 Sam says some crazy things sometimes. (a / an / bit / he's / idiot / of)
  . . . .
4 I can't park here. (a / small / space / there's / too)
  . . . .
5 I think we can win. (a / fairly / strong / team / we've got)
  . . . .
6 I can't answer that. (a / difficult / it's / question / rather)
  . . . .
7 The work will take a long time, you know. (a / big / it's / job / quite)
  . . . .
8 No wonder we're tired. (a / long / quite / way / we've walked)
  . . . .
9 It's great to see you again. (a / for / I haven't seen / long / such / time / you)
  . . . .
10 You can draw brilliantly. (a / as / as that / drawing / good / I couldn't do)
  . . . .

329 *Quite* and *rather*

▶ Finder 197

Answer the questions about these sentences.

1 The water was quite cold but not absolutely freezing cold.
   Does *quite* mean 'fairly' or 'absolutely'? . . . .

2 I don't like these new jackets. I think they look . . . . silly.
   Put in the word which is more likely here, *quite* or *rather*.

3 Before I went on the roller-coaster, I felt quite nervous.
   Does *quite* mean 'fairly' or 'extremely'? . . . .

4 Riding on the roller-coaster was quite terrifying.
   Does *quite* mean 'fairly' or 'absolutely'? . . . .

5 I don't like Oasis. ~ Oh, I quite like them.
   Does *quite* mean 'to some extent' or 'very much'? . . . .

6 We're going to move into the new building, but it's not quite ready yet.
   What does *not quite* mean here? . . . .

7 The exhibition sounds quite interesting. I'd love to see it.
   Which word has greater stress, *quite* or *interesting*? . . . .

330 *Only* and *even*

▶ Finder 198

Decide if the second sentence is correct or not. If it is correct, put a tick (✓). If it is incorrect, put a cross (X) and write the sentence correctly.

▶ I haven't seen my brother for ages. I only see him about once a year. (. . ✓ . .)
▶ Lots of horses fell. Three of them only finished the race. (. . X . .)

1 I'm not really familiar with this camera yet. I've just only bought it. (. . . . .)
2 I've looked everywhere for that letter. I've even emptied the dustbin. (. . . . .)
3 It's a very short holiday. Only I'll be away for a week. (. . . . .)
4 Slavery involved everyone. Only young children were forced to work. (. . . . .)
5 The operation is quite simple. It takes only a few minutes. (. . . . .)
6 Official notice. These seats are only for members. (. . . . .)
7 The machine has broken down again. And it was repaired even last week. (. . . . .)

   (▶) *Only three of them finished the race.*
   . . . .
   . . . .
   . . . .
   . . . .
   . . . .

331 Viewpoint, truth, and comment adverbials

▶ Finder 199–201

Put in a single-word adverb which means the same as the words in brackets.

▶ . . Clearly . ., (It's clear that) these figures are inaccurate.

1 I don't like Tom's new girlfriend much, ... (to be frank)
2 . . . . (I presume) there will be refreshments.
3 I can't help you, ... (I'm afraid).
4 . . . . (It's lucky) I've brought my phone with me.
5 . . . ., (From a cultural point of view) this place is a desert.
6 . . . ., (It could be that) it's just a rumour.
7 Do you think young people are becoming more aware . . . .?
  (of political issues)
8 . . . ., (There's no doubt that) things will be different in future.
9 . . . . (It was stupid of me, but) I told the caller my password.

332 Linking adverbials

▶ Finder 202B

Put in these words or phrases: *after all, consequently, firstly, for example, in addition, in other words, nevertheless, secondly*.

▶ The insurance company say that the payment is subject to delay. . . In other words . .,
  they're going to take a while to pay me.

1 There is lots of new building in the capital. A new government headquarters is being
  constructed, ...

2 All the staff have been put on short-term contracts, and . . . . they
  have no job security.

3 This new venture would be a big risk for us. . . . ., I believe we
  should take that risk.

4 Unemployment has risen . . . . because of the economic recession
  and . . . . because of the large number of school leavers looking
  for work.

5 You should know something about business. . . . ., you did
  business studies at university.

6 The airport authorities plan to extend the existing runway, and . . . .
  they want to build a completely new one.

Each of these sentences is incorrect. Complete the correct sentence.

▶ I don't sometimes go to bed at all.
    . . . . I sometimes don't go to bed at all. . .

1 The cable runs deeply under the ground.
The cable . . . .

2 I haven't still received the letter.
. . . . the letter.

3 I've received for two whole days no e-mails.
. . . . no e-mails.

4 I've had a so awful day.
I've had . . . .

5 At my surprise, I found the room empty.
. . . . empty.

6 We're all in the pub meeting later.
We're . . . .

7 Tom is very tall, but Mark is further taller.
Tom is . . . .

8 The situation is becoming more dangerously.
The situation . . . .

9 I saw definitely that man at the scene of the crime.
. . . . of the crime.

10 Everyone stared amazedly.
Everyone . . . .

11 I hope much that you are successful.
I hope . . . .

12 I haven't never been to Los Angeles.
. . . . Los Angeles.

13 The man is disabled, and adding to that he's got a heart condition.
The man is . . . .

14 The visit to the museum was somewhat interesting.
. . . . interesting.

334 Introduction to the comparison of adjectives

▶ Finder 203A–B

Read these two paragraphs and write down all the comparative and superlative adjectives.

GOLD AND COPPER

Gold is much softer than copper, so it is easier to hammer into shape. It is not very strong. A gold knife might look very fine, but it would not have been much use for skinning a bear, so from early times gold became the metal for ornaments. Copper is much harder; it would have been much more difficult for early man to shape, but the finished article was more durable.

(from L. Aitchison *The Story of Metals*)

MIDTOWN MANHATTAN

Midtown Manhattan, which ranges roughly from 34th to 59th Streets and river to river, is a center of superlatives. The biggest buildings, ... brightest lights, greatest concentration of big business, largest complex of theaters and concert houses, best bargain basements, most exclusive couture houses, and the most specialized services are all here.

(from *Fodor's Budget Travel in America*)

1 Comparative adjectives: *softer,* . . . .
2 Superlative adjectives: *biggest,* . . . .

. . . .

335 The comparative and superlative of adjectives

▶ Finder 203B–E

Complete this table. It may help you to look at the two paragraphs in 334.

	Adjective	Comparative	Superlative
▶	soft	*softer*	softest
1	bright	. . . .	brightest
2	difficult	more difficult	. . . .
3	exclusive	. . . .	most exclusive
4	hard	. . . .	. . . .
5	large	. . . .	. . . .
6	durable	. . . .	. . . .
7	. . . .	easier	. . . .
8	. . . .	. . . .	biggest

336 The comparative and superlative of adjectives

▶ Finder 203B–E

Look at these rules and examples. They are all about forming comparative and superlative adjectives. Which examples go with which rules?

Rules	Examples
▶ Most one-syllable adjectives end in *er/est*, e.g. . . .	a) true, truer/more true, truest/ most true
1 Some one-syllable adjectives have *more/most*, e.g. . . .	b) expensive, more expensive, most expensive
2 Some one-syllable adjectives can have either form, e.g. . . .	c) funny, funnier, funniest
3 Most two-syllable adjectives have *more/most*, e.g. . . .	d) small, smaller, smallest
4 Two-syllable adjectives ending in *y* usually have *er/est*, e.g. . . .	e) stupid, stupider/more stupid, stupidest/most stupid
5 Some two-syllable adjectives can have either form, e.g. . . .	f) real, more real, most real
6 Three-syllable adjectives have *more/most*, e.g. . . .	g) certain, more certain, most certain

▶ *a)* . .
1 . . . . .
2 . . . . .
3 . . . . .
4 . . . . .
5 . . . . .
6 . . . . .

337 The comparative and superlative of adjectives

▶ Finder 203A–E

Comment on the information using a comparative or a superlative adjective.

▶ The Excalibur Hotel in Las Vegas has over 4,000 rooms. No other hotel in the world is so large.
The Excalibur Hotel is . . *the largest hotel in the world.* . .

▶ India is quite a crowded country. It has 294 people per square kilometre. But Bangladesh has 763 people per square kilometre. Bangladesh is . . *more crowded than India.* . .

1 Telecom Tower is 180 metres tall, but Canada Tower in East London is 250 metres tall.
Canada Tower is . . . .

2 The Beatles were a very successful group. They sold over a billion discs and tapes. No other group in the world has been as successful.
The Beatles were . . . .

3 Venus has a diameter of 12,104 kilometres. It isn't as big as the Earth, which has a diameter of 12,756 kilometres.
The Earth is . . . .

4 2.6 million people visited the Tower of London last year, but it wasn't as popular as Madame Tussaud's waxwork museum, which had 2.8 million visitors.
Last year Madame Tussaud's was . . . .

5 The River Severn is 220 miles long. No other river in Britain is so long.
The River Severn is . . . .

6 Cambridge University dates from 1284, but it isn't as old as Oxford University, which dates from 1167.
Oxford University is . . . .

7 The Mona Lisa is worth many millions of dollars. No other picture in the world is so valuable.
The Mona Lisa is . . . .

8 Toby, who lived in New York, was a much-loved dog. When his owner died, she left him $75 million, which made him a world record breaker among wealthy dogs.
Toby was . . . .

338 The comparative and superlative of adjectives

▶ Finder 203A–F

Each of these sentences has a mistake in it. Cross out the wrong word or words and write the correct version.

▶ This area is becoming ~~fashionabler~~.   *more fashionable*
1 This is the boringest film I've ever seen.   . . . .
2 It was the sadest moment of my life.   . . . .
3 That hill is the most high point for miles around.   . . . .
4 As it turned out, I couldn't have been wronger.   . . . .
5 It's most expensive to go by train than by bus.   . . . .
6 How much more far is there to go?   . . . .
7 The place looks a bit tidyer now.   . . . .
8 This design is the attractivest of all.   . . . .
9 The weather was getting badder all the time.   . . . .

339 Some special comparative and superlative forms

▶ Finder 203G

Joshua and William are travelling together. They are in a strange town. Complete the conversation by choosing the correct words.

Joshua: I must post this letter to my sister. I haven't been in touch with her since (▶) last/~~latest~~ month.
William: I have to make a phone call, but my mobile needs a new battery. Do you know where the (1) next/nearest call box is?
Joshua: Well, according to this map, if we go along here and turn left at the (2) next/nearest crossroads, we'll come to the post office. Maybe you can phone from there. I can post my letter, anyway. She should get it this week.
William: Is your sister younger than you?
Joshua: No, she's (3) elder/older. She's left college and she's looking for a job. I'm sending her all the (4) last/latest news about our travels.
William: I must ring home today and find out if there's any (5) farther/further news about my mother and her operation.
Joshua: Well, I hope it's good news.
William: She didn't know she needed an operation until (6) last/latest week. It's been a shock.
Joshua: Oh, here we are. The post office. And there's a call box, look.

340 The comparative of adverbs

Complete the sentences using a verb and the comparative of an adverb.

▶ You're walking too fast. Can't you . . *walk more slowly?* . . .

1 Try not to be so careless in your work. You should try
   to . . . .

2 I thought the team played badly today. I've often seen them . . . .
   than that.

3 Must you talk so loud? Please . . . ., could you?

4 You get up too late. Why don't you . . . .?

5 I did well in this month's test. I'm pleased because I had expected to . . . .
   than last time.

6 The company is operating in a very inefficient manner. It should take immediate
   measures to . . . . ·.

341 *More, most, less, least, fewer, and fewest*

▶ Finder 20

Look at the information and complete the sentences using *more, most, less, least, fewer*
or *fewest*.

▶ Workers in the Third World don't earn as much money as those in Europe.
   Workers in the Third World . . *earn less money* . . than Europeans.

▶ Sarah took lots of photos at the wedding. No one else took as many.
   Sarah . . *took the most* . . photos.

1 There isn't as much crime in country areas as there is in cities.
   There's . . . . than in the cities.

2 The Green Party candidate didn't get many votes. All the other candidates got more.
   The Green Party candidate . . . . votes.

3 No other state of the US has as much rain as Louisiana.
   Louisiana . . . . rain.

4 Soap operas get huge numbers of viewers, but the figures for documentaries are much lower.
   Soap operas . . . . than documentaries.

5 At the moment Arsenal have 42 points. No other club has more than 37.
   Arsenal . . . . points.

6 There are lots of passengers on the buses in the daytime, but not so many in the evenings.
   In the evenings . . . . on the buses.

7 Sellco has made very little profit. In fact it has made less than any other supermarket.
   Sellco . . . . profit.

8 The Prime Minister has quite a lot of power. The Queen doesn't have as much.
   The Queen . . . . than the Prime Minister.

9 The accident rate among young drivers is higher than among older drivers.
   Young drivers . . . . than older drivers.

342 *Less, least, more, most,* and *as*

▶ Finder 206B–C

Complete the conversation. Put in *less, least, more, most,* or *as.*

Lindsay: I'm going to Zurich next week, so I'll have to book my flight. I think it'll be
(▶) . . *more* . . convenient to go by air than by train.

Peter: I'd go by train. Trains are (1) . . . . comfortable than planes.

Lindsay: But the train fare is really expensive. The plane isn't (2) . . . . expensive as
the train, which always surprises me.

Peter: I hate flying. It's my (3) . . . . favourite means of transport.

Lindsay: Well, I don't mind it. And I'm not (4) . . . . keen on trains as you are. A
short flight is (5) . . . . boring than a long train journey, I find.

Peter: I'd rather drive than fly.

Lindsay: I'm definitely not driving. No, thank you. Driving all that way would be the
(6) . . . . stressful way of getting there.

Peter: I don't think driving is (7) . . . . stressful as flying.

Lindsay: Well, it is to me.

Peter: And will you be able to get a flight at the right time? Planes are (8) . . . .
frequent than trains, aren't they?

Lindsay: Oh, there are plenty of flights. There's one at ten in the morning. That'll be the
(9) . . . . convenient.

343 Patterns expressing a comparison

▶ Finder 206

Write a second sentence so that it has a similar meaning to the previous one. Use the word
in brackets.

▶ Plastic isn't as expensive as wood. (more)
. . *Wood is more expensive than plastic.* . .

1 Dave is the same height as Mike. (tall)

. . . .

2 Sunday is less busy than other days. (least)

. . . .

3 My new job is more interesting by far. (much)

. . . .

4 For this job metal is superior to plastic. (better)

. . . .

5 The ground was very hard. (iron)

. . . .

6 Cricket is more complicated than football. (less)

. . . .

7 I've never seen a nicer view than this. (nicest)

. . . .

8 The room doesn't look as small as it did. (bigger)

. . . .

344 Comparatives with *and*

▶ Finder 207A

The MegaWare computer company was one of the success stories of the 20th century. Complete the sentences about the growth of the company.

▶ The company expanded rapidly. It grew . . *bigger and bigger* . . (big) all the time.

1 MegaWare computers became . . . . (popular).

2 . . . . (more) people bought MegaWare products.

3 The business became . . . . (profitable).

4 Its share price went . . . . (high).

5 Life got . . . . (good) for boss Bob Watts as the company became . . . . (successful).

345 Comparatives with *the ... the ...*

▶ Finder 207B

Rewrite the sentences using *the ... the ....*

▶ The crowd became increasingly angry at the long delay.
   The longer the delay was, the angrier the crowd became.
▶ The value of a picture depends on how famous the artist is.
   The more famous an artist is, the more valuable the picture is.

1 How well I sleep depends on how late I go to bed.

. . . .

2 I don't spend much time with my family because I work so hard.

. . . .

3 The traffic moves very slowly as more cars come into the city.

. . . .

4 How much you sweat depends on how hot you get.

. . . .

5 The idea becomes less attractive as I think about it more.

. . . .

6 How much petrol a car uses depends on the size of the engine.

. . . .

346 Review of comparison

▶ Finder 203–207

Complete this text about holidays. Put one word in each space.

HOLIDAYS

Where are you going for your next holiday? (▶) . . _Most_ . . people go on holiday fairly regularly, and maybe some of them have a good time. But holidays aren't (1) . . . . pleasant an experience (2) . . . . the advertisers would like us to believe. In fact, a holiday is probably the (3) . . . . stressful thing you'll experience this year. Besides the bother of choosing and organizing it, there's the worry about whether it will be worth it. (4) . . . . more money you spend, (5) . . . . more you'll feel bound to pretend that you're enjoying yourself. Anyone who has been on a holiday flight will know that airports are getting more (6) . . . . more crowded, and that long delays are common. Holidays may be a good thing, but you can be sure that staying at home is even (7) . . . . for you. It's certainly (8) . . . . dangerous. You'll be much safer at home (9) . . . . wandering around a strange place with a pocket full of money under the eyes of the local criminals. Accidents and disasters are much (10) . . . . likely to happen on holiday. If you want peace and quiet, you don't need to go any (11) . . . . than your own balcony or back garden. Have a nice time!

347 Review of comparison

▶ Finder 203–207

Complete each sentence so that it means the same as the previous one.

▶ A yard isn't as long as a metre. A metre . . _is longer than a yard._ . . .
1 The factory and the church are equally old.
  The factory is . . . .
2 This route is less interesting than the others.
  This is the . . . .
3 I'm not as clever as you.
  You're . . . .
4 A computer would calculate a more precise figure.
  A computer would calculate the figure . . . .
5 The old wallpaper wasn't as nice as the new.
  The new wallpaper is . . . .
6 How reliable a machine is depends on what it costs.
  The more a machine . . . .
7 No other city is Scotland is as big as Glasgow.
  Glasgow . . . .
8 This year the first snow has come later than last year.
  Last year the first snow came . . . .
9 I've never heard anything more ridiculous.
  That's the . . . .
10 A newspaper doesn't have as many pages as a magazine.
  A magazine . . . .

Read this true story.

AN UNFORTUNATE ACCIDENT

Bill and Barbara Hawkins live in the village of Port Isaac in Cornwall. Their house is on a hillside with a steep field above it. Bill and Barbara had had a fire at their house, and they had done some repairs to the building. When they went to France for a holiday, they employed a house-sitter called John Brown. He lived in the house during their absence and made sure everything was all right.

One morning at 9.15 am, a farmer called Robert Sloman was driving a Land Rover across the field behind the house. Suddenly he lost control of the vehicle, which skidded on the wet grass. It rolled down the hill at high speed and crashed into the house. Luckily Mr Sloman had already jumped out of the Land Rover. The vehicle went right through the roof. It landed on the bed where earlier that morning John Brown had been sleeping. 'I'd thought about a lie-in,' he said. 'Luckily I got up. But I'm worried about how to break the news to Bill and Barbara. They went to France with the idea of forgetting their problems.'

1 Read the story again and write down the first twenty prepositional phrases.

▶ . . . *in the village* . . . . i) . . . .
▶ . . . *of Port Isaac* . . . . j) . . . .
a) . . . . k) . . . .
b) . . . . l) . . . .
c) . . . . m) . . . .
d) . . . . n) . . . .
e) . . . . o) . . . .
f) . . . . p) . . . .
g) . . . . q) . . . .
h) . . . . r) . . . .

2 Write down the sentence which contains a two-word preposition.

. . . .

3 Write down the sentence which contains a preposition before an ing-form.

. . . .

4 Write down the sentence which contains a preposition before a wh-clause.

. . . .

5 Write down the sentence which contains a preposition with a modifier in front of it.

. . . .

6 Say if *down* is a preposition or an adverb in these sentences.
a) The vehicle rolled down very fast. . . . .
b) The vehicle rolled down the hill very fast. . . . .

Look at each picture and complete the sentence. Use these words.

against	her briefcase
away from	~~the circle~~
down	the dog
~~inside~~	a glass
into	the hill
onto	the office
out of	the Queen
outside	the shed
past	the stage
up	a tree

▶ The ball was
  inside the circle. . . . .

5 Joanna took some papers
  . . . .

1 The children were running
  . . . .

6 Sam waited
  . . . .

2 The soldiers marched
  . . . .

7 The dancers came
  . . . .

3 Matthew poured some water
  . . . .

8 Sarah put the ladder
  . . . .

4 A car was coming
  . . . .

9 The squirrel ran
  . . . .

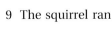

350 Prepositions of place with abstract meanings

► Finder 2090

Choose the correct preposition.

► I'm reading a book ~~into~~/on Hollywood.

1 Our message to the team is that we are all behind/beside you.
2 The government is planning a campaign against/into drugs.
3 The factory is among/with the most modern in Europe.
4 The President is regarded as behind/beyond criticism.
5 I never used to be interested in the environment, but now I'm really inside/into green issues.
6 The company is moving alongside/towards a policy of cutting back on new investment.

351 *At*, *on*, and *in* expressing place

► Finder 210

Put in *at*, *on*, or *in*.

► My flat is . . *on* . . the seventh floor.

1 I was out last night. I was . . . . . the cinema.
2 I was standing . . . . . the back of the queue.
3 The phone is . . . . . a little shelf in the hall.
4 I saw several people I know . . . . . the barbecue.
5 We could see smoke . . . . . the distance.
6 Crowds of football fans . . . . . blue shirts were coming along the street.
7 It felt really hot and stuffy . . . . . the cinema.
8 Polly is visiting some friends . . . . . Canada.
9 Let's look at the figures . . . . . the screen.
10 My brother is . . . . . university. He's doing a business course.
11 The plane landed safely . . . . . Heathrow Airport.
12 The cottage is right . . . . . the coast with views out to sea.

352 Prepositions of place

► Finder 21

Put in a prepositional phrase. Use some of these prepositions (but not all of them): *above*, ~~across~~, *among*, *between*, *in front of*, *next to*, *on top of*, *opposite*, *over*, *through*, *under*

► We drove . . *across the railway.* . . .

1 The café is . . . .

2 He's lying . . . .

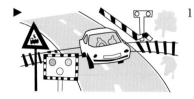   1    2

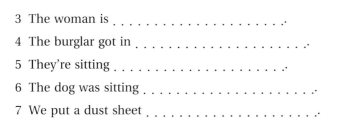

3 The woman is . . . .

4 The burglar got in . . . .

5 They're sitting . . . .

6 The dog was sitting . . . .

7 We put a dust sheet . . . .

353 Prepositions of place

▶ Finder 211

Choose the correct answer.

▶ We had a picnic ~~about~~/by the river.

1 The President was standing among/around/into his bodyguards.
2 Coventry is near/nearby/next Birmingham.
3 Karen dived down to the bottom/top of the pool.
4 Tourists were strolling along/around/between the Old Town.
5 The plane flew to/towards/up to the sun, but then it changed course.
6 Soon we crossed above/over the border into China.
7 November comes after/behind/in front of October.
8 The submarine was 200 metres above/below the surface.
9 You can get across/along/through the road more easily at the lights.
10 I couldn't help looking at the man because he was sitting right behind/next to/opposite me.

354 *At, on,* and *in* expressing time

▶ Finder 212A–D

Put in *at, on,* or *in*.

▶ My birthday is . . *in* . . February.
1 We're going to a concert . . . . . Wednesday.
2 We got home . . . . . half past eleven.
3 I'll see you . . . . . the morning.
4 My sister starts at college . . . . . the autumn.
5 The accident happened . . . . . Thursday afternoon.
6 I usually have a sandwich . . . . . lunch time.
7 Shakespeare was born . . . . . 1564.
8 You're allowed to drive . . . . . seventeen in Britain.
9 There will be lots of excitement . . . . . the coming weeks.
10 People remember the dead . . . . . the anniversary of the terrorist attack.

355 Expressions of time without a preposition

▶ Finder 212E

Some of these sentences are correct, and some have a word which should not be there. If a sentence is correct, put a tick (✓). If it is incorrect, cross the unnecessary word out of the sentence and write it in the space.

▶ There's never anyone here at the weekend. ....✓....

▶ I've got exams ~~in~~ this year. ......*in*....

1 I sometimes work on Saturdays. .....
2 It's Sophie's party on tomorrow evening. .....
3 My neighbour goes to Australia in the winter. .....
4 You've been playing computer games for all afternoon. .....
5 The weather was awful in last summer. .....
6 We're going to a gig on next Saturday. .....
7 We have no vacancies at the present time. .....
8 I found the letter in my coat pocket at six months later. .....

356 *For, since, and ago*

▶ Finder 213

Complete the second sentence so that it has a similar meaning to the first. Use the word in brackets.

▶ Amy's cold started last week, and she's still got it. (since)
Amy has . *had a cold since last week.* .

1 We moved here two years ago. (for)
We've lived . . . .

2 I last saw you at Oliver's party. (since)
I haven't . . . .

3 The film starts half an hour from now. (in)
The film . . . .

4 It's months since I've bought any clothes. (for)
I haven't . . . .

5 I spent an hour lying in the sun yesterday. (for)
I lay . . . .

6 It's six weeks now since the term began. (ago)
The term . . . .

7 I started this project in March, and I'm still doing it. (since)
I've been . . . .

357 More prepositions of time

► Finder 214

Choose the correct preposition.

► Could you do all these exercises ~~below~~/~~by~~/inside half an hour?

1 This film goes on by/during/till midnight.
2 I'll be away between/from/through Tuesday to Friday.
3 The library will be closed during/for/on a week.
4 The ticket is valid for travel inside/over/throughout the day.
5 The building won't be finished for/to/until next year.
6 There will be a limited bus service in/over/while the holiday weekend.
7 The shops close among/between/from one to two o'clock.
8 There had been a period of heavy rain close to/over/prior to the accident.
9 My grandfather was killed during/inside/throughout the war.
10 We have to complete our assignment by/through/until 15 June.

358 Prepositions: other meanings

► Finder 215A

Look at the information in brackets and complete the sentence with a prepositional phrase. Use these prepositions: *according to, by, in accordance with, in favour of, ~~instead of~~, on, on behalf of, thanks to, via.*

► (We didn't go to the beach.)
We went to the park *instead of the beach.* . . . .

1 (One of my teachers wrote the article.)
I was reading an article . . . .

2 (The speech supported the new law.)
A politician was making a speech . . . .

3 (The plane lands at Frankfurt on the way.)
We're taking a flight to Istanbul . . . .

4 (The topic was careers in computers.)
I went to a talk . . . .

5 (The newspapers say so.)
The economy is booming . . . .

6 (I'm speaking for everyone here.)
I'd like to congratulate you . . . .

7 (The candidates obeyed the rules.)
The candidates in the election all behaved . . . .

8 (It owes this increase to more aggressive marketing.)
The company has increased its profits . . . .

359 Prepositions: other meanings

▶ Finder 215B–H

Put in these prepositions: *as, by, except, for, of, like, on, with, without*. You will need to use some of the prepositions more than once.

▶ I had chips . . *with* . . my steak.

1 It'll take ages if we go . . . . bus.
2 A girl . . . . very blue eyes was staring at me.
3 Alex has gone to the supermarket . . . . some food.
4 Justin always wears old clothes. He looks . . . . a tramp.
5 I met someone I know . . . . the boat.
6 There's nothing . . . . any interest in the newspaper.
7 You cut the tiles . . . . a special tool.
8 I'm exhausted. Would you mind carrying these boxes . . . . me, please?
9 Kate was trying to use her magazine . . . . an umbrella.
10 There was just enough food. We ate everything . . . . for one sandwich.
11 Your flight is boarding. Please proceed to the gate . . . . delay.
12 You learn a language best . . . . using it to communicate.

360 Idiomatic phrases with prepositions

▶ Finder 216

Put in an idiomatic phrase beginning with a preposition.

▶ I didn't like the film much . . *at first* . ., but then it got better.

1 You'll soon find another job. You won't be . . . . for long.
2 The plane wasn't late. It arrived more or less . . . .·
3 Your friends must be moving because their house is . . . .·
4 I suppose I drink about five cups of coffee a day . . . . Sometimes it's more and sometimes it's less.
5 The players swapped shirts . . . . of the game.
6 We'd been waiting ages when . . . . something happened.
7 Luckily I was just . . . . to catch the last train.
8 There's no time to waste. We must leave . . . .·
9 I didn't do very well in the interview. . . . . I made a complete mess of it.
10 Let's get going, shall we? We can have a chat . . . . to the meeting.
11 You can't just turn up at the airport. You have to book your flight . . . .·

361 Review of prepositions

▶ Finder 208–216

Each of these sentences is incorrect. Write the correct sentence.

▶ ~~Is anyone in charge for your group?~~
  Is anyone in charge of your group?
. . . .

1 ~~The bell rings in the end of the lesson.~~

. . . .

2 ~~My friends were waiting patiently at a long queue.~~

. . . .

3 ~~We can cross the river with the ferry.~~

. . . .

4 ~~Debbie wanted to overtake the car front of her.~~

. . . .

5 ~~A woman came up at me and shook my hand.~~

. . . .

6 ~~I go to evening classes in every week.~~

. . . .

7 ~~In accordance with the referee, the ball did not cross the line.~~

. . . .

8 ~~The celebrations went on during hours.~~

. . . .

362 Review of prepositions

▶ Finder 208–216

Decide which answer is correct.

▶ It's easy to win . . *by* . . cheating.
  a) by   b) from   c) out of   d) with

1 I have to get up early . . . . Tuesday morning.
  a) at   b) during   c) in   d) on

2 Not many people live . . . . the island.
  a) at   b) in   c) on   d) to

3 We've been standing here . . . . forty-five minutes.
  a) along   b) for   c) in   d) since

4 I keep falling over this suitcase. It's really . . . . the way here.
  a) across   b) by   c) in   d) on

5 I can come any day apart . . . . Thursday.
  a) for   b) from   c) of   d) with

6 As usual, Tiger Woods is . . . . the leaders.
  a) among   b) between   c) into   d) towards

7 The cow got out . . . . a gap in the fence.
  a) across   b) along   c) between   d) through

8 The alarm rang continuously from ten o'clock . . . . half past four.
  a) along   b) at   c) in   d) till

9 The actors spoke their lines . . . . passion.
  a) by   b) for   c) of   d) with

10 I couldn't stretch my legs out because someone was sitting . . . . me.
  a) across   b) behind   c) opposite   d) over

363 Word order with phrasal verbs

▶ Finder 217A, 218A

Complete each sentence by writing the words in the correct order. Sometimes there is more than one possible order.

▶ down / everyone / sat
The meeting was about to start, so .. *everyone sat down.* ..

1 I / it / out / printed
The information looked interesting, so . . . .

2 I / my jacket / off / took
I was hot, so . . . .

3 all the litter in the park / some people / up / were picking
I noticed that . . . .

4 put / the prices / they've / up
Lunch is more expensive now that . . . .

5 away / flew / the birds
There was a sudden noise, and . . . .

6 a list of everything that's worrying you / down / should / write/ you
The book says . . . .

7 I / must / my papers / out / sort
If I'm ever going to find anything, ...

8 down / I'm going / them / to take
I don't like these posters any more, so . . . .

364 Adverbs in front position

▶ Finder 218B

Look at the information in brackets and complete the sentence. Put the adverb first to emphasize the movement.

▶ (The college principal came in.)
The door opened and .. *in came the college principal.* ..
▶ (Everyone went away.)
Everyone climbed on board, and .. *away they went.* ..

1 (The rain came down.)
We hadn't been walking five minutes when . . . .
2 (Joshua jumped up.)
Joshua's name was called, and . . . .
3 (The horses went over.)
The horses galloped to the next fence, and . . . .
4 (The balloon floated up.)
The ropes were untied, and . . . .
5 (Another player came on.)
One player left the field, and . . . .

365 Nouns formed from phrasal verbs

▶ Finder 218C

Look at the explanation and write the phrase.

▶ . . .*A take-away* . . . is a cooked meal bought in a restaurant and eaten at home.

1 . . . . is when a gunman demands money.
2 . . . . is when a car will no longer go.
3 . . . . is a page of information given to each person.
4 . . . . is someone who takes another person's place.
5 . . . . is when a company buys or gets control of another.

366 Word order with adverbs and prepositions

▶ Finder 219A–B

Put in a preposition and the pronoun. You have to decide what order they come in.

▶ My new mobile doesn't work. ~ You should take . . . .*it back* . . . . to the shop. (back)
▶ Migraines can be very painful. ~ I know. I used to suffer . . . .*from them.* . . . . (from)

1 Where's Paul? ~ He should be here soon. We're waiting . . . . (for)
2 Why don't you buy that top? ~ I've got nothing that goes . . . . (with)
3 Have you handed in your form? ~ No, but I've filled . . . . (out)
4 Mark has borrowed our CDs. ~ Well, I hope he brings . . . . (back)
5 Who's got the photos? ~ Kate. She's looking . . . . now. (at)
6 The lecture was interesting. ~ Yes, I learned something . . . . (from)
7 What happened to the TV? ~ A man came and took . . . . (away)
8 Who's Alan? ~ An old friend. I ran . . . . recently. (into)

367 Differences between phrasal and prepositional verbs

▶ Finder 219

Each pair of sentences has a different word order or a different stress pattern. Choose the correct sentence.

▶ No one interrupted. ~~To the speaker was listened in silence.~~/The speaker was listened to in silence.

1 We're going cycling tomorrow. We're hoping for fine weather./We're hoping fine weather for.
2 No, my mobile didn't ring. I'd SWITCHED it off./I'd switched it OFF.
3 They liked the food. It was all up eaten./It was all eaten up.
4 What's the answer? Can you work out it?/Can you work it out
5 There was nothing we could do. We waited patiently for news./We waited for patiently news.
6 All the rubbish has gone. It has been disposed of./Of it has been disposed.
7 No, I haven't got the job. I've applied FOR it./I've APPLIED for it.
8 I had a lie-in. I got up late this morning./I got late up this morning.

Put in a phrasal verb which expresses the meaning of the word in brackets. Make sure th●
verb is in the correct form.

▶ You've . . *left out* . . a word from this sentence. (omitted)
▶ Everyone was behaving strangely, so I knew something . . *was up.* . . (was the matter)

1 How long are you going to . . . . working? (continue)
2 I hope to . . . . who my real parents are. (discover)
3 We're going to . . . . an outing for our group. (arrange)
4 I'd like to see the new Star Wars film, but it . . . . at the moment. (isn't showing
5 Do you think this new fashion will . . . .? (become popular)
6 The old traditions are still . . . . today. (maintained)
7 I don't want to . . . . with you. (quarrel)
8 The price of new computers has . . . . quite a lot. (fallen)
9 The performance will . . . . at ten o'clock. (be at an end)
10 You can hardly . . . . on £100 a week. (manage to live)
11 For the sake of your health, you ought to . . . . alcohol. (stop drinking)
12 I'll . . . . in the morning, so could you come in the afternoon? (not be at home

369 Some common adverbs in phrasal verbs ► Finder 22

Write the meaning of each adverb.

▶ You aren't going to write **out** the report by hand, are you? . . *completely* . .

1 We always have the TV **on**, even if no one is watching it. . . . .
2 Richard is starting **off** on his trip around the world soon. . . . .
3 Joanna saw me at the bus stop, but she drove **on** without stopping. . . . .
4 I couldn't eat the food they dished **out** to us at that hotel. . . . .
5 I must get these thoughts **down** before I forget. . . . .
6 The tree outside the window blocks **out** all the light. . . . .
7 The government wants to hold inflation **down**. . . . .
8 Adam is so tall he really stands **out** in a crowd. . . . .
9 I spilled some milk, so I had to clean it **up**. . . . .
10 It's a bold plan, but can we bring it **off**? . . . .

370 Some common adverbs in phrasal verbs ► Finder 22

Put in a phrasal verb using the clue in brackets. Make sure the form is correct.

▶ I'm afraid the machine has . . *broken down.* . . . (stopped working)

1 Our phone has been . . . ., so ring me on my mobile. (disconnected)
2 The people who know the truth dare not . . . . (tell the truth publicly)
3 Some workmen . . . . all the trees. (felled)
4 The firefighters managed to . . . . the fire. (extinguish)
5 If you . . . . the radio, we'd all be able to hear. (increase the volume of)
6 We need to . . . . the situation. (fully discuss)

371 Prepositional verbs

▶ Finder 222A–B

Put in the missing preposition.

▶ Does this umbrella belong . . *to* . . you?

1 I'm absolutely dying . . . . a cup of coffee.
2 What we do at the weekend will depend . . . . . . the weather.
3 How are we going to deal . . . . . . the problem?
4 I never eat sushi. I don't care . . . . . . it at all.
5 A cricket team consists . . . . . . eleven players.
6 The artist looks . . . . . . his work as a protest against society.
7 The authorities should look . . . . . . the matter carefully.
8 A simple solution to the problem had occurred . . . . me.
9 Fortunately the latest talks have resulted . . . . a new agreement.
10 Environmental groups have called . . . . an end to the destruction
   of the rainforests.

372 Prepositional verbs

▶ Finder 222C–D

Complete the conversation. Put in the correct preposition. Sometimes there is more than
one possible answer.

Debbie: How's things, Tom?
Tom: Fine, thanks. I've just got a job.
Debbie: Oh, yes, I heard (▶) . . *about* . . that. Congratulations.
Tom: Thanks.
Debbie: I was talking (1) . . . . Rick (2) . . . . his business course, and he
         mentioned it. What company is it?
Tom: They're called Poly-Comm. They're based in Bristol.
Debbie: I have to admit I've never heard (3) . . . . them.
Tom: They're a small company, but they're very go-ahead. Just because they're not a big
         name, that doesn't mean …
Debbie: OK, OK. Fine. I'm not arguing (4) . . . . you. I'm pleased for you, Tom.
         Really.
Tom: Sorry. I'm a bit stressed about the move. How are you getting on, Debbie?
Debbie: I'm thinking (5) . . . . going to work for Macro-Byte. They've offered
         me a job.
Tom: Oh, that's great.
Debbie: The money's good, but the job isn't exactly what I want. I've got to decide soon.
         They've asked (6) . . . . an answer by the end of the week. What do you
         think I should do?
Tom: Debbie, you know your own mind. I wouldn't dream (7) . . . . telling you
         what to do.

373 Prepositional verb or verb + object?

▶ Finder 222E

Some of these sentences are correct, and some have a word which should not be there. If a sentence is correct, put a tick (✓). If it is incorrect, cross the unnecessary word out of the sentence and write it in the space.

▶ People were searching for the missing bag.   ...✓...

▶ The plane left ~~from~~ Amsterdam at 15 35.   ..*from*..

1 The train was approaching to the station.   ....
2 My sister has just married with a millionaire.   ....
3 The company paid for our hotel accommodation.   ....
4 My parents don't approve of my lifestyle.   ....
5 We finally reached to our destination after midnight.   ....
6 One company controls over the whole market.   ....
7 We were all discussing about the exam.   ....
8 We were all having a discussion about the exam.   ....

374 Verb + object + preposition

▶ Finder 223

Write a sentence with a similar meaning and include the word in brackets. Use the pattern with a verb + object + preposition.

▶ Let's look at the new plan alongside the old one. (compare)
    ..*Let's compare the new plan with the old one.*..

1 I like hip-hop better than reggae. (prefer)
    ....

2 The teacher gave the class an explanation of the theory. (explained)
    ....

3 Sarah's illness has made her unable to do anything. (action)
    ....

4 Everyone congratulated the champion when he won. (victory)
    ....

5 You should just ignore anything Mike says. (notice)
    ....

6 The winners were given a trophy. (presented)
    ....

7 Witnesses said the accident was the van driver's fault. (blamed)
    ....

8 Two boys were begging money from tourists. (asking)
    ....

9 They've made luxury apartments out of the old hospital. (turned)
    ....

10 I want to get the maximum benefit from the long weekend. (make)
    ....

375 Verb + adverb + preposition

► Finder 224

Put in these forms: *brought up against*, ~~face up to~~, *get round to*, *go out into*, *looking forward to*, *looks out over*, *looked up at*, *put up with*, *take up on*.

► I should . . *face up to* . . . my problems and not try to avoid them.

1 It was so stuffy indoors that I had to . . . . the fresh air.
2 I'm feeling nervous. I'm not . . . . giving my presentation.
3 The audience watched as Romeo . . . . Juliet on her balcony.
4 When are you going to finally . . . . tidying up?
5 The house is on top of the cliff and . . . . the English Channel.
6 I left the job because I couldn't . . . . my boss a moment longer.
7 Actually, can I . . . . you . . . . your offer of a bed for the night?
8 I had big ideas until I was . . . . the reality of the situation.

376 Adjective + preposition

► Finder 225A

Express the meaning in a single sentence. Use a preposition after the adjective.

► We were surprised. The news was unexpected.
  . . *We were surprised at the news.* . . .

1 I was worried. Where was my girlfriend?
. . . .
2 The streets were crowded. There were festival-goers everywhere.
. . . .
3 Paul was impressed. He liked your cooking.
. . . .
4 I was late. I had an appointment.
. . . .
5 I'm fed up. I've been travelling too much.
. . . .
6 The island is famous. It has standing stones on it.
. . . .

377 Adjective + preposition

► Finder 225B–C

Choose the correct preposition.

► I'm sorry at/for/~~with~~ behaving so badly.

1 I was never very good about/at/for drawing.
2 James has always been very friendly at/for/to me.
3 This first chapter of the book is concerned about/for/with the structure of the atom.
4 They say swimming is good at/for/to you.
5 I feel sorry at/for/with those people whose flights were delayed for so long.
6 Investors in the company were angry about/for/with losing their money.
7 The police are anxious about/for/of witnesses to come forward.

378 Noun + preposition

▶ Finder 226A–E

Complete the advertisement. Put in the missing prepositions.

Worried (▶) . . *about* . . break-ins? The fear (1) . . . . intruders is widespread and justified. Burglars not only steal your valuables, they can also do a lot of damage (2) . . . . your property. But there is a way (3) . . . . preventing them. SBX Security has the answer (4) . . . . your problems. Our alarms provide protection (5) . . . . burglars. We are the leading home security experts, and quality is the one reason (6) . . . . our excellent reputation. Call us on 020 737 4162 for a free visit and discussion (7) . . . . your security needs.

379 Noun + preposition

▶ Finder 226B–D

Complete the sentence so that it has a similar meaning to the previous one.

▶ I've requested a transfer to another branch of the company.
I've put in . . *a request for* . . a transfer to another branch of the company.

1 The community respects its old traditions.
The community shows . . . . its old traditions.

2 Mark is very proud of the work he does.
Mark takes great . . . . his work.

3 We're discussing the relationship between Richard and Leanne.
Richard's . . . . is what we're talking about.

4 Four men attacked a member of a rival gang.
Four men carried out . . . . a member of a rival gang.

5 Louise made a suggestion, and no one objected.
There were . . . . Louise's suggestion.

6 In what way are the two systems different?
Can you explain . . . . the two systems?

7 The country needs more investment.
There is . . . . more investment in the country.

8 The number of murders has gone down ten per cent.
There has been . . . . ten per cent . . . .
of murders.

380 Phrasal verbs and prepositional idioms

▶ Finder 217–226

Decide which answer is correct.

▶ I'm not watching TV because there's nothing . . on. . .
a) in   b) off   c) on   d) up

1 Why are you so angry . . . . a little mistake?
a) about   b) for   c) of   d) with

2 Unfortunately all my plans fell . . . .
a) away   b) off   c) out   d) through

3 Try to concentrate . . . . your work.
a) at   b) on   c) in   d) to

4 The shoes felt too tight, so I took . . . . and tried a larger size.
a) away them   b) off them   c) them away   d) them off

5 I've just e-mailed my application . . . . the job.
a) for   b) in   c) into   d) to

6 What we do next depends . . . .
a) from you   b) on you   c) you from   d) you on

7 You go on ahead and then I'll catch . . . . you.
a) along with   b) forward to   c) on to   d) up with

8 Our landlady provided us . . . . a packed lunch.
a) for   b) on   c) to   d) with

9 There was a sign, but I couldn't . . . . what it said.
a) hang on   b) look up   c) make out   d) see off

10 The matter is being . . . . by the police.
a) into looked   b) on looked   c) looked into   d) looked on

11 So you don't care . . . . the environment? You should, you know.
a) about   b) for   c) of   d) with

12 The child doesn't . . . . either of her parents.
a) resemble   b) resemble at   c) resemble to   d) resemble with

381 Phrasal verbs and prepositional idioms

Each of these sentences is incorrect. Write the correct sentence.

▶ ~~I was listening a concert to.~~

. . . . *I was listening to a concert.* . . .

1 ~~Next week the hospital will close out for good.~~

. . . .

2 ~~I've met her before, but I just can't think about her name.~~

. . . .

3 ~~They've had to put away the game because of the weather.~~

. . . .

4 ~~The patient suddenly cried in pain out.~~

. . . .

5 ~~I must thank Alice my present for.~~

. . . .

6 ~~Are you satisfied on your progress?~~

. . . .

7 ~~We saw our friends away at the airport.~~

. . . .

8 ~~We're just going to around travel for a while.~~

. . . .

9 ~~I had to describe the police the woman.~~

. . . .

10 ~~The authorities won't give any reason about their decision.~~

. . . .

11 ~~The workers are demanding for more money.~~

. . . .

12 ~~In his speech the PM didn't refer at the recent scandal.~~

. . . .

13 ~~Some of the UN delegates staged an outwalk.~~

. . . .

14 ~~I'm surprised you put over with these awful conditions.~~

. . . .

382 Types of clause

Answer the questions. Tick the correct answer.

► Which of these is a complete sentence?
a) As there was a lot of traffic.
b) As usual there was a lot of traffic. ✓

1 Which is correct?
a) I didn't think you would finish so early.
b) I didn't think you would so early finish.

2 Which sentence has a non-finite clause?
a) I was tired after doing all that work.
b) I was tired because I had been working.

3 Which is correct?
a) We can walk up the stairs or can take the lift.
b) We can walk up the stairs or take the lift.

4 Which of these has two co-ordinate clauses?
a) I felt really angry, but I kept my temper.
b) I was glad that I kept my temper.

5 Write down the non-finite clause in this sentence.
Louise was ill in the night, and in the morning she didn't look any better, so we decided to call the doctor, and he came at ten o'clock.

. . . .

383 What comes after the verb?

► Finder 228

Match the two parts of the sentence.

► I wonder	the alarm to sound.
1 No one believes	falsifying its accounts.
2 Well, I warned you	for our luggage to be sent on ahead.
3 The company admitted	how to samba.
4 You can teach me	~~if the weather is going to be all right~~.
5 We arranged	in repairing the damage.
6 I don't understand	not to touch that wire.
7 They succeeded	that the earth is flat.
8 Smoke will cause	why you're so angry with me.

► . . *I wonder if the weather is going to be all right.* . . .

1 . . . .
2 . . . .
3 . . . .
4 . . . .
5 . . . .
6 . . . .
7 . . . .
8 . . . .

384 What comes after the verb?

▶ Finder 228

Complete each sentence using a sub-clause.

▶ The company was in trouble. We all knew.
  We all knew *that the company was in trouble.*
▶ We all wanted to have the lesson outside, and the teacher agreed.
  The teacher agreed *to have the lesson outside.*

1 Matthew copies all his files to disk. He insists.
  Matthew insists . . . .
2 You don't need to work overtime. We don't expect it.
  We don't . . . .
3 The man wouldn't give up his seat. He refused.
  The man refused . . . .
4 I might apply for the job. I'm considering it.
  I'm . . . .
5 Everything will be OK. I promise you.
  I . . . .
6 Yes, you can bring your problems to me. Of course I don't mind.
  Of course I . . . .
7 The children sat inside the fire-engine. The fireman let them.
  The fireman . . . .
8 You have to book in advance. That's what I assume.
  I . . . .
9 I can't use this operating system. I've never learned how.
  I've never . . . .
10 Will the office be open now? I doubt it.
   I . . . .
11 They don't want people to get in free. They're trying to prevent that.
   They're . . . .
12 What time shall we meet? I don't mind.
   I . . . .

385 Clause combinations

▶ Finder 229

Put the clauses in the right order to form a sentence.

▶ flying to more than 1,000 airports / scattered around the world / there are over 50 airlines
  There are over 50 airlines flying to more than 1000 airports scattered around the world.

1 the gallery has decided / painted by local artists / to buy more pictures

  . . . .
  . . . .
2 because I didn't want to offend him / but Mark invited me / I don't really like opera / so I
  went with him

  . . . .
  . . . .
3 but it didn't work / but they wouldn't give him his money back / a man bought a TV / so he
  threw the TV through the shop window / so he took it back to the shop

  . . . .
  . . . .

Combine the clauses into one sentence, keeping them in the same order. Try not to overuse the word *and*. Do not use it more than once in a sentence.

▶ The couple left the wife's parents. Her parents looked after the children. The couple set off in the car. They headed for London. *The couple left the wife's parents to look after the children, and they set off in the car heading for London.*

1 I don't mind. I'll help. I've got plenty of time.

. . . .

2 The two leaders had no common language. They had an interpreter. She was present at all their meetings.

. . . .

. . . .

3 I'm a waitress. I just work in the afternoons. I serve teas.

. . . .

4 The President knew. His wife was ill. She wouldn't live long.

. . . .

5 Eventually we took off. We didn't land at Heathrow. We had to go to Manchester instead. This made the journey home much longer.

. . . .

. . . .

6 Did you know? There's a museum in Detroit. You can see the car. John F. Kennedy was riding in it. He was shot.

. . . .

. . . .

387 The unreal present and past and the subjunctive ▶ Finder 230–231

Some of these sentences have a mistake in them. Find the mistakes and write the sentences correctly.

a) Suppose someone stole your credit card.
b) I would rather you are completely honest with me.
c) Supposed all your dreams came true.
d) If I'm you, I'd certainly complain.
e) Emily looked as if she'd seen a ghost.
f) It is essential that no one give any information to the press.
g) I'm sure the train leave at six tomorrow morning.
h) Supposing the letter doesn't get there in time.
i) It's time I go to bed.
j) Suppose your new friend were some kind of spy.

▶ *b) I would rather you were completely honest with me.*

1 . . . .
2 . . . .
3 . . . .
4 . . . .

388 Verbs after *wish* and *if only*

▶ Finder 232

Complete what people are saying about their situation.

▶ It rains every weekend, and Sarah is getting fed up with it.
Sarah: I wish . . *it wouldn't rain every weekend.* . .

1 Amy isn't as confident as Laura, but she would like to be.
Amy to Laura: I wish . . . . you.
2 Julia drove to the airport, but she missed her plane because she didn't get up early enough.
Julia: If only . . . . earlier.
3 Rick and Emily can't afford a new computer, but Rick would really like one.
Rick to Emily: I wish . . . .
4 Chloe very much wants to contact an old friend, but she doesn't have the address.
Chloe: If only . . . . the address.
5 Nicola and Kirsty had a secret, but Nicola is annoyed because Kirsty told everyone.
Nicola to Kirsty: I wish . . . .
6 Adam never locks the front door, and Oliver is complaining to him about it.
Oliver to Adam: I wish . . . .
7 The DVD player won't work, and Carl is desperate to play his DVD.
Carl: If . . . . work.
8 Unfortunately Kate couldn't be at Tim's wedding, although she regrets not being there.
Kate to Tim: I wish . . . .

389 Words meaning 'and' and 'or'

▶ Finder 233–234

Put one of these words into each sentence: *addition, alternatively, besides, both, either, more, neither, only, otherwise, well, with.*

▶ I can't afford to go to the ballet. . . *Besides* . ., I wouldn't enjoy it.

1 Is it possible to do a full-time job and look after small children
as . . . . ?
2 Fast food isn't especially good for you. What's . . . ., it's expensive.
3 The government will . . . . confirm nor deny the report.
4 The burglars took the TV and video recorder, along . . . . all
my jewellery.
5 The film star has beautiful homes . . . . in Los Angeles and in Paris.
6 Ian had better return my car in one piece, ... I'm never going to
speak to him again.
7 There's no post, and I haven't had any e-mails . . . .
8 We're cooking for four guests in . . . . to everyone else.
9 The company not . . . . lost the case, but they also had to pay all the
legal costs.
10 We can go on the motorway, or . . . . we could drive across country,
which is slower but more direct.

390 Words meaning 'but'

▶ Finder 235

Link each pair of sentences without changing their order. Use the word in brackets. Sometimes you have to expand the word into a longer phrase.

▶ The man was very helpful. I felt suspicious of him. (even)

   The man was very helpful. Even so, I felt suspicious of him.

1 I'd had a good night's sleep. I felt tired. (same)

   . . . .

2 Alice felt optimistic. She had a few problems. (despite)

   . . . .

3 I couldn't speak. I was conscious. (although)

   . . . .

4 It was freezing cold. People were in T-shirts. (even though)

   . . . .

5 I'm in a wheelchair. I'm not stupid, you know. (in spite)

   . . . .

6 Yes, I do eat meat. My flat-mate is a vegetarian. (other hand)

   . . . .

391 Words meaning 'so'

▶ Finder 236

Match the two parts of the sentence.

▶ The company was mismanaged,	and consequently the fish have died.
1 I didn't need the bike any more,	~~and as a result it went bankrupt.~~
2 I was so annoyed	as a result of overwork.
3 My health was getting worse	she'll know what to do.
4 Hannah is such an expert	so I sold it.
5 All the candidates were hopeless,	that I completely lost my temper.
6 They've polluted the river,	and therefore I didn't vote.

▶ . . *The company was mismanaged, and as a result it went bankrupt.* . . . . .

1 . . . .

2 . . . .

3 . . . .

4 . . . .

5 . . . .

6 . . . .

392 Review of *and, or, but, so*, etc

▶ Finder 233–236

Look at each sentence or pair of sentences and decide if the second of the two ideas is an addition, an alternative, a contrast, or a result.

▶ The flat is too small. Furthermore, it's in a horrible area.   *addition* . . . .

1 The computers are down. Consequently, everything is in chaos. . . . .
2 I might do business studies or work in my parents'company. . . . .
3 The plan was approved in spite of all the objections. . . . .
4 I don't think I fancy a picnic. Besides, I've got work to do. . . . .
5 Not only did we see the tower, but we went up to the top. . . . .
6 At least you're safe. Even so, you took a big risk. . . . .

393 Review of *and, or, but, so*, etc

▶ Finder 233–236

Decide which answer is correct.

▶ It was . . *such* . . a shock that I didn't know what to say.
  a) big b) so c) such d) very

1 There was a bomb scare in the resort, and . . . . tourists stayed away.
  a) consequently b) however c) though d) while
2 My uncle is . . . . the owner and the manager of the hotel.
  a) as well b) both c) either d) neither
3 It's a nice coat. It doesn't fit me . . . .
  a) although b) but c) despite d) though
4 Friday was a sunny day, ... Saturday was wet.
  a) as well as b) besides c) however d) while
5 The man had a motive for the murder. . . . ., he was seen in the area at the time.
  a) Consequently b) However c) Moreover d) Nevertheless
6 I'd better post the parcel today, ... it won't get there in time.
  a) alternatively b) despite c) furthermore d) otherwise
7 Not everyone is happy about the new timetable. There are, ... ,
a number of advantages to it.
  a) consequently b) furthermore c) however d) moreover

394 Review of *and, or, but, so*, etc

▶ Finder 233–236

Write a sentence of similar meaning using the word or words in brackets.

▶ This product is cheap, and it's effective. (as well as)
  This product is cheap as well as effective. . . .

1 I haven't got a car, and I haven't got a bike. (either)
. . . .

2 The answer was obvious, but I just couldn't see it. (although)
. . . .

3 The party isn't very popular, and its policies aren't very popular. (neither, nor)

. . . .

4 I felt very emotional, and I almost burst into tears. (so, that)

. . . .

5 You'll love this film. Or will you hate it? (either)

. . . .

6 I was quoted in the newspapers and interviewed on TV. (not only, but, also)

. . . .

7 I have to book the hotel, and I have to make the travel arrangements. (in addition to)

. . . .

8 The meal was excellent, but the surroundings were depressing. (though)

. . . .

9 The affair became public even though they attempted to conceal it. (despite)

. . . .

10 Wage cuts have led to people rioting on the streets. (as a result of)

. . . .

395 Review of *and, or, but, so*, etc ▶ Finder 233–236

Complete these two paragraphs.

Put in: *also, but, despite, or, that, therefore*.

CAR PROBLEMS

I was having a lot of problems with my car. The engine kept cutting out, and I (1) . . . .
had trouble starting it. I got so fed up with it (2) . . . . I took it to a garage. They told me
it was going to cost hundreds of pounds to repair, (3) . . . . unfortunately I didn't have
the money, and I (4) . . . . decided to get rid of the car (5) . . . . needing it for
work. Now I get the bus to work (6) . . . . a colleague gives me a lift.

Put in: *alternatively, as a result of, consequently, furthermore, in spite of, on top of*.

UNIVERSITY STUDENTS

(7) . . . . their aim to get more young people into universities, the government
has put financial difficulties in their way. Nowadays most students get a loan instead of a grant,
and some have to pay tuition fees (8) . . . . that. (9) . . . .,'
many of them run up huge debts, or (10) . . . . their parents have to support
them. (11) . . . . these obstacles, some school leavers are discouraged from
applying to go to university. (12) . . . ., an increasing number are dropping out
before completing the course.

396 Introduction to adverbial clauses ▶ Finder 237

Read this story and then write the answers.

WHEELCHAIR GETAWAY

If you find this story hard to believe, that's understandable, but it really is true, and it happened in Glasgow. Two men, one of whom is confined to a wheelchair, decided to steal a television set from a shop. The able-bodied man went into the shop. Snatching a TV set, he ran out and gave it to his friend, who held it while being pushed along at speed. The pair managed to travel about a quarter of a mile before police caught up with them.

1 Write down the two finite adverbial clauses. (They begin with a conjunction and a subject.)

. . . .

. . . .

2 Write down the two non-finite adverbial clauses.

. . . .

. . . .

397 Clauses of time ▶ Finder 238A–B

Some of these sentences are correct, and some have a word missing from them. If a sentence is correct, put a tick (✓) after it. If it is incorrect, put the word in the right place.

▶ I'd like to talk to you before you go. ✓

▶ I was tired after I'd *been*ᴧ working all day.

1 I've been to that restaurant once since opened.

2 Once built, the tunnel will cut an hour off the journey.

3 Be careful when put these glasses away.

4 The player was injured soon after start of the game.

5 You're supposed to keep dancing until the music stops.

6 So, finished my work, I sat down to watch TV.

398 *When, while,* and *as* ▶ Finder 238C

Put in *when, while,* or *as.*

▶ . . *As* . . I was chatting away to my friend, the line suddenly went dead.
1 . . . . the door slammed, the birds all flew away.
2 . . . . night slowly fell, people were hurrying home.
3 . . . . I ride in a car, I always feel sick.
4 . . . . I was younger, my parents had a farm.
5 I was reading a book . . . . I waited to see the doctor.

6 Debbie always says hello . . . . she sees me.
7 Just . . . . we raced onto the platform, the train pulled away.
8 . . . . we finally arrived at our destination, it was after midnight.
9 I was crossing the road . . . . I suddenly saw someone I know.
10 The atmosphere grew more and more tense . . . . we approached the frontier.

399 Clauses of time

▶ Finder 238

Rewrite each sentence replacing the adverbial phrase with an adverbial clause.

▶ In wet weather, water comes in through the roof.
   When it rains, water comes in through the roof.

1 Tom felt nervous before his appearance on TV.
....

2 We had to wait to the end of the performance.
....

3 Our visitors had to leave immediately after breakfast.
....

4 After the death of our cat we felt very sad.
....

5 At twenty I started my first real job.
....

6 By the time of our arrival at the hotel, it'll be midnight.
....

7 It's a month since your last visit to us.
....

8 Immediately after the start of the film, I realized I'd seen it before.
....

9 Leanne's flat was burgled during her holiday.
....

10 At the exact moment of our departure, my mobile rang.
....

400 Clauses of reason

▶ Finder 239

Combine each pair of sentences without changing their order. Put the word in brackets either at the beginning or in the middle.

▶ The player had an injury. He had to leave the field. (due to)
   Due to an injury, the player had to leave the field.
▶ I'm going to move abroad. The weather is so awful here. (because)
   I'm going to move abroad because the weather is so awful here.

1 My father gave up his job. His health is poor. (on account of)
....

2 I'd worked all weekend. I had Monday off. (seeing)
....

3 I didn't buy the coat. It was so expensive. (as)
....

4 I feel much more confident. I'm qualified. (now)

. . . .

5 The car is in excellent condition. It's a bargain. (because of)

. . . .

6 I can't talk now. I'm working. (because)

. . . .

7 There is so much street crime. You had better take a taxi. (since)

. . . .

8 Joshua helped us. He was being kind. (out of)

. . . .

9 People are staying at home. They are afraid of terrorism. (because of)

. . . .

401 Clauses of purpose

▶ Finder 24(

Find the sentences that belong together. Then combine the sentences using the word ir brackets in one of the clauses.

▶ I want to leave my options open.	I needed a paper. (for)
▶ People need to feed their families.	I wanted to watch a film. (to)
1 I stayed up late.	It is increasing production. (in order to)
2 Put plenty of glue on the paper.	~~Then I can do whatever I want. (so that~~
3 We talked quietly.	Then I don't lose them. (to avoid)
4 The company is trying to meet demand.	Then it'll stick properly. (so that)
5 I had to go to the newsagent's.	~~They have to earn money. (in order to)~~
6 I hang my keys around my neck.	We didn't want to wake the baby. (so as
7 A spade is a tool.	You dig with it. (for)
8 You want to understand the political situation.	You need to know some history. (in ord

▶ . . *I want to leave my options open so that I can do whatever I want.* . .
▶ . . *In order to feed their families, people have to earn money.* . .

1 . . . .
2 . . . .
3 . . . .
4 . . . .
5 . . . .
6 . . . .
7 . . . .
8 . . . .
. . . .

402 Clause meanings

▶ Finder 238–240

Read each sentence and decide if the adverbial clause is one of time, reason, or purpose.

▶ What did you think when you saw the exam questions? . . *time* . .

1 I'm saving up so that I can buy a motor-bike. . . . .
2 As I was waiting my turn, I was reading a book. . . . .
3 Having paid the bill, we sat there chatting a while longer. . . . .
4 You should know the answer as you're so clever. . . . .
5 We had to hurry to get here on time. . . . .
6 Being an only child, I was good at amusing myself. . . . .
7 I've lived here since I was a child. . . . .
8 I use this computer for surfing the web. . . . .
9 The soldiers were exhausted for they had marched a long way. . . . .
10 Since I was obviously expected to make a speech, I rose to my feet. . . . .

403 As and *like*

▶ Finder 241

Put in *as* or *like*.

▶ Mark looks . . *like* . . he's in a hurry to be off.

1 . . . . we've learned, the cheapest option isn't always the best.
2 The guests rushed to grab their food . . . . animals.
3 You look . . . . though you've had a shock.
4 We never looked . . . . winning the game.
5 I felt . . . . if I'd been kicked by a horse.
6 The stock market has performed exactly . . . . financial analysts had forecast.

404 *Whoever, whatever*, etc

▶ Finder 242A

Rewrite each sentence using *whoever, whatever*, etc.

▶ No matter when I ring Louise, her phone is switched off.
. . *Whenever I ring Louise, her phone is switched off.* . .

1 No matter where we looked, there were flags flying.
. . . .

2 I don't care who does the cooking, it won't be me.
. . . .

3 I don't care when that man comes here, I'm going to be out.
. . . .

4 It makes no difference what's happened, the newspapers will invent their own story.
. . . .

5 It doesn't matter which method you use, the result is the same.
. . . .

6 You should never neglect a customer, no matter how busy you are.
. . . .

405 Review of adverbial clauses

► Finder 238–24:

Complete this true story. Put in these words: *after*, *as if*, *because*, *because of*, *however*, *in order to*, *no sooner*, *since*, *than*, *when*, *while*.

SLOW WALK FOR CANCER HERO

40-year-old Lloyd Scott crossed the finishing line of the London Marathon yesterday
(►) . . *after* . . walking for 128 hours in a deep sea diver's suit weighing 54 kilos. He did it
(1) . . . . raise money for children with cancer. Mr Scott once had cancer
himself and has been living under its shadow (2) . . . . he was 27.
(3) . . . . he was moving very slowly on his way, his helpers were busy
collecting money from the public. Our hero spent five days on the road and the nights in a
camper van. (4) . . . . he got to the finish, he was greeted by Paula Radcliffe
winner of the women's race on Sunday. 'It was very tiring (5) . . . . the weigh
of the suit,' said Mr Scott. I often felt (6) . . . . I just couldn't go any furthe
But I was determined to finish, (7) . . . . hard it was And I'm pleased
(8) . . . . I've raised £100,000 for children with cancer.' But Mr Scott isn't
going to rest there. (9) . . . . had he finished the marathon
(10) . . . . he was talking about his next project – a bike ride across Australia

406 Review of adverbial clauses

► Finder 238–24

Each of these sentences is incorrect. Write the correct sentence.

► I did it carefully that I wouldn't make a mistake.
. . *I did it carefully so that I wouldn't make a mistake.* . . .

1 Like you can imagine, I've been very worried.

. . . .

2 Please ring me momently you arrive.

. . . .

3 How hard Justin tried, he couldn't hit the target.

. . . .

4 The matter was kept secret not to alarm the public.

. . . .

5 We look as though getting approval for the plan.

. . . .

6 While the day of the exam approached, I felt more and more nervous.

. . . .

7 I must have my passport back by I leave the country.

. . . .

8 The journey always takes ages because the amount of traffic.

. . . .

407 Review of adverbial clauses

▶ Finder 237–242

Write a sentence of similar meaning using the word in brackets.

▶ I'd like to go out and have a meal. (for)
. . . *I'd like to go out for a meal.* . . .

1 The teacher came in and everyone stopped talking. (when)
. . . .

2 I wish the team had played the same way they did last week. (like)
. . . .

3 There was no evidence, so the police couldn't make an arrest. (since)
. . . .

4 Let's have lunch after our game of mini-golf. (we've)
. . . .

5 Come and see me any time you like. (whenever)
. . . .

6 Our sales are declining, and cheap imports are the cause. (due)
. . . .

7 I want everything to be ready so that I won't be delayed. (avoid)
. . . .

8 The clock struck, and immediately the doors opened. (soon)
. . . .

408 Open and unreal conditions

▶ Finder 243A

Say if these conditions are open or unreal, and give the reason.

▶ If you look in the market, you'll find some bargains.
. . *open – You may look in the market.* . . .
▶ If I'd seen you at the bus stop, I'd have given you a lift.
. . *unreal – I didn't see you at the bus stop.* . . .

1 If I lived in the country, I'd die of boredom.
. . . .

2 If you vote for me, I'll be your friend for ever.
. . . .

3 If everyone comes to the party, there won't be room for them.
. . . .

4 If you'd asked politely, you might have got what you wanted.
. . . .

5 If I could understand computers, my life would be a lot simpler.
. . . .

6 If I hear any news, I'll let you know.
. . . .

409 The use of conditional sentences

▶ Finder 243D

Write down the use of each conditional sentence. Choose from these uses: ~~advising~~, criticizing, offering, requesting, suggesting, threatening, warning.

▶ If I were in your position, I'd make a formal complaint. . . *advising* . .

1 If you don't open the door, I'll break it down. . . . .
2 If I open a bottle of wine, would you like some? . . . .
3 If you've got a moment, would you mind helping us? . . . .
4 We could go out somewhere tonight if you feel like it. . . . .
5 If you hadn't wasted so much time earlier, we wouldn't be in such a hurry now, would we? . . . .
6 If you're going out this evening, don't wear any jewellery or you might get mugged. . . . .

410 Type 0 conditionals

▶ Finder 244A

Write sentences from the notes using a Type 0 conditional.

▶ drop something → falls to earth
. . . *If you drop something, it falls to earth.* . . .

1 pour oil on water → floats
. . . .

2 air gets warmer → rises
. . . .

3 heat chocolate → melts
. . . .

4 lift a heavy object → use up energy
. . . .

5 water freezes → expands
. . . .

411 Type 1 conditionals

▶ Finder 245A

Rewrite these advertisements using a Type 1 conditional.

▶ Choose a Sunbright holiday and have a wonderful time.
. . . *If you choose a Sunbright holiday, you'll have a wonderful time.* . . .
▶ Be in touch. Use a Commex mobile phone.
. . . *You'll be in touch if you use a Commex mobile phone.* . . .

1 Know the right time. Wear a Minuta watch.
. . . .

2 Live a life of luxury. Fill your home with Superstyle furniture.
. . . .

3 Read the Daily Dirt and enjoy all the latest gossip.

. . . .

4 Take a Kodex camera with you and take better pictures.

. . . .

5 Wear Regal jewellery. Be noticed.

. . . .

6 Save money by buying a Maestro computer.

. . . .

412 Type 2 conditionals

► Finder 246

What do people say in these situations? Use Type 2 conditionals.

► Simon has a lot of homework. Otherwise going out with you would be a good idea.
Simon: *If I didn't have so much homework, I'd go out with you.*
► Without a car, getting to work would be impossible for Peter.
Peter: *If I didn't have a car, I couldn't get to work.*

1 Kate doesn't want to tell you the truth because it would result in you getting angry.
Kate: . . . .
2 Sarah is afraid of flying. Otherwise it's possible she would go to Disney World.
Sarah: . . . .
3 For Karen life isn't boring, but with no surprises it would be.
Karen: . . . .
4 Adam hasn't got any money. Otherwise paying all his bills would be the thing to do.
Adam: . . . .
5 It's raining, just when Matthew wants to go to the beach.
Matthew: . . . .
6 Mark is injured, so he isn't playing tennis right now.
Mark: . . . .
7 Jo and Cristos don't have a common language. Jo wishes it was easier to communicate.
Jo: . . . .
8 Nicola can't afford a flat, although she would like to buy one.
Nicola: . . . .

413 Type 3 conditionals

► Finder 247A

Read this true story of crime and rewrite each underlined sentence as a Type 3 conditional.

LAST-MINUTE BOOKING

Alan and his girlfriend had a big fight. (►) Alan hadn't behaved very well, and so he needed to put things right. What could he do? (1) He didn't want to break up with his girlfriend, so he booked a holiday for the two of them. It was for two weeks in Benidorm, Spain, and he paid for the holiday by cheque. (2) When the cheque bounced, he turned to crime. In the twenty-four hours before their departure, he successfully held up three banks. (3) The money from the first hold-up wasn't enough, so he carried on. He got the money and paid it to the travel agency at the very last moment. (4) Because he had left it so late, they didn't have any time to spare. They were the last passengers to board the plane. (5) But Alan had made a silly mistake which meant that he was found out. In the first hold-up he had written his demand for money on the back of an envelope which had his name and address on the front. (6) He left the envelope in the bank, and so the police discovered his identity. Meanwhile Alan and his girlfriend were enjoying the holiday. (7) But when they returned to England, Alan was arrested at once. Later he went to prison. His lawyer said that(8) he committed the crimes because the holiday was so important to him.

▶ *If Alan had behaved well, he wouldn't have needed to put things right.*

1 ....

2 ....

3 ....

4 ....

5 ....

6 ....

7 ....

8 ....

414 Review of conditional Types 1-3

▶ Finder 245–247

Put in the correct form of each verb in brackets.

▶ If I ask Paul nicely, . . *he'll help* . . (he/help) us.

1 . . . . (you/make) yourself ill if you don't eat properly.

2 If the ball . . . . (cross) the line, that would have been the end of the game.

3 If . . . . (you/drink) up all the orange juice that was in that carton, you ought to go out and get some more.

4 If everyone . . . . (work) an extra hour a day, it would greatly increase production.

5 If you're a lucky winner, a prize . . . . (be) on its way to you soon.

6 If I'd seen anything suspicious, ... (I/call) the police.

7 If I slipped quietly out of the room in a few minutes' time, no one . . . . (notice).

8 If . . . . (you/not/mind) waiting a moment, I'll see if the manager is free.

9 If . . . . (I/drive), I would hire a car to drive round the island..

10 If . . . . (I/let) you know in time, I would have done.

11 If someone knocked a candle over, ... (it/start) a fire.

12 A moisturizer is what you need. If you use one, ... (you/not/get) dry skin.

13 If . . . . (I/not/agree) with you, I would say so.

14 Even if there had been an SOS message on the radio,
. . . . (I/not/listen) at the time.

415 *Should, were, had,* and inversion   ▶ Finder 248

Match the two parts of the sentence.

▶ If you should lose your credit card,	he would have little useful information.
1 If it hadn't been for the rain,	I wouldn't have understood a word.
2 If we were to win the contract,	~~please contact the bank immediately.~~
3 If a spy should be captured,	the crops would have died.
4 If anyone had spoken to me,	there would be more deaths.
5 If the speed limit were higher,	we might need more staff.

▶ . . *If you should lose your credit card, please contact the bank immediately.* . . .
1 . . . .
2 . . . .
3 . . . .
4 . . . .
5 . . . .

Then rewrite sentences 1-4 using inversion.

▶ . . *Should you lose your credit card, please contact the bank immediately.* . .
6 . . . .
7 . . . .
8 . . . .
9 . . . .

416 Review of conditional sentences   ▶ Finder 244–248

Look at these rules and examples. Which examples go with which rules?

Rules	Examples
▶ We can use an imperative in a conditional sentence.	a) If I was a bit taller, I could reach.
1 This sentence refers to an imaginary action in the past.	b) If I got a hundred per cent in my next test, would you be impressed?
2 Sometimes we can leave out *if* and invert the subject and verb.	c) If you mix black and white, you get grey.
3 This sentence is a mixture of Type 2 and Type 3 conditionals.	d) If I'd hit that stupid idiot, it would have served him right.
	(continues over page)

4 The past tense can express a theoretical possibility in the future.
5 This if-clause expresses an open condition, something that may or may not happen.
6 The past tense often expresses an unreal condition.
7 We can use *will* in an if-clause to make a request.
8 This type of sentence means that one thing follows automatically from another.

e) If we win the game, we'll go through to the next round.
f) If you don't like the product, don't buy it.
g) If you'll kindly come through into the next room.
h) If I knew where the treasure was buried, I'd have dug it up by now.
i) Should you have any queries, could you contact the office?

▶ *f)*

1 . . . . . 3 . . . . . 5 . . . . . 7 . . . . .
2 . . . . . 4 . . . . . 6 . . . . . 8 . . . . .

417 Review of conditional sentences

▶ **Finder 244–24**

Correct the clause that has a mistake in it.

▶ ~~If I have my wish~~, I'd be a film star.
  . . *If I had my wish,* . .

1 If I had a camera, ~~I can take a photo~~.

. . . .

2 ~~If they would have bought a group ticket~~, it would have been less expensive.

. . . .

3 If you're joking, ~~I going to be angry~~.

. . . .

4 ~~If you can go to the concert~~, you'd have enjoyed it, I'm sure.

. . . .

5 The alarm rings ~~if anyone will approach the house~~.

. . . .

6 Just keep quiet about it. Mention it to anyone ~~or you'll regret it~~.

. . . .

7 ~~If anything shall go wrong~~, give me a ring.

. . . .

8 If we drove through the town centre, ~~it will take longer~~.

. . . .

9 A bank will lend you money only ~~if they knew you can pay it back~~.

. . . .

10 If I had trusted my instincts, ~~I had refused~~.

. . . .

11 ~~Have we delayed any longer~~, we would have been too late.

. . . .

12 If the material gets very hot, ~~it would burst into flames~~.

. . . .

418 Review of conditionals Types 1–3 ▶ Finder 245–247

Complete the conversation. Put in the correct form of each verb in brackets.

Lucy: I'm going to watch a documentary on fashion tonight if no one (▶) _wants_
          (want) anything else.
Emily: What time is that?
Lucy: Half past eight.
Alice: If it goes on after nine o'clock, (1) . . . . (we/miss) the
          start of the film.
Emily: I'd like to see the film too.
Lucy: Well, if you're both watching the film, (2) . . . . (I/watch)
          it with you. If (3) . . . . (I/record) the documentary, I can
          watch it tomorrow.
Alice: I don't think we've got another tape. You know, if we bought a few new ones,
          (4) . . . . (we/not/keep) having this problem.
Emily: If (5) . . . . (I/think), I could have bought some at the
          supermarket this afternoon.
Lucy: Chloe has recorded some tennis on this one, but that doesn't matter. If she really
          wanted to, (6) . . . . (she/watch) it by now.
Emily: Chloe (7) . . . . (be) annoyed if you record over her tennis.
Alice: I'd be annoyed if someone (8) . . . . (do) that to me.
Lucy: I'm sure if I explain, (9) . . . . (she/not/mind).
Emily: Well, if (10) . . . . (there/be) a row, I'm going to keep
          out of it.

419 *When* and *if* ▶ Finder 249A

Put in *when* or *if*.

▶ I'm getting the lunch now. I'll call you . . _when_ . . it's ready.

1 I might move in with a couple of friends. . . . . I do, I'll be quite near a tube station.

2 I've given up hope of ever finding work. . . . . I ever get a job, it'll be a miracle.

3 Everything should be OK, but . . . . something does go wrong, you'll have to deal
   with it yourself.

4 Turn left, and . . . . you get to the end of the road, you'll see the house on your left.

5 The report will be published soon. . . . . it comes out, we will study it carefully.

420 More details about *if*

▶ Finder 249

Choose the correct form.

▶ Even as/~~but~~/though she's my neighbour, I hardly ever see her.

1 If no one wants to watch the film, but/so/then it can't be much good.
2 Suppose/Then/What if we all get together and buy one big present?
3 I don't think I'll be going out, but if/though/when I do, I'll leave you my key.
4 At least we can watch the parade, but/even/what if we can't take part in it.
5 If is wet/If it wet/If wet, the sale will be held inside the hall.

421 *Unless*

▶ Finder 250

Look at these sentences with *if*. Some can be changed into sentences with *unless*, and some cannot. Write the sentences with *unless*.

▶ You can't see anyone if you haven't got an appointment.

1 The hostages will be killed if the ransom isn't paid today.
2 If the computer hadn't crashed, I wouldn't have lost all my work.
3 I'll be very annoyed if the parcel doesn't arrive today.
4 The problem will get worse if we don't tackle it now.
5 If you don't practise regularly, you'll never learn to play the piano.
6 If the shops weren't so crowded, you could get around more quickly.
7 Don't try to do electrical work if you're not sure of what you're doing.

. . (▶) *You can't see anyone unless you've got an appointment.* . . . .
. . . .
. . . .
. . . .
. . . .

422 Ways of expressing a condition

▶ Finder 251

Choose the correct form.

▶ ~~Otherwise~~/~~Provided~~/With a bit of luck, we might get the four o'clock train.

1 Eat these sandwiches up, in case/otherwise/providing they'll be wasted.
2 The man was released in/on/with condition that he reported to the police every day.
3 I'll put the alarm clock on if/in case/unless I don't wake up in time.
4 I don't mind you having a party as long as/in case/with I'm invited.
5 As long as/In case/Without your help I would never have succeeded.
6 But for/In the event of/Provided that a breakdown, you would receive immediate assistance.
7 You can give a file any name condition/provided/supposing that the name has not already been used.

423 Ways of expressing a condition

▶ Finder 248–251

Say what kind of meaning is expressed by the sub-clause or by a prepositional phrase. It might be a condition (6x), time (2x), reason, contrast, or a wish.

▶ You can book in advance providing you give your credit card number. _condition_

1 Should you change your mind, you can always cancel the booking.
. . . .

2 When I think of flying, my heart sinks. . . . .

3 Although the food was nice, the background music was driving me mad.
. . . .

4 But for all the noise, it would have been a perfect place to stay. . . . .

5 If only we didn't have to climb all these stairs! . . . .

6 They won't turn the music off unless you ask them. . . . .

7 Had I not complained, we wouldn't have got our money back. . . . .

8 As soon as I lay down, I felt better. . . . .

9 We didn't do much shopping on account of the prices. . . . .

10 I'll go anywhere in the world as long as it's sunny. . . . .

424 Ways of expressing a condition

▶ Finder 249–251

Complete these sentences by putting in the missing words. Use these words: *as long as, if, in case, otherwise, then, unless, without.*

▶ I can come back later . _if_ . necessary.

1 I'll take an umbrella with me now . . . . it rains later on.

2 You shouldn't make promises . . . . you mean to keep them.

3 If it's my turn to wash up, ... I suppose I'd better do it.

4 You shouldn't ride a bike . . . . a helmet.

5 A picnic would be nice, ... it's warm enough.

6 I have to take a sleeping pill, ... I can't sleep.

425 Review of conditional sentences

▶ Finder 244–25

Write a sentence of similar meaning using the word in brackets.

▶ We haven't got satellite TV, so we can't watch the game. (if)
      If we had satellite TV, we could watch the game.

1 But for the view, this would be a lovely room. (if)

. . . .

2 The police are already on the streets because the protest may get violent. (in case)

. . . .

3 Please give the book back to me some time – I'd be grateful. (if)

. . . .

4 I might lose my job, but they'd have to pay me a month's wages. (should)

. . . .

5 We might have received all the replies by the weekend. Then we'll know who's coming. (if

. . . .

6 I'm not going to play if you don't keep to the rules. (unless)

. . . .

7 Simon was ill, so he didn't go to the party. (if)

. . . .

8 You can ring me in the middle of the night – it may be necessary. (if)

. . . .

9 If you don't leave the building immediately, I'll call security. (or)

. . . .

10 Imagine a situation where sea levels rise dramatically. (what)

. . . .

11 Six and eight are fourteen. (if)

. . . .

12 The sun isn't shining, so I'm not lying on the beach. (if)

. . . .

Read this true story and then write the sentences below.

HIGH SECURITY

In September 2001, there were a number of terrorist attacks on America. Americans soon realized how much more important security was becoming. More and more often people had to show an identity card with their photo on it. At the time of the attacks the singer Bob Dylan was on tour. He demanded that security should be increased at his concerts. But he obviously didn't realize the possible problems involved. His next venue was a showground in Oregon. When Dylan arrived, two security guards, a man and a woman in their thirties, asked for his identity card. Unfortunately he didn't have one, and when he tried to explain, the guards laughed in his face and refused to let him in. Dylan completely lost his temper. It is not clear whether he was angry at their rudeness or at their failure to recognize him. The fact that they didn't know him can't have helped. That his career should have made so little impact on them is surprising. The showground manager was called, and eventually the star was allowed in. The result of the incident was that the two guards were sacked – 'relocated', as the manager put it. Later he said they had done a good job.

▶ Write a sentence from the story that has a noun clause as its subject.
   That his career should have made so little impact on them is surprising.

1 Write a sentence that has as its object a clause beginning with *that*.
   ....
   ....

2 Which sentence has a noun clause as its complement?
   ....
   ....

3 Which has a noun clause coming after an adjective?
   ....
   ....

4 And which has a noun clause coming after a noun?
   ....
   ....

5 Which sentence has a noun clause beginning with a question word?
   ....
   ....

6 And which has a that-clause but without the word *that*?
   ....
   ....

427 Noun clause as object

▶ Finder 25

Combine the two sentences into one. Use a noun clause as object.

▶ The children can go to the zoo. I promised them.
   I promised the children they can go to the zoo.
▶ Why can't we use the computers? I don't understand.
   I don't understand why we can't use the computers.

1 You didn't mean to be rude. I realize that.

. . . .

2 When will you be back? I'd like to know.

. . . .

3 Mark is telling the truth. He convinced me.

. . . .

4 We're doing a survey. I explained that to the manager.

. . . .

5 We won't leave Amy on her own. I've reassured her.

. . . .

6 Why don't we go to the park? That's what I suggest.

. . . .

7 The President intends to run for re-election. He announced this to the media.

. . . .

. . . .

428 Noun clause with *it*

▶ Finder 254A–I

These sentences begin with a noun clause. Rewrite them beginning *It ...* .

▶ That Oliver is popular with his colleagues is obvious.
   It's obvious that Oliver is popular with his colleagues.

1 That no one claimed the prize was surprising.

. . . .

2 Whether I'll be able to sell these books is doubtful.

. . . .

3 That we have to change trains twice is a nuisance.

. . . .

4 That everyone is enjoying themselves is good to know.

. . . .

5 How this information got onto the Internet is a mystery.

. . . .

6 What you can find down the back of an old sofa is amazing.

. . . .

429 Noun clause after a preposition

▶ Finder 255A

Comment on each situation. Use a structure with a preposition + noun clause.

▶ Paul: What did you say?
  Steve: I can't remember exactly, but people are objecting to it.
  People are . . *objecting to what Paul said.* . . .

1 Kate: Where are you going to park?
  Simon: I don't know. That's what I'm worried about.
  Simon is . . . .

2 Louise: How are we going to pay our debts?
  Martin: Yes, that's what we should concentrate on.
  Louise and Martin should . . . .

3 Matthew: How awful the band were.
  Lauren: I know. My boyfriend kept making comments about it.
  Lauren's boyfriend . . . .

4 Gemma: What grades will you get?
  Jodie: I don't know. But my whole future depends on it.
  Jodie's whole future . . . .

5 James: My area of study is how waste is recycled.
  Lucy: Well, I wouldn't be interested in that.
  Lucy wouldn't . . . .

6 Sarah: Do you take a gamble or not, Kirsty?
  Kirsty: That's the question.
  Kirsty is faced with the . . . .

430 Noun clauses and prepositions

▶ Finder 255B

Look at each sentence and decide if it is correct or not. If it is correct, put a tick (✓) after it. If it is incorrect, put in the missing preposition.

▶ I don't care whether we go out or not. ✓

▶ I'm writing a report _on_ where our marketing should be targeted.

1 I wasn't really aware what was going on.

2 I'm doing research how children learn to talk.

3 Aren't you interested how the special effects were produced?

4 We need to decide where we're going to put the files.

5 This new law might have an effect whether our business can survive.

431 Noun clause after an adjective

▶ Finder 256A

Match the two parts of the sentence.

▶ I'm annoyed that	I was dreaming or not.
1 I'm so glad	people might be injured.
2 I was surprised how	quickly the time passed.
3 We are very concerned that	the weather will improve.
4 We are hopeful	you got home safely.
5 I wasn't sure whether	~~you threw my magazine away.~~

▶ *I'm annoyed that you threw my magazine away.* . . . .

1 . . . .

2 . . . .

3 . . . .

4 . . . .

5 . . . .

432 Noun clause after a noun

▶ Finder 256B

Combine the two sentences into one.

▶ The factory is to close. The news has shocked the town.
   The news that the factory is to close has shocked the town. . . . .

1 Would the war end? The hope proved false.

. . . .

2 The Vikings landed in America. There is plenty of evidence.

. . . .

3 Was Diana murdered? The theory convinced many people.

. . . .

4 Did God create the world? Science has challenged the idea.

. . . .

5 We should stop destroying the rainforests. I share that view.

. . . .

6 The President had not resigned. The reports were untrue.

. . . .

433 Review of noun clauses

▶ Finder 252–256

Each of these sentences is incorrect. Write the correct sentence.

▶ I wonder I've put my keys.
  I wonder where I've put my keys. . . . .

1 We've decided on we're going on strike.
. . . .

2 The fact of that we were lost didn't seem to matter.
. . . .

3 The song will go to number one is certain.
. . . .

4 I explained your sister what was happening.
. . . .

5 Let's see if are you right.
. . . .

6 I was confused where I was supposed to go.
. . . .

7 If they're going to give us permission is in some doubt.
. . . .

8 The news taxes were to go up caused an outcry.
. . . .

434 Review of noun clauses

▶ Finder 253–256

Combine the sentences into one.

▶ I was late. It was my own fault.
  . . . *It was my own fault that I was late.* . . .

1 We have to fill in all these forms. It's ridiculous.
  It's . . . .
2 You're upset. I realize that.
  I . . . .
3 How have the animals managed to escape? It isn't obvious.
  It . . . .
4 The figures had been checked. That's what I assumed.
  I . . . .
5 Everything will be all right. I'm confident of that.
  I'm . . . .
6 My visa has run out. That's the problem.
  The . . . .
7 I'm going home tomorrow. I told you that.
  I . . . .
8 What questions are they going to ask me? I'm quite anxious.
  I'm . . . .

435 Nominalization

Combine the two clauses into one by nominalizing the first one. Use the preposition in brackets.

When you change a verb into a noun, sometimes you can use the same word, and sometimes the noun has a special ending like *-tion*. Use these nouns: *damage, education, emergence, influence, lack, legalization, movement, need, over-production, request, respect.*

▶ People lack clean water. This is a major cause of disease. (of)
  The lack of clean water is a major cause of disease.

1 Children are being educated. This is an investment in the future. (of)

   . . . .

2 Old people aren't respected. This is no longer important in Western societies. (for)

   . . . .

3 My car was slightly damaged, but this will be paid for by the insurance company. (to)

   . . . .

4 Certain drugs may be legalized. This is being discussed in Parliament. (of)

   . . . .

5 They are suddenly moving troops, and this has increased tension. (of)

   . . . .

6 The company needs greater profits, which has led to some aggressive marketing. (for)

   . . . .

7 The National Party has emerged. It is a threat to the present government. (of)

   . . . .

8 They have massively over-produced coffee, and this has pushed down prices. (of)

   . . . .

9 Advertisements influence our behaviour enormously. This is well known. (of, on)

   . . . .

10 We requested more help, but we were refused. (for)

   . . . .

436 Verbs of reporting

▶ Finder 259B–D

Look at the direct speech and then complete the indirect speech. Put in the verb in brackets and add the name of the person spoken to if necessary.

▶ Alison to Karen: I'm being ignored.
  Alison _felt_ that she was being ignored. (felt)
▶ James to Sarah: I don't really own a castle.
  James _admitted to Sarah_ that he didn't really own a castle. (admitted)

1 Boss to Rick: I have a special project for you.
  The boss . . . . that she had a special project for him. (informed)

2 Paul to Laura: Something's wrong.
  Paul . . . . something was wrong. (knew)

3 Teacher to class: I'll be leaving.
  The teacher . . . . that she would be leaving. (explained)

4 Chloe to Simon: I saw a ghost.
  Chloe . . . . she saw a ghost. (thinks)

5 Hotel to Amy: There is a vegetarian menu.
  The hotel . . . . that there was a vegetarian menu. (assured)

6 Oliver to Elaine: I'm going to Scotland.
  Oliver . . . . that he was going to Scotland. (mentioned)

437 Verbs of reporting in the passive

▶ Finder 259B–C

Rewrite each sentence using a verb of reporting in the passive.

▶ They announced that the train would be delayed.
  It _was announced that the train would be delayed._
▶ A letter reminded us that the bill is overdue.
  We _were reminded that the bill is overdue._

1 The boss has told us that we have to work late.
  We . . . .

2 Someone suggested we should form a protest group.
  It . . . .

3 The police have warned people that a lion has escaped.
  People . . . .

4 Someone pointed out that there was a mistake in the exam paper.
  It . . . .

5 No one informed the residents that there had been a nuclear accident.
  The residents . . . .

438 *Tell, say,* and *ask*

▶ Finder 260

Put in *told*, *said*, *asked*, or *talked*.

▶ Someone . . *said* . . there's been a fire.
▶ Lauren . . *told* . . everyone she was going to win the prize.

1 Adam . . . . me he felt nervous.

2 Has Emily . . . . who she's invited to the party?

3 I . . . . you if you wanted a coffee.

4 The men . . . . about football all evening.

5 So I . . . . to the waiter, 'I think you're very rude.'

6 Elaine has . . . . her boyfriend she wants to split up.

7 Has Matthew . . . . you what he intends to do?

8 I needed an aspirin, so I . . . . where the nearest chemist's was.

9 I had a really interesting time and . . . . to lots of people.

10 Steve . . . . a joke, but no one laughed.

11 Who . . . . that we now live in a global village?

12 The security guard . . . . me what was in my briefcase, so I . . . . him there were some papers in it.

439 Changes in indirect speech

▶ Finder 261

Put in the missing words. Write either one or two words in each space.

1 Unfortunately you missed a bus yesterday. 'It left only a moment ago,' someone standing at the bus stop told you. You were late meeting your friend, and you explained what had happened. 'I must have only just missed it. Someone told . . . . it had left only a minute . . . .'

2 When you saw Alice a couple of days ago, she told you she was very busy that day. Her actual words were, ' . . . . very busy . . . .'

3 Last Friday Anna told you she had a date the following evening, but she wouldn't tell you who with. She just said, ' . . . . got a date . . . . evening.

4 Last week Richard told you, 'I bought a new mobile yesterday.' Now you're telling a friend, 'When I last saw Richard, he told me . . . . had bought a new mobile the . . . .'

5 One day about a month ago, you went to see Amy at her office, but someone there told you, 'She's away all this week.' Yesterday you said to a friend, 'I went to see Amy the day after our meal out, but she . . . . away all . . . . week.'

6 Yesterday your boss asked you to find out some information. 'Can you do it **now**, please?' he said. Now you're telling your friend, 'I had to find out some information for my boss. He said . . . . had to do it . . . .'

440 Tense change or not?

▶ Finder 262A–C

Complete the indirect speech. Decide if you need to change the tense or not.

▶ 'I feel cold.' → Emily says she .. *feels* .. cold.
▶ 'I've got a headache.' → I told you yesterday I .. *had* .. a headache, but you weren't listening.

1 'Doesn't Nicola study art?' → I don't know why, but Steve thought you . . . . art.
2 'United are going to win.' → Richard thinks United . . . . going to win.
3 'United are going to win.' → You thought United . . . . going to win, but you were wrong.
4 'I knew the answer all the time.' → Paul says he . . . . the answer all the time.
5 'I always sleep on the floor.' → Joanna says she always . . . . on the floor.
6 'I'm worried about my interview.' → You told me before the interview that you . . . . worried about it.

441 The tense change

▶ Finder 262C–D

These people were all talking to you at a barbecue last week. Now you're talking about the barbecue to a friend who has just got back from a trip away. Report what was said using the time change where necessary.

▶ Jake: I want a better job.
1 Max: I'm going to Paris.
2 Polly: I've had an e-mail from Karen.
3 Mike: I don't like the new trainee.
4 Jane: I have a new boyfriend.
5 Andrew: I'm being spied on.
6 Mrs Lucas: I wish I was young again.
7 Angela: I've found a place to live.
8 Celia: I've been invited to a reception.
9 Alan: I know a secret.

▶ . *Jake said he wanted a better job.* . . . .
1 . . . .
2 . . . .
3 . . . .
4 . . . .
5 . . . .
6 . . . .
7 . . . .
8 . . . .
9 . . . .
. . . .

442 The tense change

▶ Finder 262C–E

Ten years ago an African freedom fighter called Harrison Tengo was released from prison and became President of his country. You are writing an article about him. Read the speech that Mr Tengo made after his release and then report what he said. You do not need to repeat 'He said'.

'I have high hopes for the future. I have spent many years in prison, but I do not feel bitter. The world is changing and I want to change with it. I love my country, and I believe it is a great nation. In my youth I fought for its freedom. I wish I could work miracles, but it would be foolish to think so. It will be a long hard road. I urge my people to join me in this task. We can do it together.'

Mr Tengo said that he had high hopes for the future. He had . . . .

443 Reporting questions

▶ Finder 263A–C

An Englishman made a solo cycle journey round the world. In one country he was arrested and taken to a police station, where the police asked him lots of questions. Afterwards they let him go. Months later, when he was back home, he told a reporter all about the incident. How did he report the questions from the police? Use the verbs of reporting in brackets.

▶ 'What have you got in your luggage?' (want to know)
They wanted to know what I had in my luggage.

▶ 'Are you a spy?' (ask me)
They asked me if I was a spy.

1 'Do you have a notebook?' (ask)
. . . .

2 'Where are you going?' (want to know)
. . . .

3 'Where have you come from?' (want to know)
. . . .

4 'How long have you been in the country?' (inquire)
. . . .

5 'Have you spoken to anyone on your journey?' (wonder)
. . . .

6 'Who paid for your journey?' (ask)
. . . .

7 'Are you carrying any drugs?' (inquire)
. . . .

8 'Where do you plan to sleep?' (ask me)
. . . .

Decide which sentence is spoken by which person. Then report what was said.

▶ Can you all sit down in your seats, please?	Boss told employee.
1 I want you to learn the new words.	~~Bus driver asked passengers.~~
2 You ought to go on a diet.	Doctor told patient.
3 Don't be late tomorrow morning.	Hotel guests asked porter.
4 Can you move your car out of the way, sir?	Security guard asked travellers.
5 Could you take our luggage, please?	Teacher told class.
6 You mustn't leave your bags unattended.	Traffic warden told motorist.

▶   *The bus driver asked the passengers to sit down in their seats.*

1 ....

2 ....

3 ....

4 ....

5 ....

6 ....

445 Reporting statements, questions, and requests

▶ Finder 262–264

The sentences below were all addressed to you yesterday. How would you report them Use *said, told,* or *asked.*

▶ Debbie: I bought a cake.
   Debbie said she'd bought a cake.

▶ Waiter: Would you mind moving to another table?
   The waiter asked me to move to another table.

1 Oliver: I'd love to do a parachute jump.

2 Shop assistant: What's your postcode?

3 Linda: Would you mind looking after my luggage?

4 Policeman: Does anyone else live in the house?

5 Sarah: I can drive a minibus.

6 Landlord: Don't park your car in the yard, OK?

7 Tom: Have you finished with the computer?

8 Librarian: Could you turn the music off, please?

9 Louise: Where are you going?

10 Jack: I've been dropped from the basketball team.

446 Reporting offers, warnings, etc

▶ Finder 26!

Decide which sentence of indirect speech goes with which direct speech.

▶ 'All right. I'll go.'   a) I advised them to go.
1 'No, I certainly didn't go.'   b) I agreed to go.
2 'I'm really sorry I went.'   c) I apologized for going.
3 'You really should go.'   d) I assured them that I would go.
4 'I'm just not going.'   e) I criticized them for going.
5 'Don't worry, I'll go.'   f) I denied going.
6 'Let's go.'   g) I insisted on going.
7 'I really must go.'   h) I refused to go.
8 'You shouldn't have gone.'   i) I suggested going.

▶ b)   3 . . . . .   6 . . . .
1 . . . . .   4 . . . . .   7 . . . .
2 . . . . .   5 . . . . .   8 . . . .

447 Reporting offers, warnings, etc

▶ Finder 265

Combine the clauses into a single sentence with the verb of reporting in the first clause.

▶ I might go camping. My friends have invited me.
. . *My friends have invited me to go camping.* . .

1 Lisa is going to fax the information. She's promised.

. . . .

2 The weather forecast was awful, James warned me.

. . . .

3 Gemma won the competition. We all congratulated her.

. . . .

4 We might get a group ticket. Someone suggested it.

. . . .

5 The money must be paid by tomorrow, the office has reminded us.

. . . .

6 Prices will remain steady. That's what the government is forecasting.

. . . .

7 The visitors had to wait in the rain. They were complaining about it.

. . . .

8 I'll probably sit the exam again. That's what my tutor has advised.

. . . .

448 Review of indirect speech

▶ Finder 261–265

Look at the indirect speech and write the direct speech.

▶ Lauren said she was feeling fine.
▶ Lauren: . . *I'm feeling fine.* . . .

1 Peter said he couldn't get the door open.
Peter: . . . .

2 Jodie asked me whether I was ready to go.
Jodie: . . . .

3 Matthew said he likes all kinds of music.
Matthew: . . . .

4 Adam apologized for getting the message wrong.
Adam: . . . .

5 Chloe says she forgot her ticket.
Chloe: . . . .

6 Alison told me not to spoil the fun.
Alison: . . . .

7 Your brother shouldn't have asked Mark how much money he earns.
Your brother: . . . .

8 Emma said she would ring me the following week.
  Emma: . . . .

9 My friends told me they'd just seen Madonna in the street.
  My friends: . . . .

10 Tim refused to climb the ladder.
   Tim: . . . .

11 The receptionist asked us to wait for a moment.
   Receptionist: . . . .

12 The couple told immigration officers that they had got married the previous month.
   Couple: . . . .

449 Review of indirect speech

▶ Finder 259–265

Decide which answer is correct.

▶ I pointed out . . *to* . . the manager that we had already paid the bill.
  a) at   b) by   c) on   d) to

1 Someone told us . . . . sit on the stairs.
  a) don't   b) not   c) not to   d) to not

2 Martin said his hair was wet because . . . .
  a) he'd been swimming   b) he's been swimming   c) he swam   d) he swims

3 Did anyone . . . . what time we have to be there?
  a) say   b) speak   c) talk   d) tell

4 I was wondering . . . . you've got a moment, please.
  a) how   b) if   c) that   d) what

5 All the students . . . . knowing anything about the matter.
  a) apologized   b) denied   c) promised   d) refused

6 I thought I . . . . get away with my basic Russian, but I was wrong.
  a) can   b) could   c) may   d) will

7 A company spokesperson said that the accusations . . . . completely untrue.
  a) are   b) be   c) should be   d) were

8 No one has . . . . us why our application has been unsuccessful.
  a) explained   b) informed   c) mentioned   d) said

450 Review of indirect speech

▶ Finder 259–265

Complete the indirect speech.

▶ Sarah: I need a good night's sleep.
Yesterday Sarah told . . . *me she needed a good night's sleep.* . . .

1 Mark: Do you believe in God?
Mark once asked me . . . .

2 Tom: I came out of hospital only an hour ago.
When I saw Tom last week, ...
. . . .

3 Kate: Could I have my key, please?
Kate . . . .

4 Lisa: You'll be sorry.
When Lisa first learned that Oliver was investing in the scheme, ...
. . . .

5 Leanne: When will I be getting my money?
Leanne wants . . . .

6 Alan: Hey! Why should I do all the work?
Alan objected . . . .

7 Simon: Please don't laugh at me, Emily.
Simon is asking . . . .

8 Rick: It's your turn next, Jessica.
Rick reminded . . . .

9 Hannah: I'm waiting for Lucy.
I wanted to take Hannah for a coffee yesterday, but she explained . . . .
. . . .

10 Charlotte: Listen, Paul. The secret address is hidden in …
Charlotte told . . . .

451 Introduction to relative clauses

▶ Finder 266A

Read this story and underline the relative clauses. There are seven of them, not including the example.

Here's a true story <u>which teaches us to guard our secrets carefully</u>. It's about a man whose house front collapsed one day. As a result, his secrets were embarrassingly revealed for all the world to see. Colin Campbell, who lives in the English Midlands, wasn't very pleased when a lorry rolled down a hill and crashed into his house. The damage it did was spectacular. The front of the house collapsed, which was bad enough in itself. Even worse, a life-size model of Elvis Presley, which was standing in an upstairs bedroom, became visible to passers-by. Colin said, 'It was something I bought on impulse. Then I hid him away in the spare bedroom because I didn't want anyone to see him. Now people are laughing at me. In future I'll always be the man who bought Elvis Presley.'

452 Ways of modifying a noun

▶ Finder 266B

Combine the information in the shortest way possible.

▶ a house (it has a garden) *a house with a garden*
▶ some boys (they are playing football) *some boys playing football*
▶ the man (he won the competition) *the man who won the competition*

1 the shop (it is on the corner) . . . .
2 a car (it is red) . . . .
3 the woman (she missed her train) . . . .
4 a book (it was published last month) . . . .
5 a woman (she was waiting for someone) . . . .
6 a chair (it is comfortable) . . . .
7 the people (they have heard the story before)
. . . .
8 a man (he has a gun) . . . .
9 a face (it is recognized everywhere) . . . .

453 The use of commas with relative clauses

▶ Finder 266D

Decide if there are any commas missing from these sentences. If the sentence is correct
put a tick (✓) after it. If there are commas missing, put them in.

▶ Students who get below-average exam results do not have the best prospects. ✓

▶ Only about 70 people live on Lundy Island , which lies off the coast of Devon.

1 I'm having a visit from my favourite aunt who lives in London.

2 This is the room that we've just decorated.

3 The people who invested in the company have all lost their money.

4 The match will be played at Lord's which is the home of English cricket.

5 Accidents that happen at night usually involve fewer people.

6 Marian Evans who wrote under the name of George Eliot was a great novelist.

7 The new college which cost £80 million to build opens this week.

8 People who live in glass houses shouldn't throw stones.

454 Types of relative clause

▶ Finder 267A–E

Read the story and say what type each relative clause is: identifying, classifying, for emphasis, adding, or connective.

If you're one of those people (▶) **who might find accidents amusing**, then this is the story for you. It happened somewhere in England, and it's about a motorist (▶)**who was approaching a level crossing**. (A level crossing is a barrier (1) **that prevents traffic from driving across the railway line when a train is coming**.) As he approached the crossing, the motorist suddenly saw in front of him a girl on a horse and an old man with a dog. He had to brake quite suddenly. There was a motor-bike behind the car, and the motor-cyclist, (2) **who wasn't paying attention**, crashed into the back of the car. This frightened the horse, (3) **which reared up and threw its rider into a hedge**. The old man, (4) **who was a helpful sort of person**, decided to come to the rescue by catching the horse. But first he tied his dog to the level crossing barrier, (5) **which was the nearest suitable thing**. The train (6) **which everyone had been expecting** then passed through the crossing, and the barrier (7) **that the dog had been tied to** began to rise. It was this (8) **that really made things interesting**. The old man rushed back to release the dog, (9) **which promptly bit the motor-cyclist**, (10) **who was still lying on the ground**. This scene, (11) **which certainly has its funny side**, was nominated the most bizarre accident of the year by the insurance company (12) **which handled the horse rider's claim**.

▶ classifying

▶ identifying

1	5	9 ....
2	6	10 ....
3	7	11 ....
4	8	12 ....

455 Relative clauses without commas

▶ Finder 268A–B

Look at each conversation and then write the information in a sentence with a relative clause. Use *who* or *that*.

▶ Martin: Well, we met that man, anyway.
  Emily: What man?
  Martin: You know who I mean. He works at the post office.
  .. *Martin and Emily met the man who works at the post office.* ..

▶ Alice: I like the jacket.
  Simon: What jacket do you mean?
  Alice: Your new jacket. You wore it yesterday.
  .. *Alice likes the jacket that Simon wore yesterday.* ..

1 Tom: I know the girl.
  Sarah: What girl?
  Tom: That girl over there. She appeared on television.
  . . . .

2 Louise: I like those people.
  Rick: What people?
  Louise: The people we're talking about. You've invited them to the party.

. . . .

3 Leanne: I wish I still had the camera.
  James: What camera are you talking about?
  Leanne: My camera. You broke it, remember?

. . . .

4 Adam: I saw them carry off that player.
  Mark: Oh, why did they do that?
  Adam: He was injured, of course.

. . . .

5 Kate: I'm going to complain about that burglar alarm.
  Nicola: Was it ringing?
  Kate: It wouldn't stop ringing.

. . . .

6 Paul: The company still hasn't received the letter.
  Laura: What letter?
  Paul: My letter to the company. I posted it on Tuesday.

. . . .

7 Steve: I couldn't understand that woman?
  Hannah: What woman is that?
  Steve: You know. You were interviewing her.

. . . .

8 Lisa: I was reading about the bridge.
  Karen: The bridge?
  Lisa: Yes, it collapsed in a hurricane.

. . . .

456 Prepositions in relative clauses without commas

▶ Finder 268

Rewrite the sentences and make them more suitable for a piece of formal writing.

▶ Religion is a subject that people hold very firm opinions on.
  . *Religion is a subject on which people hold very firm opinions.* . .
▶ No one cares about the starving people that the aid is intended for.
  . *No one cares about the starving people for whom the aid is intended.* . .

1 The photographs show the floor that many of the victims were trapped on.

. . . .

2 The Sales Manager is a young woman we have great confidence in.

. . . .

3 We entered the territory that so many battles have been fought over.

. . . .

4 Nearby are the Roman baths that the city of Bath gets its name from.

. . . .

5 Washington is the man Americans owe their independence to.

. . . .

457 Leaving out the relative pronoun ▶ Finder 268E

Rewrite the sentences using a relative clause without a pronoun.

▶ You took some photos, and they were great.
   The photos you took were great.
▶ I've been waiting for a train, but it's been cancelled.
   The train I've been waiting for has been cancelled.

1 We stayed at a hotel, and it was perfect.

. . . .

2 We were watching a programme, and it was really interesting.

. . . .

3 I'm wearing these shoes, and they're the latest fashion.

. . . .

4 We were looking at some jewellery, but it was rather expensive.

. . . .

5 You were playing some music, and it sounded very familiar.

. . . .

6 I was telling you about a club, and it's called the Palace, I've remembered.

. . . .

458 Leaving out the relative pronoun ▶ Finder 268

Some of these sentences are correct, and some have a relative pronoun missing. If a sentence is correct, put a tick (✓). If it is incorrect, put the pronoun in the right place.

▶ The pills I took have had no effect at all. ✓

▶ Something ⋏*that* happened yesterday has been worrying me.

1 People smoke are endangering their health.

2 None of the people I talked to could give me any useful information.

3 There was a bad accident closed the motorway.

4 No one has said anything would persuade me to change my mind.

5 I've been having a look at that website you mentioned.

6 The police wouldn't tell us the source of the information on they were acting.

7 I'm beginning to think this CD I heard about doesn't exist.

8 Immigrants are in jobs could not be filled from the existing workforce.

9 He was the leader in the population placed all their hopes.

10 It's no use passing a law nobody takes any notice of.

459 Relative clauses with commas

▶ Finder 269

Read this paragraph about Nelson Mandela.

Fifty years ago South Africans lived under the apartheid system. The best jobs went to white people, and the worst jobs were done by black workers. Mandela was a lawyer. He joined the African National Congress. Things got even worse at Sharpeville in 1960 when police fired into a crowd of black people. Mandela played his part in the struggle for equal rights. He was found guilty of sabotage. He stayed in prison for many long years. In fact Mandela became the most famous prisoner in the world. He was finally released in 1990. Soon he was President of the new South Africa. But although he had suffered for so long, he did not want to take his revenge on the white minority.

Now improve the text by adding more details. Find the best place for the following information and rewrite the text putting in relative clauses with commas.

- White people lived in nice homes with gardens and swimming-pools.
- Many of the black workers had to live apart from their families.
- The African National Congress was leading the fight against apartheid.
- The black people were protesting peacefully.
- The fact that Mandela played his part in the struggle led to his imprisonment.
- He was sent to prison for life for sabotage.
- Mandela's 70th birthday was celebrated with a concert in London.
- By 1990 he had spent 27 years in prison.
- He would have had every reason to hate the white minority.

> Fifty years ago South Africans lived under the apartheid system. The best jobs
> went to white people, who lived in nice homes with gardens and swimming-pools, and
> the worst jobs

460 *Who* and *whose* ▶ Finder 268A, 269F, 270A–B

Match the two parts of each sentence and put in *who* or *whose*.

▶ The Queen's eldest son is Charles,	... have been forced out of their homes.
▶ The manager sent on his new striker,	... soon disappeared.
1 There are quite a few artists	... ~~scored a brilliant goal~~.
2 I have a secretary	... products have a reputation for quality.
3 The camp is full of refugees	for ... support I am extremely grateful.
4 I wish to thank a number of people	... job is to arrange my appointments.
5 We are a first-class company	... paintings are worth millions.
6 My sister married a conjuror,	... ~~marriage to Diana ended in 1996~~.

▶ *The Queen's eldest son is Charles, whose marriage to Diana ended in 1996.*

▶ *The manager sent on his new striker, who scored a brilliant goal.*

1 . . . .
2 . . . .
3 . . . .
4 . . . .

5 . . . .

6 . . . .

461 *Of which* ▶ Finder 270C

Combine each pair of sentences using *of which*.

▶ We saw a house. Its roof had been blown off in the storm.
   We saw a house, the roof of which had been blown off in the storm.

1 It's a very exclusive club. Its members are wealthy business people.

. . . .
. . . .

2 The fire destroyed many treasures. Their value is incalculable.

. . . .

3 Tom told me a complicated story. I've forgotten the details.

. . . .

4 The Romans built a huge fort. Its remains are still visible today.

. . . .
. . . .

5 My flat-mates had an angry argument. The result is that they aren't speaking to each other.

. . . .
. . . .

6 We saw a film. Its plot was totally incomprehensible.

. . . .

7 The chairman made a speech. By the end of it most of us were asleep.

. . . .

462 Relative adverbs, *what,* and *whoever*

▶ Finder 271–27:

Put in these words: *way, what, when, where, which, whoever, why.*

▶ The police have moved into areas . . *where* . . trouble is expected.

1 There isn't a moment . . . . I'm not thinking of you.
2 I hate the . . . . you never look at me when you speak to me.
3 There must be a reason . . . . no one has replied to our message.
4 . . . . gets home first cooks the tea.
5 We ate most of the food and threw away . . . . we couldn't eat.
6 I can't remember the name of the island on . . . . the aircraft landed.
7 Unfortunately we live in a part of the city . . . . there's no underground line.

463 Participle relative clauses

▶ Finder 274A–I

Combine the two sentences into one. Change the first sentence into a noun phrase + relative clause, as in the examples. Use a participle clause if possible. Otherwise use a finite relative clause.

▶ The students were complaining about high rents. They were on the streets.
. . *Students complaining about high rents were on the streets.* . .
▶ A woman was injured in the accident. She is a German tourist.
. . *The woman injured in the accident is a German tourist.* . .
▶ An inventor gave us the telephone. He was a Scot.
. . *The inventor who gave us the telephone was a Scot.* . .

1 The dam was holding back the water. Then it suddenly gave way.

. . . .

2 Some buildings were hit by bombs. They are still burning.

. . . .

3 Some people want to smoke. They have to leave the building.

. . . .

4 A plane crashed into the sea. It may have been a terrorist target.

. . . .

5 A shot was fired that day. It signalled the start of the American Revolution.

. . . .

6 The letter accused me of theft. It hadn't been signed.

. . . .

7 Tourists take the train from London to Stratford. They have to change at Coventry.

. . . .

8 A scientist discovered the neutron. He was James Chadwick.

. . . .

9 People were walking across the bridge. They could feel it swaying.

. . . .

10 One man is tipped to become the new President. He is little known outside his own country.

. . . .

. . . .

464 Infinitive relative clauses
▶ Finder 275

Comment on each situation using an infinitive relative clause.

▶ The US dropped an atom bomb. No other country had done that before.
. . *The US was the first country to drop an atom bomb.* . . .

▶ The protesters had no weapons. They couldn't defend themselves.
. . *The protesters had no weapons with which to defend themselves.* . . .

1 Henry VIII of England married six times. No other king did that.

. . . .

2 John F. Kennedy was assassinated, which hasn't happened to any US President since.

. . . .

3 The government has little money. It can't tackle the many social problems.

. . . .

4 New Zealand gave women the right to vote. No other country had done that before.

. . . .

5 I think China will host the Olympic Games soon. It'll be their turn next.

. . . .

6 Voters are faced with a lot of parties. They can choose from a large number.

. . . .

7 At 24, William Pitt became Prime Minister. No one else so young has ever done that.

. . . .

465 Review of relative clauses
▶ Finder 266–275

Read this paragraph about a military exercise.

The army held a military exercise recently. It took place on Bleak Moor. Colonel Phillips was in charge of the exercise, which began at seven o'clock in the morning. The press were interested, and several journalists and photographers tried to witness the exercise, although in fact they were forbidden from going anywhere near it. There were a number of photographers, including Bill, Terry and Steve. Bill was arrested by the military police. As for Terry, his camera was confiscated. Steve was working with a journalist called Angela. He didn't get any photos. No one managed to get any except Sandra of the Daily Vision. The Vision always has the best pictures. Otherwise the exercise was a success, and that pleased the colonel.

Now complete these sentences using a relative clause.

▶ The area . . *where the exercise took place* . . . is called Bleak Moor.

1 The man . . . . is called Colonel Phillips.
2 Seven o'clock in the morning was the . . . .
3 Bill was the photographer . . . .

4 Terry was the photographer ....
5 Angela was the journalist ....
6 Sandra was the only person ....
7 The Vision is the paper ....
8 The exercise was a success, ...

466 Review of relative clauses

▶ Finder 266–27!

Each of these sentences is incorrect. Write the correct sentence.

▶ ~~The man which saved a boy from drowning got an award.~~
  The man who saved a boy from drowning got an award.

1 ~~There were rushing about everywhere people.~~
  ....

2 ~~Where's that magazine at I was looking?~~
  ....

3 ~~I'm quite happy with that I've got, thanks.~~
  ....

4 ~~They live in Pensford, that lies just south of Bristol.~~
  ....

5 ~~Peter was the only person notice my new hairstyle.~~
  ....

6 ~~The weather has been far too wet to go out that we've had lately.~~
  ....

7 ~~We've got a light always comes on automatically in the evening.~~
  ....

8 ~~I can't see any reason for it shouldn't work.~~
  ....

9 ~~There were 35 passengers on the coach, almost all who were British.~~
  ....

10 ~~Who dumped this rubbish here doesn't care about the environment.~~
  ....

11 ~~There was an accident in that four people were killed.~~
  ....

12 ~~They are the generation who's fathers fought in the Vietnam War.~~
  ....

Combine the two sentences into one.

▶ This is the bus. It goes to the university.
   This is the bus that goes to the university.
▶ The park was full of people. They were strolling around.
   The park was full of people strolling around.

1 Do you remember the place? We all used to meet there?
. . . .

2 There are a number of options. We are considering them.
. . . .

3 We took in a dog. It had been abandoned by its previous owner.
. . . .

4 I rang the police. They came immediately.
. . . .

5 In the corridor there was a notice board. Several students were looking at it.
. . . .

6 She is an artist. I am quite familiar with her work.
. . . .

7 You always disapprove of anything I do - it doesn't matter what it is.
. . . .

8 My favourite street is Clark Avenue. It has lots of pavement cafés.
. . . .

9 It isn't much evidence. You can't base a whole theory on it.
. . . .

Key to Exercises

The numbers after the arrows tell you which part of the *Grammar Finder* book has the relevant explanation. ▶ 42A–B means that you should look at sections 42A and 42B if you need information on the grammar point.

The symbol / (slash) between two words means that either answer is possible. *Went/had gone* means that *went* and *had gone* are both correct answers.

Brackets ( ) around a word or phrase means that it can be left out. *I've been here (for) a week* means that there are two possible answers: *I've been here for a week* and *I've been here a week*.

1
1 'Candidate' is a noun.
2 'Her' is a pronoun.
3 'About' is a preposition.
4 'Ear' is a noun.
5 'Hoping' is a verb.
6 'Because' is a conjunction.
7 'Crossly' is an adverb.
8 'Was' is a verb
9 'Same' is an adjective.
10 'Lenses' is a noun.
11 'Very' is an adverb.
12 'That' is a conjunction.
13 'Of' is a preposition.
14 'Simple' is an adjective.
15 'One' is a determiner.
16 'Wear' is a verb.
▶ 1

2
1 verb, noun   4 noun, verb
2 noun, verb   5 adjective, noun
3 noun, adjective   6 adjective, verb
▶ 2

3
1 often   6 by Thursday
2 on the bus   7 have been happening
3 really nice   8 so slowly
4 must have   9 you
5 all these old   10 hot
  magazines
▶ 3

4
1 complement   8 adverbial
2 adverbial   9 complement
3 verb   10 adverbial
4 subject   11 subject
5 object   12 (indirect) object
6 (object) complement 13 verb
7 adverbial   14 (object) complement
▶ 4

5
1 gave the driver a tip.   2 are delicious.
3 put the car in the garage.   4 was shining.
5 is in Tokyo.   6 built some new flats.
7 keeps the team fit.
▶ 4

6
1 We've painted the walls bright yellow.
2 I like my coffee very strong.
3 The members elected Alice president.
4 The long journey (had) made me tired.
5 They call their cat 'Biscuit'.
6 The ice-packs will keep the food cool.
▶ 5D

7
1 One Saturday morning, in a small English town
2 For a few minutes, carefully   3 Then, on the floor   4 now, on his feet   5 Luckily, immediately   6 soon, too slowly   7 very fast, in two right-foot boots
▶ 5E

8
1 My boyfriend is going to cook me a meal. ▶ 6A
2 Uncle Robert promised his nephews and niece a trip to the zoo. ▶ 6A
3 They gave the job to a young man from Glasgow. ▶ 6B
4 Patrick made some sandwiches for his guests. ▶ 6B
5 The guide handed me a list of hotels. ▶ 6A
6 The company mailed us the information. ▶ 6A
7 Lucy's parents are going to buy her a car. ▶ 6A
8 The protestors have sent a message to the Prime Minister. ▶ 6B
9 The organizers have saved seats for our group ▶ 6B

9
1 to   2 for   3 to   4 to   5 for   6 to   7 for
▶ 6C

10
1 you more money. ▶ 6E
2 all her money to an animal hospital. ▶ 6D
3 six numbers for my little sister. ▶ 6D
4 most of it to the dog. ▶ 6D
5 me fifty pounds. ▶ 6E
6 all their employees a free holiday. ▶ 6D

1 1 b) Caroline described her symptoms to the doctor.
2 d) The artist's family have donated the picture to the National Gallery.
3 f) Lucy explained the rules of the game to us.
4 g) The government must communicate its message to the public.
▶ 6F

2 1 a statement, asking for information ▶ 7B
2 an imperative, a request ▶ 7A
3 an exclamation, expressing a feeling ▶ 7A
4 a question, asking for information ▶ 7A
5 an imperative, good wishes ▶ 7B
6 a question, a request ▶ 7B
7 a statement, giving information ▶ 7A
8 a statement, an order/a request ▶ 7B

3 1 giving information, predicting, expressing sympathy
2 making a suggestion, not agreeing with a suggestion, offering, thanking
▶ 8

4 1 agree ▶ 9A   4 advise ▶ 9B
2 insist ▶ 9B   5 promise ▶ 9A
3 refuse ▶ 9A   6 apologize ▶ 9A

5 1 isn't improving
2 You haven't put them/things right.
3 It hasn't been modernized.
4 It doesn't lead the world in technology.
5 They shouldn't be grateful to you.
6 You didn't save it from ruin.
7 They aren't/Our ideas aren't ridiculous.
8 You won't win it/win the next election.
▶ 10A–B

6 1 Not many companies/Not a lot of companies
2 Not much/Not a lot   3 not more than five minutes.   4 Not far away   5 not long ago.
6 Not everyone/everybody has
▶ 10C

7 1 There weren't many seats left.
2 None of these problems are major ones.
3 There was hardly any traffic on the road.
4 No one/Nobody disagrees with your suggestion.
5 Louise doesn't like Mark, and neither do I.
6 I suppose we will never know the truth.
7 The new computer is no more expensive than the old one.
8 We no longer go to that club.
▶ 10D

18 1 least   3 whatsoever   5 far
2 absolutely   4 not   6 at
▶ 10E

19 1 Only in the fantasies of news reporters is the President corrupt.
2 At no time has he broken the law.
3 Never in his whole life did he do anything wrong.
4 Not since 1997 has the President been late with his tax payments.
5 In no way are these rumours true.
6 Seldom does Mr Curtis think about his own finances.
7 The President does not cheat the people, and neither does he tell lies.
▶ 10F

20 1 Open   3 Write/Put   5 leave
2 Don't make   4 Don't look   6 Close/Shut
▶ 11A

21 1 Could I have a coffee, please? ▶ 11C
2 Would you mind holding my bag for a minute, please? ▶ 11B
3 Could I have/Could you give me a clean glass, please? ▶ 11C
4 Could you move your bicycle out of the way, please? ▶ 11B
5 Can I have/Can you give me a receipt, please? ▶ 11C
6 I'd like you to sit/Would you like to sit over here, please? ▶ 11B

22 1 an instruction 2 a piece of advice 3 wishing someone well 4 an advertisement 5 a slogan
6 an invitation
▶ 11D

23 1 Turn it down, can't you? ▶ 11E
2 Enjoy your game, won't you? ▶ 11E
3 Let's play mini-golf, shall we? ▶ 11F
4 Shut the window, can you? / could you? / will you? / would you? ▶ 11E
5 Don't drop those plates, will you? ▶ 11E

24 1 what   3 What a   5 How
2 How   4 What   6 What a
▶ 12B

25 1 asking for information 2 an offer
3 a complaint 4 asking for information
5 a request
▶ 13

26 **Yes/no questions:**
Will it be fine tomorrow?
Did you bring some money with you?
Are you doing anything tonight?
Have you had a holiday this year?
Has anything interesting happened lately?
Wh-questions:
When does the film start?
Why is everyone laughing?
How are you feeling?
Where can we park the car?
Who did you ring on your mobile?
▶ 14A–B

27 1 Where did they   2 How did they book a
3 Where did they think they were   4 How did
they go/get/travel there/to Gerona?   5 Why were
they puzzled?   6 When did they realize (that)
something was wrong?   7 Who did they ask for
help?   8 What did the couple tell Michael and
Kate?   9 Which box had they clicked?
▶ 15A

28 1 Who broke the world record?
2 What has Mark broken?
3 Who called the police?
4 What does Susan keep in the safe?
5 What made Susan late for work?
6 Who did Emma mail for advice?
7 Who mailed Emma with some advice?
8 Who are the police interviewing?
9 How much (money) have we spent?
10 How many people are coming?
11 What happened?
12 Who did Leanne meet?
▶ 15B

29 1 Who are those people looking for?
2 What has Laura decided on?
3 What is the picture frame made of?
4 Who did Sarah dance with?
5 What are you worried about?
6 What could people object to?
7 What was Sam apologizing for?
▶ 15D

30
1 What ▶ 16A–B   6 What ▶ 16A–B
2 Which ▶ 16A–B   7 Which ▶ 16A–B
3 Which ▶ 16A–B   8 Which ▶ 16A–B
4 What ▶ 16C   9 What ▶ 16C
5 Who ▶ 16B   10 Who ▶ 16B

31 1 How ▶ 16D, What time ▶ 16C
2 What ▶ 16D, What colour ▶ 16C

3 What else ▶ 16F, What ▶ 16C
4 How old, How long, How often ▶ 16C
5 What kind, What about, How much ▶ 16C

32 1 What does she look like? ▶ 14A–B, 16D
2 When was/What time was she last seen? ▶ 14A–
B, 15A
3 Where was she? ▶ 14A–B, 15A
4 Has someone kidnapped her?/Has she been
kidnapped? ▶ 14A–B
5 Is she in trouble? ▶ 14A–B
6 Has she (ever) gone missing before? ▶ 14A–B
7 Where are you/people looking (for her)? ▶ 14A–
B, 15A
8 Would you like people to help?/Would you like
(some/any) help? ▶ 14A–B
9 Are you optimistic? ▶ 14A–B
10 How do Kirsty's/her/the parents feel?
▶ 14A–B

33 1 What have scientists discovered? ▶ 14A–B, 16A–
B
2 How many people were killed in the accident?
▶ 15B
3 Is National Bank in crisis? ▶ 14A–B
4 How long have the fires been burning? ▶ 14A–B,
16C
5 How much did the new building cost? ▶ 14A–B,
16C
6 Where should new houses be built? ▶ 14A–B,
15A
7 Does the Prime Minister speak French? ▶ 14A–B
8 What has the government decided to do?
▶ 14A–B, 15A
9 When will the factory close down? ▶ 14A–B, 15A
10 Why are the workers protesting? ▶ 14A–B, 15A

34 1 wondering what time the next guided tour
starts.
2 Do you know how I can get to/how to get to
City Airport?
3 I'm trying to find out if/whether I need a visa?
4 Could you tell me where the toilets
are,(please)?
5 I need to know if/whether the palace is open
today.
6 I'm trying to find out if/whether I can buy these
goods tax-free.
▶ 17

35 1 Didn't you like it/the film?
2 Haven't you got/Don't you have a mobile
(phone)?
3 Can't/Don't you remember it/the number?

4 Have you never been to London/visited London?/Have you never seen (any of) the sights of London?

5 Why don't you (try to) sell it?
▶ 18A–B

36 1 What couldn't you find (in the dictionary), Carlos?

2 Who hasn't given in their homework?

3 Which word can't you understand, Christian?

4 What doesn't make sense to you, Isabel?/What don't you understand, Isabel?

5 Which lesson won't you be able to attend, Sven?
▶ 18B

37 1 What are you looking at? ▶ 15D

2 Did you watch the football on TV? ▶ 14B

3 Do you know what time the shop opens? ▶ 17

4 Whose coat is this? ▶ 15A

5 Which foot did you drop your bag on? ▶ 16B

6 Who else have you told the news to? ▶ 16F

7 Isn't it time we started? ▶ 18B

8 Should we have checked the timetable first?
▶ 14B

9 What on earth/What ever/Whatever were you thinking of? ▶ 16G

10 What type of phone should we buy? ▶ 16C

38 1 Yes, it is. ▶ 19B

2 Of course (you can). ▶ 19C

3 I'm worried about my exam. ▶ 19A

4 (I'm) sorry. (I'd like to, but) I've got a headache. ▶ 19C

5 Two./I've got two. ▶ 19A

6 Yes, please. (Thank you.) ▶ 19C

7 No, (I didn't). I forgot. ▶ 19B

8 (No,) I'm sorry, it isn't working. ▶ 19C

39 1 wasn't it? ▶ 20A, E   6 are you? ▶ 20B, F

2 will they? ▶ 20B, F   7 is there? ▶ 20B, C, F

3 didn't we? ▶ 20A, E   8 don't they? ▶ 20A, E

4 are you? ▶ 20B, G   9 does he? ▶ 20B, G

5 hasn't he? ▶ 20A, E   10 can I? ▶ 20B, F

40 1 disbelief   3 disbelief   5 agreement

2 interest   4 agreement   6 interest
▶ 21B

41 1 f) ▶ 19C   4 h) ▶ 18C   7 g) ▶ 18C

2 j) ▶ 21B   5 b) ▶ 19C   8 k) ▶ 21A

3 a) ▶ 19C   6 d) ▶ 16D   9 e) ▶ 19B

10 i) ▶ 19B

42 1 b) ▶ 19B   4 b) ▶ 18C   7 b) ▶ 19C

2 a) ▶ 21B   5 c) ▶ 20E   8 b) ▶ 16C

3 b) ▶ 16C   6 a) ▶ 15B

43 1 (that) it's too big   3 some apples

2 supermarket   4 those apples
▶ 22A

44 That holiday, sixty photos, some photos, as many photos, the funniest photo, a few jokes
▶ 23

45 1 coming   2 sees him   3 tried to get Peter on his mobile.   4 keep it switched on.   5 keeps his promises.
▶ 24

46 1 d) ▶ 25A   4 g) ▶ 25A   7 a) ▶ 25A

2 h) ▶ 25B   5 b) ▶ 25B   8 c) ▶ 25B

3 j) ▶ 25A   6 i) ▶ 25B   9 e) ▶ 25A

47 1 Are you keeping busy? ▶ 26C

2 There's lots to do at the office. There's a big panic on at the moment. ▶ 26B

3 I'm sorry to hear that. ▶ 26B

4 It doesn't bother me. I'm loving it, actually. Well, I must dash. ▶ 26B

5 I'll see you again. ▶ 26B

48 1 too   3 too   5 either

2 either   4 too   6 too
▶ 27A

49 1 Alan hasn't got a job, and neither has his father.

2 The hotel was nice, and so was the beach.

3 Karen doesn't like jazz, and nor does James.

4 The students (all) enjoyed the trip, and so did the teachers.

5 My mother can't speak French, and neither can my father.

6 Laura won't be at school tomorrow, and nor will I.

7 Cars cause pollution, and so do planes.

8 Gemma isn't (very) well, and nor is her boyfriend.
▶ 27B

50 1 We did   2 You are   3 it has   4 you will

5 It doesn't   6 it isn't   7 She wasn't
▶ 27C

51 1 I suppose so. ▶ 28A   5 It seems so. ▶ 28A

2 I don't expect so. ▶ 28B   6 I believe so ▶ 28A

3 I told you so ▶ 28A   7 I'm afraid not. ▶ 28B

4 I hope not. ▶ 28B   8 He didn't say so. ▶ 28B

52 1 do so   2 done it   3 do so   4 doing it/that
5 do that   6 did so
  ▶ 29A

53 1 not ▶ 28B   5 that way ▶ 29C
2 the same ▶ 29D   6 not ▶ 28D
3 so ▶ 29A   7 so ▶ 28C
4 the same ▶ 29D   8 so/that way ▶ 29C

54 on Sunday. We are all having a marvellous time.
The weather is perfect. I am writing this on the
beach. The children are playing in the sea. The
water is nice and clean. We are going on a tour of
the island tomorrow.
  ▶ 30D

55 1 So do I. ▶ 27B   8 So they say. ▶ 28C
2 Yes, I am. ▶ 26B   9 Well, I hope to. ▶ 25B
3 Of course not. ▶ 28E   10 And did you? ▶ 25A
4 Who did? ▶ 25A   11 You shouldn't do that.
5 Oh, so I have. ▶ 28C   ▶ 29A
6 Neither do I. ▶ 27B   12 I guess not. ▶ 28B
7 Thanks. Same to you. ▶ 29D

56 1 No, they aren't. ▶ 24A, C
2 I can't (cycle), really. ▶ 24A, C
3 I'd like to, but there isn't a very good route.
  ▶ 25B
4 Yes, I suppose so/I suppose it is. ▶ 28A
5 Oh, does she? ▶ 25A
6 So is mine./Mine is, too. ▶ 27B
7 And her husband doesn't either. ▶ 27A
8 I hope not. ▶ 28B
9 You mustn't do that. ▶ 29A

57 1 The kitchen is in a mess, and so is the living-
room. ▶ 27B
2 My friends all rode on the roller-coaster, but
I couldn't (do it/that). ▶ 29A
3 Which way is the quickest? ▶ 23
4 I went to the party, although I didn't really want
to. ▶ 25B
5 You don't need to tell me I'm late because I
know (I am). ▶ 28A
6 I'm not certain the trains are running, but they
should be. ▶ 24C
7 The women sat on one side of the room, and
the men on the other (side). ▶ 25C
8 The weather is lovely, and it's going to stay
that way all weekend. ▶ 29C
9 My girlfriend doesn't like sport, but I do.
  ▶ 24A, C
10 I didn't get here as quickly as you did.
  ▶ 24A, C

11 The book isn't very funny, and the film isn't
either/neither is the film. ▶ 27B
12 There could be problems, but I hope not. ▶ 28B

58 1 is made up of tiny particles. These particles are
called atoms. An atom consists of even smaller
particles. There is a nucleus in the middle of
each atom. Around this nucleus a number of
electrons are in constant orbit.
2 I'm really fed up at the moment. It's because of
my boyfriend. He never tells me where he is,
and he's out late most nights. Last night he went
to a club with some friends, but he didn't want
me there. All this is making me very depressed.
3 Mike Roots, a 57-year-old teacher from
Colchester in Essex, is cycling round the world.
But 'cycling' means that Mr Roots rides an
exercise bike at home and uses maps to plot his
imaginary journey. This began in Norway, and
he has now reached West Africa. The next
country he will be passing through is Sierra
Leone. His route through the country is on a
map pinned on his bedroom wall.
  ▶ 32

59 1 in King Street. ▶ 31 The houses in this street are
quite old. ▶ 32 Our house is on two floors. ▶ 32
Downstairs we've got a living-room, dining-
room, kitchen and bathroom. ▶ 32, 34 Upstairs
there are three bedrooms. ▶ 34 My bedroom is
at the front. ▶ 32, Behind the house (there) is
quite a big garden. ▶ 32, 34 The garden is my
mum's hobby. ▶ 32 She spends a lot of time
looking after it. ▶ 32 It looks beautiful in summer.
  ▶ 32 On sunny days we like to sit there. ▶ 32 We
usually sit under the apple tree. ▶ 32

60 1 The price includes the battery.
2 This topic will be discussed by a panel of
experts.
3 The new Olympic Stadium is the biggest in the
country.
4 They were built in the summer.
5 The delay caused us to miss our connecting
flight.
6 The story appeals to people of all ages.
  ▶ 33

61 1 on Friday news came through.
2 sometimes we eat at home.
3 in a village everyone knows you.
4 stupidly I missed the turning.
5 perhaps we should go home.
  ▶ 34A

2
1 At the entrance stood a man in uniform. ▶ 34B
2 this I have to do right now. ▶ 34D
3 Everywhere people were celebrating. ▶ 34A
4 Here comes the bus. ▶ 34C
5 Marcus I wouldn't trust. ▶ 34D
6 One slight problem was the lack of time. ▶ 34D
7 There it goes. ▶ 34C
8 On the screen was a message in code. ▶ 34B

3
1 There might be something valuable in the safe. ▶ 35A–C
2 There were lots of people on the beach. ▶ 35A–C
3 Soon there arose/There soon arose a further difficulty. ▶ 35G
4 Is there life after death? ▶ 35D
5 There have to be fire doors in a hotel. ▶ 35A–C
6 There have been no other messages for you. ▶ 35A–C
7 There was a parade last week, wasn't there? ▶ 35D
8 There seems to be a problem with the heating. ▶ 35G
9 There should be someone waiting for me at the airport. ▶ 35F
10 Will there be time for a proper discussion? ▶ 35D
11 There was a gust of wind that/which blew some tiles off the roof. ▶ 35F
12 There have been a number of people mugged/There have been a number of muggings in this area recently. ▶ 35A-C, F

4
1 game it looked ▶ 36C
2 is it now ▶ 36A
3 ✓
4 make it possible ▶ 36B
5 Look, it really ▶ 36A
6 Luckily, it appears ▶ 36C
7 ✓
8 Actually, it amuses ▶ 36B
9 think it is/think it's ▶ 36B
10 consider it absolutely ▶ 36B

5
1 It, There   3 It, There   5 there, there
2 it, it   4 It, there   6 there, it
▶ 37

6
1 I am an American citizen.   2 they do live in Australia.   3 she does work   4 she has orbited the earth   5 I do know lots of famous people.
6 I did once meet the President.
▶ 38C

67
1 What I'm worried about is the money. ▶ 38E
2 It's/It was the poor service I was complaining about. ▶ 38D
3 What Kate expected was a friendy welcome. ▶ 38E
4 It was four years ago that we went to Greece ▶ 38D
5 It was Charles Dickens who/that wrote *Oliver Twist*. ▶ 38D
6 What I want is some peace and quiet. ▶ 38E
7 What happened earlier was that Paul and Steve had an argument. ▶ 38E
8 It was *Titanic* (that) we saw in London ▶ 38D
9 What Lewis and Clark did was (to) explore the American West. ▶ 38E
10 It was after I'd been jogging that I first felt ill. ▶ 38D
11 It's/It was me who/that did all the work. ▶ 38D
12 What really annoyed me is/was the fact that no one offered to help. ▶ 38E

68
1 But then there was a sudden shout. ▶ 35A–C
2 I did lock it. ▶ 38C
3 Oh, here it is. ▶ 34C
4 I find it hard to understand English people. ▶ 36B
5 The people (who/that) we saw just now aren't students. ▶ 38E
6 There seems to be no way out of the building. ▶ 35G
7 To our left (there) were steep cliffs. ▶ 34B, 35A–C
8 But there are two cinemas. ▶ 35A–C
9 It's two weeks since/It's/It was two weeks ago that you received it. ▶ 38C
10 The meat he left on his plate. ▶ 34D
11 It looked as if the party was over. ▶ 36C
12 There shouldn't be any more problems. ▶ 35A–C

69
1 are taking   2 have admitted   3 have been discussing   4 enjoyed   5 were searching
6 had wheeled   7 had been feeling
▶ 39

70
1 now ▶ 41B   4 ever ▶ 40B
2 sometimes ▶ 40B   5 three times a day ▶ 40B
3 at the moment ▶ 41B 6 just ▶ 41B

71
1 are you doing ▶ 41, 42A
2 I'm working ▶ 41, 42B
3 I don't think ▶ 40, 42D
4 are you going ▶ 41, 42A
5 I'm taking ▶ 41, 42A
6 I'm going ▶ 41, 42A
7 I'm not working ▶ 41, 42A
8 I suggest ▶ 42G

9 They serve ▶ 40, 42A
10 do/don't you want ▶ 40, 42D
11 doesn't matter ▶ 40, 42D
12 I want ▶ 40, 42D
13 it always takes ▶ 40, 42C
14 does the café open ▶ 40, 42A
15 I don't know ▶ 40, 42D

72 1 I usually go to work by train. ▶ 40, 42A
    2 The telephone is ringing. ▶ 41, 42A
    3 This cake contains nuts. ▶ 40, 42D
    4 I'm travelling to India. ▶ 41, 42A
    5 The children like ice-cream. ▶ 40, 42D
    6 I think it's a lovely painting. ▶ 40, 42D
    7 My sister is reading that book. ▶ 41, 42A
    8 Hot air always rises. ▶ 40, 42C
    9 Nicola doesn't eat meat. ▶ 40, 42A

73 1 He speaks ▶ 42A, I only speak ▶ 42A, he travels
      ▶ 42A, he's travelling ▶ 42B
    2 she's improving ▶ 42A, She hates ▶ 42D, always
      take ▶ 42C
    3 are you doing ▶ 42A, I'm just putting ▶ 42A,
      I collect ▶ 42A
    4 Do you go ▶ 42A, I'm doing ▶ 42B, does it cost
      ▶ 42A

74 1 tells, reporting the written word ▶ 42G
    2 I'm driving, in the middle of something ▶ 42A
    3 I agree, a performative verb ▶ 42E
    4 shoots, an instant action ▶ 42E
    5 I'm living, a temporary routine ▶ 42B
    6 arrives, a timetable ▶ 42I
    7 You click, an instruction ▶ 42H
    8 He's always talking, annoyingly often ▶ 42C
    9 I usually get, a permanent routine ▶ 42B
    10 finds, an action in a story ▶ 42F

75 1 were   13 followed
    2 disappeared   14 was
    3 ran   15 didn't/did not
    4 didn't/did not come   seem
    5 didn't/did not know 16 phoned
    6 rang   17 took
    7 began   18 gave
    8 called   19 allowed
    9 spent   20 wanted
    10 fell   21 said
    11 found   22 saw
    12 raced   23 had
                          24 scared

    ▶ 43A

76 1 hasn't/has not stopped, Have you ever seen
    2 have we had, We've had
    3 I've forgotten, I haven't brought
    4 Has anyone ever jumped, I've never heard.
    ▶ 44A

77 1 held ▶ 43B, 45A
    2 've had/have had ▶ 44B, 45B
    3 organized ▶ 43B, 45A
    4 's been/has been ▶ 44B, 45B
    5 suffered ▶ 43B, 45B
    6 campaigned ▶ 43B, 45B
    7 started ▶ 43B, 45A
    8 finished ▶ 43B, 45A
    9 had ▶ 43B, 45A
    10 wanted ▶ 43B, 45B
    11 enjoyed ▶ 43B, 45A
    12 've decided/have decided ▶ 44B, 45A
    13 has/have just completed ▶ 44B, 45A
    14 were ▶ 43B, 45B
    15 has increased ▶ 44B, 45A
    16 has improved ▶ 44B, 45A
    17 has simply moved ▶ 44B, 45A
    18 did not have/didn't have ▶ 43B, 45B
    19 've told/have told ▶ 44B, 45C
    20 have now asked ▶ 44B, 45A
    21 have not received ▶ 44B, 45A

78 1 I gave ▶ 43B, 45A
    2 I've had ▶ 44B, 45B
    3 did you decide ▶ 43B, 45A
    4 I got ▶ 43B, 45A
    5 It was ▶ 43B, 45B
    6 I didn't believe ▶ 43B, 45B
    7 I decided ▶ 43B, 45A
    8 I applied ▶ 43B, 45A
    9 they gave ▶ 43B, 45A
    10 it's been/it has been ▶ 44B, 45B
    11 I haven't/I have not regretted ▶ 44B
    12 I knew ▶ 44B, 45B
    13 I've changed ▶ 44B, 45A
    14 you haven't heard ▶ 44B, 45A
    15 it's/it has doubled ▶ 44B, 45A
    16 have you been ▶ 44B, 45B
    17 I joined ▶ 43B, 45A
    18 I left ▶ 43B, 45A
    19 I've just remembered ▶ 44B, 45A

79 1 Inflation has risen again. Prices went up 4 per
      cent last year.
    2 The firemen have decided to return to work
      tomorrow. Earlier today the union accepted an
      improved offer.
    3 Four climbers have died in an accident in the
      Alps. They fell 200 metres when a rope broke.

4 A new traffic-charging scheme has started in Manchester. It came into operation at seven o'clock this morning.

5 The England football captain has broken his leg. He received the injury in a match at Newcastle earlier this evening.
▶ 45D

0 1 once ▶ 46B   4 for ▶ 46D   7 this ▶ 46C
2 just ▶ 46A   5 ever ▶ 46B   8 since ▶ 46D
3 last ▶ 46C   6 already ▶ 46A

1 1 b) ▶ 46E   3 a) ▶ 46B   5 b) ▶ 46C
2 b) ▶ 46C   4 b) ▶ 46D   6 b) ▶ 46D

2 1 I've always lived in this house. ▶ 45B
2 Karen lay in hospital for weeks. ▶ 45B
3 I've just switched the computer on. ▶ 45A, 46A
Also possible: I just switched the computer on.
4 As a child I hated school. ▶ 45B
5 The parcel has arrived. ▶ 45A
6 The parcel arrived two hours ago. ▶ 45A
7 And Anderson has won this year's Grand Prix!
▶ 45A, C
8 My grandfather won three Olympic medals.
▶ 45A, C
9 I haven't flown since April. ▶ 46D
10 By the time he was twenty, the young entrepreneur already had a million pounds.
▶ 46A

3 1 b) ▶ 47C 3 a) ▶ 47C 5 b) ▶ 47C 7 b) ▶ 47C
2 a) ▶ 47E 4 a) ▶ 47C 6 c) ▶ 47E 8 b) ▶ 47C

4 1 When Alice was riding the pony, she had a bad fall.
2 We were driving along when suddenly we noticed a police car behind us.
3 Someone stole Adam's clothes while he was swimming in the lake.
4 When Tom woke up, sunlight was streaming in through the curtains.
5 The player dropped his racket as he was running towards the net.
6 I was eating a yogurt when I discovered a dead insect in it.
▶ 47C

5 1 saw ▶ 47B, was catching ▶ 47E
2 didn't understand ▶ 47D, gave ▶ 47B
3 injured, was playing, fell ▶ 47C
4 married ▶ 47B, had ▶ 47D, was working ▶ 47E
5 hated ▶ 47D, thought ▶ 47D, were laughing
▶ 47B

6 rang, picked, was listening ▶ 47C, didn't seem
▶ 47D

86 1 playing the piano for 32 days.
2 been questioning a man since early this morning.
3 has been barking for half an hour.
4 have been preparing (for their holiday in India) for months.
5 have/has been discussing (the problem of) rising crime since last year.
▶ 48A–B

87 1 I didn't come on the train.
2 I just couldn't stop turning the pages.
3 I'm about halfway through.
4 We're in the dark now.
5 We sometimes have to sit in the dark.
6 He can speak it perfectly.
7 He can already say a few words.
8 There are none left, I'm afraid.
9 They're delicious.
▶ 48C

88 1 'd/had counted   5 had taught
2 hadn't slept   6 hadn't paid
3 had stopped   7 'd/had expected
4 hadn't received   8 had destroyed
▶ 49A–B

89 1 fell, landed   2 had started   3 started   4 saw
5 had inspected, handed   6 woke, had dawned, looked, saw, had he got, had taken, felt, didn't think, had suffered, tried, had disappeared
▶ 49C

90 1 Nicola was exhausted. She'd been working hard all day.
2 Andrew finally found his keys. He'd been searching everywhere for them.
3 The soldiers were filthy. They'd been crawling through the mud.
4 Karen suddenly felt sick. She'd been eating chocolates all evening.
5 Our friends were still in fancy dress. They'd been wearing it at a party.
6 The reporter was finally allowed a short interview with Madonna. He'd been waiting all day.
▶ 50A–B

91 1 I've been cooking.   2 you were driving, I was waiting   3 I'd been looking   4 They were playing   5 they'd been playing   6 I'd been looking, I'd seen
▶ 50B–C

92 1 I don't care ▸ **51B**
2 I'm still having ▸ **51B**
3 appeared ▸ **51B**
4 It tastes ▸ **51B**, didn't cost ▸ **51C**
5 is costing ▸ **51C**, we're enjoying ▸ **51C**
6 are you doing ▸ **51A**, I'm fitting, it fits ▸ **51B**
7 Do you think ▸ **51B**, I don't expect ▸ **51B**, doesn't seem ▸ **51A**
8 are you looking ▸ **51B**, it looks ▸ **51B**

93 1 heard   5 saw
2 'm/am seeing   6 see
3 was feeling   7 could feel Also possible: felt
4 could hear Also possible: heard
▸ **51E**

94 1 d)   4 h)   7 c)   10 i)   13 j)
2 g)   5 f)   8 l)   11 o)   14 m)
3 a)   6 b)   9 n)   12 k)
▸ **52**

95 1 I remember 2 have completed 3 was doing
4 didn't slow 5 crashed 6 killed 7 had been taking/had taken 8 had been 9 I've/I have seen 10 I think 11 they had put/they put
12 I usually take 13 I don't like 14 I had
15 I went 16 They're digging 17 is coming
18 have been getting/have got
▸ **52**

96 1 I didn't take the money. ▸ **43A**
2 I've been ready for ten minutes. ▸ **45B**
3 I was cooking the supper. ▸ **47B**
4 I've/I have been waiting here for twenty minutes. Also possible: I've/I have waited here for twenty minutes. ▸ **48B**
5 Do you know where it is? ▸ **40A**
6 I did them ages ago. ▸ **49C**
7 I've peeled about twenty. ▸ **48C**
8 She had achieved all her aims. ▸ **49B**
9 It isn't working properly. ▸ **41A**
10 I've had it for ages. ▸ **45B**
11 What are you doing now? ▸ **41B**
12 We haven't eaten out since your birthday. ▸ **46D**
13 So I'm working in here this week. ▸ **42B**

97 1 has done ▸ **44B**   15 saw ▸ **47C**
2 lives ▸ **40B**   16 had only just started ▸ **49B**
3 was lying
  Also possible: lay ▸ **47C**   17 hadn't been burning ▸ **50B**
4 started ▸ **47C**   18 had got/got ▸ **49C**
5 noticed ▸ **43B**   19 called ▸ **43B**
6 had forgotten ▸ **49B**   20 brought ▸ **43B**
7 jumped ▸ **43B**

8 ran ▸ **43B**   21 owe ▸ **51A**
9 scratched ▸ **43B**   22 didn't/did not run ▸ 4
10 were sleeping ▸ **47B** 23 saved ▸ **43B**
  Also possible: **slept**   24 love ▸ **40B**
11 woke ▸ **43B**   25 he's/he is having ▸ 51
12 opened ▸ **49C**   26 we've/we have been making ▸ **48B**
13 saw ▸ **49C**
14 was carrying ▸ **47C**   27 we've heard ▸ **44B**

98 1 freezes ▸ **40B**
2 has known ▸ **46D**
3 been sending ▸ **48B**
4 are, making ▸ **42C**
5 gets ▸ **40B**
6 mother has, two books ▸ **45C**
7 were eating/having a picnic ▸ **47B**
8 he died, had been ill ▸ **49B**

99 Future time: get, will be, are going to be, don't get, will be, are to bring, won't ruin, 'll be able t do, will have, begins, will be, is broadcasting, wi be running
Present or past time: have taken, have had, are warned, are, says, found, have
▸ **53A–B**

100 1 Shall ▸ **54E**   7 won't ▸ **54D**, 'll ▸ **54C**
2 will ▸ **54B**   8 'll/shall ▸ **54B**, 'll ▸ **54C**
3 'll ▸ **54C**   9 will, won't ▸ **54B**
4 Will, won't ▸ **54C**   10 'll ▸ **54C**, will ▸ **54D**
5 shall ▸ **54E**, 'll   11 Shall ▸ **54E**, won't ▸ 54
  ▸ **54B**   12 'll ▸ **54C**
6 'll, Will ▸ **54B**

101 1 He's going to cook (a meal) (this evening). ▸ **55A, C**
2 It's going to/The train is going to stop (at a/th station). ▸ **55A–B**
3 He's going to be/feel hot (in his coat). ▸ **55A–B**
4 She's going to fail (the exam/the geography exam). ▸ **55A–B**
5 They're going to play tennis. ▸ **55A, C**
6 She's going to call/phone/ring the police (on her mobile). ▸ **55A, C**

102 1 I'm going ▸ **56A**
2 are travelling ▸ **56A**
3 goes Also possible: is going ▸ **56B**
4 are you coming ▸ **56A**
5 finishes ▸ **56B**
6 leaves Also possible: is leaving ▸ **56B**
7 Are you doing ▸ **56A**
8 I'm visiting ▸ **56A**

103 1 We're visiting/We're going to visit ▶ 57
2 it'll be/it's going to be ▶ 57
3 We're going to take/We're taking ▶ 57
4 That'll be/That's going to be ▶ 57
5 are going to do ▶ 57
6 ends ▶ 56B
7 we fly ▶ 56B/we're flying ▶ 57

104 1 're going to   6 'll
2 's going to   7 's going to
3 'll   8 'll
4 's going to   9 's/is going to
5 're going to   10 'm going to
   ▶ 57

105 1 to ▶ 58B   6 to ▶ 58A
2 not ▶ 58B   7 is ▶ 58B
3 is ▶ 58A   8 Future events: 3, 5, 6
4 be ▶ 58B   9 Instructions: 1, 2, 4, 7
5 are ▶ 58A

106 1 The company is on the point of going bankrupt.
2 The football season is about to begin.
3 The country is about to join the European Union.
4 I think our boss is on the point of resigning.
5 I'm (just) about to go home.
   ▶ 58C

107 1 You will receive a warning when the PM is five minutes away. ▶ 59A
2 You will be given a second warning as soon as the PM enters the stadium. ▶ 59A
3 You will be on full alert when the PM gets out of his car. ▶ 59A
4 You will stay on alert while the PM is in the stadium. ▶ 59A
5 You will be responsible for taking care that nothing happens. ▶ 59A
6 You must take action immediately if there is trouble. ▶ 59A
7 You must stop people who try to get too close to the PM. ▶ 59A
8 After the match you will wait until everyone leaves/has left. ▶ 59A–B

108 1 'll/will have dried ▶ 61A
2 won't be wearing ▶ 60B
3 'll/will be revising ▶ 60B
4 'll/will have spent ▶ 61A
5 'll/will be coming ▶ 60C
6 won't have finished ▶ 61A
7 'll/will be playing ▶ 60C
8 'll/will have passed ▶ 61A
9 will you be using ▶ 60C

109 1 she'll have drunk 64 litres (of milk). ▶ 61A
2 she'll have eaten 128 bars of chocolate. ▶ 61A
3 she'll have worn out eight pairs of socks. ▶ 61A
4 she'll have used about 21 (or 22) films/at least 20 films. ▶ 61A
5 she'll have been walking for 64 days. ▶ 61B

110 1 Adam was going to have a bath, but there was no hot water.
2 The girls were going to look round the museum, but there was no time.
3 Tony was going to buy some flowers, but he forgot.
4 We were going to play golf, but then it started to rain.
5 Linda was going to take some photos, but she didn't have a film.
6 Gary was going to take driving lessons, but he couldn't afford it.
7 We were going to work in the library, but it was closed.
   ▶ 62A

111 1 about ▶ 62C   4 going ▶ 62A
2 seeing ▶ 62A   5 was ▶ 62C
3 wouldn't ▶ 62B   6 would ▶ 62B

112 1 c) will be ▶ 54B
2 b) I'll have done ▶ 61A
3 a) we'll win ▶ 59C
4 c) We're having ▶ 56A
5 b) It's going to ▶ 55B
6 b) have been working ▶ 61B
7 a) I'll be walking ▶ 60B
8 c) to report ▶ 58B
9 b) we meet ▶ 59A
10 c) on the point of ▶ 58C
11 b) shall ▶ 54E
12 a) was going to ▶ 62A

113 1 This time tomorrow we'll be flying over the Atlantic. ▶ 60B
2 You'll definitely pass the test. ▶ 53D
3 We were going to get up at six in the morning. ▶ 62A
4 The ferry is due to leave at ten thirty tonight. ▶ 58D
5 They're about to close the flight. ▶ 58C
6 I'm having next week off work. ▶ 56A
Also possible: I'm going to have next week off work.
7 We'll probably get a message when we arrive at the hotel. ▶ 59A
8 All (of) the guests will have gone/left (by) tomorrow. ▶ 61A

9 When I finally go into hospital, I'll have been waiting for ten months. ▶ 61B

10 The government will not/won't comment on the affair. ▶ 54D

114 1 she is going to move ▶ 55C /she will be moving ▶ 60C

2 she will have to ▶ 54B Also possible: she is going to have to

3 would happen ▶ 62B Also possible: was going to happen

4 I'll have to ▶ 54B Also possible: I'm going to have to

5 I'll tell ▶ 54C

6 I was going to leave ▶ 62A

7 she'll be paying ▶ 60B Also possible: she's going to pay

8 she'll have spent ▶ 61A

9 Will they throw ▶ 54B / Are they going to throw ▶ 55B–C

10 runs ▶ 59A/has run ▶ 59B

11 will not disappear ▶ 54B / is not going to disappear ▶ 55B

12 will find ▶ 54B / are going to find ▶ 55B

13 are meeting ▶ 56A / will be meeting ▶ 60C/will meet ▶ 54B / are going to meet ▶ 55C

14 will continue ▶ 54B / are going to continue ▶ 55B

15 will be able to ▶ 54B Also possible: is going to be able to

115 1 ordinary verb ▶ 64B   7 auxiliary verb ▶ 64A
2 auxiliary verb ▶ 64A   8 ordinary verb ▶ 64B
3 ordinary verb ▶ 64B   9 ordinary verb ▶ 64B
4 auxiliary verb ▶ 64A   10 auxiliary verb ▶ 64A
5 ordinary verb ▶ 64B   11 ordinary verb ▶ 64B
6 ordinary verb ▶ 64B   12 auxiliary verb ▶ 64A

116 1 We've been ▶ 65A   5 isn't/is not ▶ 65A
2 Is ▶ 65B   6 I'm/I am ▶ 65B
3 wasn't/was not ▶ 65A   7 being ▶ 65C
4 had been ▶ 65A

117 1 They're being very noisy. 2 He was being very unpleasant. 3 He's being rather selfish. 4 She was being awkward. 5 They're being very secretive. 6 They were being patient. ▶ 65C

118 1 gone 2 gone 3 been 4 been 5 been 6 gone ▶ 65D

119 1 Emma had the money. ▶ 66B, D
2 They've got time. ▶ 66C
3 We haven't got the address. ▶ 66D
4 Lisa had (got) a cat. ▶ 66B

5 Mark hasn't got/doesn't have a cold. ▶ 66B, D

6 Did I have an umbrella? ▶ 66B, D

7 Does Sarah have a bike? ▶ 66D

8 I don't have/I haven't got a map. ▶ 66D

9 They've had/They have had the best seats. ▶ 66B

120 1 I haven't got/I don't have ▶ 66D
2 You've got/You have ▶ 66B–C
3 I've never had ▶ 66B, E
4 not having/not to have ▶ 66E
5 I didn't have/I hadn't got/I hadn't ▶ 66B, D
6 I had/I'd got ▶ 66C

121 1 ~~got~~ ▶ 66D   5 ~~got~~ (in the reply) ▶ 66E
2 ~~got~~ ▶ 66E   6 ✓ ▶ 66B
3 ✓ ▶ 66E   7 ~~got~~ ▶ 66D
4 ~~got~~ ▶ 66D   8 ✓ ▶ 66E

122 1 has had his motor-bike ▶ 66B
2 I had ▶ 66B, F
3 has (got) a CD ▶ 66G
4 had (got) a suitcase ▶ 66G
5 you've got my/you have my ▶ 66A
6 The material has Also possible: The material has got ▶ 66B, F
7 has (got) a pond at the ▶ 66G

123 1 Did Paul have a letter this morning?
2 I'm going to have some water.
3 What did you have for breakfast?
4 I never have dreams.
5 I've had an invitation.
▶ 67

124 1 I usually have ▶ 67
2 He doesn't have ▶ 66C
3 We're having ▶ 67
4 Have you got ▶ 66C, F
5 We didn't have ▶ 67
6 No, I don't. ▶ 66D

125 1 do, doing   3 done, do
2 done, did   4 does, do
▶ 68A

126 1 does ▶ 68C   6 doing ▶ 68C
2 made ▶ 68C   7 do ▶ 68C
3 makes ▶ 68C   8 make ▶ 68C
4 do ▶ 68B   9 done ▶ 68B
5 making ▶ 68C   10 made ▶ 68C

27 1 I usually have a swim ▶ 69A–B
  2 I'd better have a quick wash ▶ 69C
  3 made a rather silly suggestion ▶ 69B–C
  4 was able to give a description of his attacker
    ▶ 69B
  5 should take immediate action ▶ 69B–C
  6 make use of the Internet facilities ▶ 69B
  7 made a significant contribution to ▶ 69B–C
  8 will have an adverse effect on ▶ 69B–C

28 1 got ▶ 66A   8 been ▶ 65A
  2 go ▶ 69B   9 had ▶ 69B
  3 doing ▶ 68A   10 done ▶ 68A
  4 did ▶ 64A   11 make ▶ 69B
  5 made ▶ 69B   12 has ▶ 64A
  6 didn't ▶ 66C   13 makes ▶ 68C
  7 having ▶ 67   14 being ▶ 65C
                15 have ▶ 66D

29 1 a) would carry   d) can run
    b) might operate   e) may take
    c) must show   f) will please
  ▶ 70A–B

  2 a) has to reach b) have to do c) were able to
    complete
  ▶ 70F

  3 a) must be joking b) should have happened
    c) should be put d) will not please
  ▶ 70E

30 1 Could I have a lift?
  2 What time will/When will the guests arrive?
  3 You shouldn't do/should not do anything
    illegal.
  4 Can all birds fly?
  5 A new computer wouldn't be/would not be a
    waste of money.
  6 How long would the journey take?
  7 The plan (just) won't work/will not work.
  8 There mightn't be/might not be any tickets.
  ▶ 70C

31 1 future   4 past   7 past
  2 past   5 future   8 present
  3 present   6 present   9 future
                    10 past

  ▶ 70D

32 1 have to ▶ 71A, C   4 had to ▶ 71A
    Also possible: must   5 having to ▶ 71A
  2 must ▶ 71D   6 have to ▶ 71A
    Also possible: have to   7 must ▶ 71D
  3 have to ▶ 71A

133 1 has to/'ll have to retake 2 didn't have to
    apply for 3 don't/won't have to get up
    4 doesn't have to get out of 5 have to/'ll
    have to book 6 won't have to paint
  ▶ 71A–B

134 1 ~~got~~ ▶ 72C   3 ✓ ▶ 72C   5 ~~got~~ 72C
    2 ✓ ▶ 72A   4 ~~got~~ ▶ 72B   6 ✓ ▶ 72C
                    7 ~~got~~ 72B

135 1 You needn't shout. ▶ 73A
  2 He doesn't have to clean it. ▶ 73A–B
  3 We mustn't ring her now. ▶ 73D
  4 We don't need to stop here. ▶ 73A–B
  5 He mustn't clean it. ▶ 73D
  6 We mustn't stop here. ▶ 73D
  7 You needn't stay any longer. ▶ 73A–B
  8 We don't need to ring her now. ▶ 73A–B
  9 You mustn't shout. ▶ 73D

136 1 didn't need to take
  2 needn't have watered/didn't need to water
  3 needn't have put/didn't need to put
  4 didn't need to buy
  5 didn't need to wait
  ▶ 73C

137 1 He shouldn't be chatting to his friends. He
    should be studying.
  2 She ought to make her mind up. She shouldn't
    put off the decision.
  3 He should have sent her a card. He shouldn't
    have forgotten.
  4 She shouldn't be lying in bed. She should be
    doing a practice run.
  5 They should have complained. They shouldn't
    have suffered in silence.
  6 She shouldn't burst into other people's rooms.
    She ought to knock.
  ▶ 74A

138 1 You ought ▶ 74A   5 supposed to ▶ 74C
  2 supposed to ▶ 74C   6 better take/have ▶ 74B
  3 not leave/not put ▶ 74B   7 should have ▶ 74A
  4 to do ▶ 74A   8 He wasn't/isn't ▶ 74C

139 1 Can I/Could I/May I take your photo/take a
    photo of you?
  2 Can I/Could I/May I come in?
  3 Can I/Could I/May I sit down?
  4 Can I/Could I/May I borrow/take/use your/the
    umbrella?
  ▶ 75A

140 1 isn't/is not allowed to stay
2 they weren't/were not allowed to open
3 I'm/I am allowed to use
4 You won't be/You'll not be/You will not be allowed to take
5 We were allowed to hold/have
6 Will we be allowed/Are we allowed to ask
► 75C

141 1 I can/I'm allowed to take photos because I'm a professional photographer. ► 75C
2 Will I/we be allowed to take a dictionary into the exam? ► 75C
3 You can watch TV in my room if you want to. ► 75B
4 I hope to be allowed to interview Robbie Williams. ► 75C
5 Can I/Could I/May I borrow your bicycle (, please)? ► 75A
6 A century ago people could travel/were allowed to travel around Europe without a passport. ► 75C
7 So far no one has been allowed to use the new machine. ► 75C
8 When I was young I couldn't go/I wasn't allowed to go out alone. ► 75C
9 My brother was allowed to swim in the river. ► 75C
10 you can't use the computer. I'm using it myself. ► 75B

142 1 be real; (the words) 'Great Britain' on it; it must be a fake ► 76B
2 They can't be playing lacrosse; they aren't carrying/they haven't got sticks (with nets on them); they must be playing netball ► 76C
3 They can't have seen *Nights of Terror* because they aren't 18. So they must have seen *Disney Fun*. ► 76C
4 It can't be a taxi because it looks like any other car. So it must be a minicab. ► 76B
5 It can't have been taken in the Netherlands because there are no mountains there. So it must have been taken in Switzerland. ► 76C

143 1 a) ► 77 2 b) ► 77 3 b) ► 74A 4 b) ► 77

144 1 It may/might be ► 78A
2 may/might have filed ► 78B
3 may/might have taken ► 78B
4 They may/might be showing ► 78B
5 It may/might have fallen ► 78B
6 It may/might have been thrown ► 78B
7 You may/might find it ► 78A
8 may/might make ► 78A

145 1 c) could have been ► 79C
2 b) may ► 78A
3 a) can ► 79D
4 c) might have seen ► 78B
5 a) Could ► 79B
6 c) may be having ► 78B
7 b) might ► 78C
8 a) can't ► 79E
9 c) might as well ► 78D
10 a) could ► 79A

146 1 We could take a taxi. ► 79A
2 Louise may be waiting for us at the airport. ► 78B
3 The story can't be true. ► 79E
4 You might take off your wet shoes before you come in. ► 78C
5 The others could be looking for us now. ► 79▪
6 Matthew might have forgotten all about it. ► 78B
7 Polly can be very rude. ► 79D
8 Could you fill in this form (, please?) ► 79B
9 We might not/We mightn't have enough money. ► 78A
10 I could have done a parachute jump, but I wa▪ too scared. ► 79C

147 1 were able to   4 was able to
2 could/were able to 5 couldn't/weren't able t▪
3 could/was able to
► 80C

148 1 I simply cannot/can't understand it. ► 80A
2 Are you able to study/Can you study with the TV on? ► 80B
3 I could play/I was able to play the piano when ▪ was five. ► 80C
4 I could have gone to the party, but I was just ▪ too tired. ► 80C
5 I'll be able to retake/I can retake the exam ne▪ year. ► 80B
6 I am afraid we are not able to/we are unable t▪ help you. ► 80B

149 1 could hear police sirens ► 80C
2 was able to save ► 80C
3 can't remember/isn't able to remember ► 80A–B
4 couldn't be ► 80C/wouldn't be able to be ► 80▪
5 won't be able to wear it ► 80B
6 could have gone on ► 80C
7 haven't been able to go ► 80B
8 could run a mile / was able to run a mile in four minutes. ► 80C
9 to be able to choose ► 80B

150 1 like to go home now. ▶ 81B
2 we left early. ▶ 81D
3 would laugh at me if I wore that hat. ▶ 81A
4 mind seeing the parade. ▶ 81C
5 hate to work in this place. ▶ 81B

151 1 I'd like 2 I like 3 I want 4 I'd like 5 I like
▶ 81C

152 1 used to being ▶ 82C
2 used to live ▶ 82B, C
3 used to hearing ▶ 82C
4 used to vote ▶ 82A, C
5 didn't use to forget/never used to forget ▶ 82B
6 used to making ▶ 82C
7 used to starting ▶ 82C
8 didn't use to have/never used to have ▶ 82B

153 1 No one dare argue with the President./
No one dares (to) argue with the President./
No one would dare (to) argue with the
President.
2 We daren't go out after dark./
We don't/wouldn't dare (to) go out after dark.
3 People didn't dare (to) resist the invaders./
People dared not resist the invaders.
4 Dare you step into the unknown?/
Do/Would you dare (to) step into the
unknown?
5 How dare you come in here without knocking?
▶ 83

154 1 should be allowed to take/ought to be
allowed to take a short break.
2 will have to possess/have a driving licence.
3 may be allowed to see/might be allowed to
see the documents.
4 should be able to find accommodation.
5 may have to prove/might have to prove their
identity.
▶ 84

155 1 Can/Could/May ▶ 75B   8 wouldn't ▶ 81A–B
2 needn't ▶ 73A   9 ought ▶ 74A
3 should ▶ 74A   10 can ▶ 79D
4 must ▶ 76B   11 couldn't ▶ 75C
5 couldn't ▶ 80C   12 can't ▶ 76B/
6 may/might ▶ 78A   won't ▶ 76A
7 mustn't ▶ 73D/shouldn't ▶ 74A

156 1 k) ▶ 71C   4 g) ▶ 74A   7 e) ▶ 76B
2 j) ▶ 81E   5 b) ▶ 79A   8 h) ▶ 73D
3 a) ▶ 75B   6 i) ▶ 83   9 d) ▶ 77
                            10 c) ▶ 79B

157 1 I'm afraid the photos might not be/mightn't be
ready. ▶ 70C, 78A
2 You must renew/You'll have to renew your visa
soon. ▶ 71A
3 We ought to visit Phil in hospital. ▶ 74A
4 Someone must have taken your bike last night.
▶ 76C
5 Would Charlotte be willing/Is Charlotte willing
to help? ▶ 70C
6 That old man used to be a professional boxer.
▶ 82B
7 I would love to be able to sing, but I just can't.
▶ 80B

158 1 I'm/I am allowed to use this room. ▶ 75C
2 I daren't go/I don't dare (to) go out on my own.
▶ 83
3 You didn't need to leave ▶ 73C / didn't have to
leave a tip. ▶ 71A
4 I used to play tennis regularly. ▶ 82B
5 You ought to have accepted the offer. ▶ 74A
6 The parcel should arrive soon. ▶ 77
7 Mark had to go to hospital. ▶ 71A
8 The child must have run away. ▶ 76C

159 1 the prisoners   4 the subject   7 by
2 passive   5 active
3 no   6 no
▶ 86

160 1 have heard 2 has not been revealed
3 was eaten 4 were waiting 5 were being served
6 had taken 7 had been left 8 will be jettisoned
▶ 87A

161 1 shows Also possible: has shown ▶ 87A
2 are being driven Also possible: are driven ▶ 87A
3 have been increasing/have increased ▶ 87A
4 were made ▶ 87A
5 include/included Also possible: have included
▶ 87A
6 can be heard ▶ 87C
7 do ... have to be used ▶ 87C
8 are ... carried ▶ 87A
9 is still increasing ▶ 87A
10 starts/is starting ▶ 87A
11 stay/are staying ▶ 87A
12 must be tackled ▶ 87C
13 can be driven ▶ 87C
14 is ... done/is ... being done/has ... been
done ▶ 87A
15 has paid ▶ 87A
16 is needed ▶ 87A
17 will not be ignored/are not ignored ▶ 87A, B

162 1 action   4 state   7 state
     2 action   5 state   8 action
     3 action   6 state
     ▶ 87E

163 1 aren't respected. ▶ 87A
     2 is cutting the grass. ▶ 87A
     3 is going to be repaired. ▶ 87A
     4 was lost ▶ 87E / had been lost. ▶ 87A
     5 the mistakes been corrected? ▶ 87A, B
     6 should have locked the door behind us. ▶ 87C
     7 will be broadcast on Sunday. ▶ 87A
     8 was torn ▶ 87E / had been torn. ▶ 87A
     9 has to be done. ▶ 87C
     10 is being looked into. ▶ 87D
     11 are just laughed at. ▶ 87D
     12 must have been delayed. ▶ 87C

164 1 a) ▶ 88D   3 a) ▶ 88A   5 b) ▶ 88B
     2 b) ▶ 88C   4 b) ▶ 88C   6 b) ▶ 88B

165 1 which was invented in Canada. ▶ 87A, ▶ 88A
     2 It has been completely renovated. ▶ 87A, ▶ 88A
     3 It cost millions of pounds. ▶ 88A
     4 They can be mixed to make other colours.
       ▶ 87C, ▶ 88B
     5 It is listened to (by people) all over the world.
       ▶ 87D, ▶ 88A
     6 It has taken over its main competitor. ▶ 88A
     7 which lacks proper facilities. ▶ 88C

166 1 *Jurassic Park* was directed by Steven Spielberg.
     2 The Harry Potter books were written by J.K.
       Rowling.
     3 The telephone was invented by Alexander
       Graham Bell.
     4 The pyramids were built by the Egyptians.
       ▶ 89A

167 1 no, ~~by the TV companies~~
     2 yes
     3 no, ~~by a window cleaner~~
     4 no, ~~by the wind~~
     5 no, ~~by the police~~
     6 yes
     ▶ 89

168 1 get killed ▶ 90A   4 got left ▶ 90A
     2 getting married ▶ 90B   5 getting lost ▶ 90B
     3 get changed ▶ 90B   6 gets thrown ▶ 90A
                          7 get started ▶ 90B

169 1 This photo should be shown to the police.
     2 My grandmother gave me this jumper.
     3 Polly has been promised a rise (by the boss).

     4 The leftover meat can be fed to the dogs.
     5 The shop assistant handed Simon the receipt
       handed the receipt to Simon.
     6 The lawyers are paid large fees.
     7 Our group is going to be taught skiing by a
       handsome instructor.
     ▶ 91

170 1 It is rumoured that the company is in
       difficulties.
     2 It was believed that the Emperor was a god.
     3 It was reported that the fighting had just begun
     4 It will be shown that poverty is increasing.
     5 It is estimated that 200 people were killed by
       the pollution.
     6 It was agreed that wages would be raised by fiv
       per cent.
     7 It has been decided that the project will have t
       be cancelled.
     8 It was suggested that the tickets should cost fiv
       pounds.
     ▶ 92A

171 1 is rumoured to be in difficulties. 2 was
     believed to be a god. 3 The fighting was reporte
     to have just begun. 4 Poverty will be shown to b
     increasing. 5 200 people are estimated to have
     been killed by the pollution.
     ▶ 92B

172 1 The workers have been persuaded to accept
       lower wages. ▶ 93A
     2 Two young men were seen fighting. ▶ 93B
     3 The victims have been advised (by their
       lawyers) to take legal action. ▶ 93A
     4 The children were made to pick up all the litte
       ▶ 93A
     5 The woman was caught smuggling cigarettes
       into the country. ▶ 93B
     6 The refugees aren't allowed to/won't be
       allowed to get a job. ▶ 93A
     7 £50,000 was/were spent (on) decorating the
       ballroom. ▶ 93B
     8 You were warned not to drive so fast. ▶ 93A

173 1 Angela is having her flat decorated. ▶ 94B
     2 Lisa had her car damaged last week. ▶ 94C
       Also possible: Lisa's car got damaged (by vandal
       last week. ▶ 90A
     3 My friends had a house built (for them). ▶ 94
     4 I really must get my homework finished/don
       soon. ▶ 94B
     5 Mark has had his credit card withdrawn (by th
       bank). ▶ 94C
     6 Where did Tom have/get his hair cut? ▶ 94B

7 Karen is having/is going to have her carpets cleaned. ▶ 94B

74 1 being seen 2 to be promoted 3 to have been delivered 4 being tested/having been tested 5 to be transferred 6 being informed 7 to have been mislaid 8 being moved/having been moved ▶ 95

75 1 to be laid ▶ 96B
2 cutting ▶ 96A
3 to do ▶ 96B
4 are selling ▶ 96C
5 to write ▶ 96B
6 to solve ▶ 96B
7 to be understood ▶ 96B
8 seeing to ▶ 96A

76 1 having/getting ▶ 94B
2 to ▶ 92B
3 be ▶ 96B
4 had ▶ 94A
5 being ▶ 87A
6 by ▶ 89A
7 having ▶ 95
8 seen/filmed ▶ 93B
9 been ▶ 87C
10 it ▶ 92A
11 get ▶ 90B
12 did ▶ 94B

77 1 were sold ▶ 87A
2 applied ▶ 88C
3 were promised ▶ 91
4 were spent ▶ 87A
5 had to be approved ▶ 87C
6 had ... renovated ▶ 94B
7 created ▶ 86
8 to do ▶ 96B
9 seemed ▶ 88C
10 is ... admired ▶ 87A
11 is said to be ▶ 92B
12 have been preserved ▶ 87A /are preserved ▶ 87E
13 is now used/is now being used ▶ 87A
14 can be visited ▶ 87C
15 are asked not to come ▶ 93A
16 being disturbed ▶ 95

78 1 We got/had the rubbish removed. ▶ 94B
2 They've put up a new bus shelter. ▶ 88D
3 The building was designed by an American architect. ▶ 89A
4 Meals always have to be prepared. ▶ 87C
5 It's terrible to be ignored. ▶ 95
6 The story is going to be published. ▶ 87A
7 Does the document have to be printed out? ▶ 87C, D
8 The actress was awarded an Oscar. ▶ 91 /They awarded the actress an Oscar. ▶ 88D

79 1 perfect 2 perfect, continuous 3 simple, passive 4 continuous 5 perfect, negative ▶ 97B

80 1 to go on holiday. ▶ 98A

2 to think about. ▶ 98B
3 to send an e-mail. ▶ 98A
4 to be better. ▶ 98A
5 to fly from. ▶ 98B

181 1 It might be dangerous to hitch-hike on your own. 2 It is a basic human right to have an education. 3 It is the duty of every Muslim to visit Mecca. 4 It is not easy to fully understand the theory of relativity. 5 It costs a great deal of money to keep a racehorse.
▶ 99A

182 1 to post a/the parcel.
2 to protect his hands/to protect himself.
3 to get rid of (the/some) mice.
4 to keep in the cows/cattle/to keep the cows/ cattle in.
5 to keep/stay/get fit
▶ 100A

183 1 to find an angry crowd. (B) ▶ 100B
2 to warm them. (A) ▶ 100A
3 to be honest. (C) ▶ 100C
4 To see the pictures (D) ▶ 100D
5 To stay awake (A) ▶ 100A
6 to fall at the last fence. (B) ▶ 100B
7 to hear him talk. (D) ▶ 100D

184 1 Our neighbours threatened to call the police.
2 MPs have voted to change the law. 3 Those people seem to be arguing about something.
4 I refuse to apologize for something I haven't done. 5 The man claims to have been Julius Caesar in an earlier life.
▶ 101A

185 1 to make/to be making ▶ 101C
2 to do ▶ 101C
3 to avoid ▶ 101C
4 losing ▶ 101B–C
5 solving ▶ 101C
6 to open ▶ 101C
7 to buy ▶ 101C
8 to have/to be having ▶ 101C
9 to relax ▶ 101C
10 thinking ▶ 101C
11 to do ▶ 101C
12 to be ▶ 101C

186 1 working nights. ▶ 102B
2 to be winning. ▶ 102A
3 hearing gunshots. ▶ 102F
4 to stay in and watch TV. ▶ 102A
5 to start a business. ▶ 102G
6 to be improving. ▶ 102C
7 to have been trodden on. ▶ 102A
8 allow singing ▶ 102I
9 mind waiting for you. ▶ 102H
10 to see the photos. ▶ 102B

187 1 ✓ hate hearing ▶ 103A
2 starting to come ▶ 103A
3 like to have ▶ 103B
4 ✓ continued to throw ▶ 103A
5 (would) like to welcome ▶ 103B
6 ✓ prefer doing ▶ 103A

188 1 repairing/to be repaired ▶ 104I, to study ▶ 104I, fiddling ▶ 104E
2 to say ▶ 104B, to tell ▶ 104H, talking ▶ 104E
3 to go ▶ 104A, to get ▶ 104A, meaning ▶ 104A, to get ▶ 104F, to chat ▶ 104E, writing ▶ 104D, driving ▶ 104F, to decide ▶ 104D

189 1 I need you to come with me (, please). ▶ 105E
2 The animals have been trained to do tricks. ▶ 105C
3 The police were ordered to use water cannon. ▶ 105B
4 Paul's doctor advised him to go on a diet. ▶ 105B
5 Scientific tests have proved the drug (to be) harmful. ▶ 105D
6 This card enables you to get a discount. ▶ 105C
7 The law requires there to be a doctor present./ The law requires a doctor to be present. ▶ 105C
8 The road was known to be dangerous. ▶ 105D

190 1 It is too dangerous to swim in the sea. ▶ 106D
2 You'll be lucky to wait less than an hour. ▶ 106E
3 Good restaurants are hard to find. ▶ 106B
4 It is foolish not to buy insurance. ▶ 106A
Also possible: It is foolish not to have bought insurance.
5 The shops are liable to close for lunch. ▶ 106F
6 The town is an interesting place to visit. ▶ 106C
7 It is important to book in advance. ▶ 106A
8 It is too long a journey to make/to be made on foot. ▶ 106D
9 You would be wise not to carry too much cash. ▶ 106E
10 The view is dramatic enough to attract thousands of visitors. ▶ 106D

191 1 People's desire to breathe clean air has led to a flight from the city. 2 The company's failure to modernize caused its decline. 3 Matthew's decision not to take the exam is quite understandable. 4 Simon's reluctance to spend any money annoyed Emma. 5 The President's promise to end the war surprised everyone.
6 The government's ability to run the country is seriously in doubt.
▶ 107A

192 1 wondering who to ask for help. 2 to know where to put the flowers. 3 Nicola wasn't sure how much money to take (with her). 4 Adam has no idea whether to accept the offer (or not). 5 Lucy didn't know what to do next. 6 Hannah is trying to find out how to download the software.
▶ 108

193 1 It's dangerous for cars to come along here at top speed. ▶ 109A, D
2 My mother taught me to ride a pony. ▶ 105C
3 I wouldn't mind paying (for) a decorator to smarten this place up. ▶ 109A, C
4 It was very nice of your friend to invite me to the party. ▶ 109E
5 My brother persuaded me to do a parachute jump. ▶ 105B
6 It takes ages for them to update the website. ▶ 109A, C
7 There's absolutely no need (for anyone) to get up early tomorrow. ▶ 109A, D
8 It was very rude of you not to speak to my friends. ▶ 109E
9 My ambition is/It's my ambition for my genius to be recognized/for people to recognize my genius. ▶ 109A–B

194 1 hurry ▶ 110B　　4 have ▶ 110C　　7 have ▶ 110B
2 land ▶ 110D　　5 to be ▶ 110A　　8 to answer ▶ 110B
3 to lend ▶ 110C　　6 copy ▶ 110C　　9 lie ▶ 110E

195 1 to take ▶ 110A　　5 have looked ▶ 110B
2 be playing ▶ 110A　　6 to have lost ▶ 97B
3 to be doing ▶ 97B, 110A　7 have been waiting ▶ 110A
4 wear ▶ 110B

196 1 ✓ ▶ 102G　　4 ✓ ▶ 97B　　7 ✓ ▶ 103B
2 it ▶ 98B　　5 ✓ ▶ 109E　　8 them ▶ 106B
3 of ▶ 108A　　6 for ▶ 100A　　9 to ▶ 110C

197 1 You must have forgotten to lock the door. ▶ 104A
2 I want you to trust me. ▶ 105E
3 We set off really early so as not to be late/so that we wouldn't be late. ▶ 100A
4 It was kind of you to make me feel so welcome ▶ 109E
5 There are some important rules (for you) to follow. Also possible: There are some important rules to be followed. ▶ 106C, 109D
6 I'm not sure whether to buy this CD. ▶ 108A
7 The builders agreed to do the work/The builders accepted (that) they should do the work all over again. ▶ 102E

8 That joke Tom told really made me laugh.
  ▶ 110C
9 I'd love to have met Albert Einstein. ▶ 97B
10 It was amazing to fly over the Grand Canyon.
  ▶ 98A
11 That's too difficult a question to answer. ▶ 106D
12 There are picnic tables for people to sit at.
  ▶ 109B

98 1 where to go on holiday. ▶ 108A
  2 is to keep the audience happy. ▶ 99B
  3 rather walk. ▶ 110B /prefer to walk ▶ 103A
    Also possible: prefer walking
  4 far to walk. ▶ 106D
  5 to move to Ireland soon. ▶ 101C
  6 the power to arrest people without reason.
    ▶ 107A
  7 me to get around OK. ▶ 105C
  8 a product to sell ▶ 109B
  9 We happened to ▶ 102A

99 1 not knowing 2 being stared (at) 3 having
  sailed 4 having been injured
    ▶ 111

00 1 My doing all the cooking isn't fair.
  2 Our inviting everybody to Carl's party wasn't a
    good idea.
  3 Your wearing these strange clothes amuses
    everyone.
  4 Does my sitting here bother you?
    ▶ 112B

01 1 I had problems getting to work. ▶ 113B
  2 Travelling by train can be relaxing. ▶ 113A
  3 It was a nuisance not having a map. ▶ 113B
  4 There was no difficulty getting tickets. ▶ 113B
  5 Seeing Madonna was quite a thrill. ▶ 113A
  6 We can have fun going out to discos. ▶ 113B
  7 Sitting at a computer can be bad for you.
    ▶ 113A
  8 It is no use trying to repair the machine. ▶ 113B

02 1 destroying ▶ 113E   7 to oppose ▶ 105B
  2 to build ▶ 105C   8 happening ▶ 113E
  3 to fly ▶ 105C   9 to change ▶ 105B
  4 wanting ▶ 113E   10 to put ▶ 105E
  5 being constructed ▶ 113E 11 going ▶ 113E
  6 causing ▶ 113E   12 flying ▶ 113E

03 1 The prisoners escaped by digging a tunnel.
    ▶ 114A
  2 On hearing the news, my sister fainted. ▶ 114C
  3 Always look in your mirror before driving off.
    ▶ 114A

4 Far from enjoying the film, I was totally bored
  by it. ▶ 114A
5 In borrowing money, we added to our
  problems. ▶ 114C
6 I'm sure you'll have a great time without me/
  my being there. ▶ 114B
7 I bought this special brush for painting ceilings
  (with). ▶ 114C
8 Since being mugged/Since the/my mugging,
  I've been afraid to go out on my own. ▶ 114A
9 Sending an e-mail is quicker than posting a
  letter. ▶ 114D
10 My friend is in trouble on account of (him/his)
  not renewing his visa. ▶ 114A

204 1 to going ▶ 115A, with working ▶ 115A, of/about
    getting ▶ 115A, from leaving ▶ 115B
  2 with clearing ▶ 115A, in sharing ▶ 115A, in
    avoiding ▶ 115A, to doing ▶ 115A
  3 from using ▶ 115B, on getting ▶ 115A, in
    waiting ▶ 115B, for sitting ▶ 115A
  4 for making ▶ 115B, for getting ▶ 115B, of cheating
    ▶ 115B, of trying ▶ 115A, like giving ▶ 115A

205 1 I wasn't very good at climbing the rope.
  2 The parcels are ready for loading into the van.
  3 I'm worried about forgetting the number.
  4 Emily is quite capable of photocopying the
    document.
  5 Jodie is responsible for messing up the
    arrangements.
  6 I'm annoyed at having to do all this work again.
  7 My friend was involved in organizing/in
    helping to organize the event. / My friend was
    involved with organizing/with helping to
    organize the event.
  8 We're fed up with/of always being told to do
    the boring jobs.
    ▶ 116

206 1 I'm thrilled by the prospect of starting a new
    life.
  2 Have you got a good excuse for taking
    yesterday off?
  3 I had the unpleasant task of breaking the bad
    news.
  4 What's the reason for (them/their) keeping
    everything secret?
  5 I've conquered my fear of flying.
  6 We (all) share your interest in promoting our
    products.
  7 There's no hope of finding those people alive.
  8 The boss has got a reputation for chasing after
    women.

9 I admire the company's success in dominating the market. ▶ 117

207 1 about saying
2 to post
3 of falling
4 to admit
5 about seeing
6 in making
7 to accept
8 for behaving
9 delivering
▶ 118B

208 1 to be ▶ 101B
2 to ... taking ▶ 119
3 to bursting ▶ 119
4 to help ▶ 105B
5 to having ▶ 119
6 to read ▶ 106A
7 to not liking ▶ 119
8 to living ▶ 119
9 not to have been killed ▶ 95, 106E

209 1 on ▶ 115A
2 with ▶ 116
3 to ▶ 115A
4 of/about ▶ 115A
5 from ▶ 115B
6 of ▶ 116
7 of ▶ 116
8 on ▶ 116
9 to ▶ 116
10 at/about ▶ 116
11 of ▶ 117
12 to ▶ 115A

210 1 no/No ▶ 120A
2 cleaning ▶ 120A
3 some ▶ 120A
4 of ▶ 120B
5 running ▶ 120A
6 the ▶ 120A
7 wearing ▶ 120B

211 1 It was quite an experience riding/to ride in a racing-car. ▶ 113B
2 Everyone congratulated Emma on passing her test. ▶ 115B
3 I don't remember having written a cheque. ▶ 111B
4 Let's do some fishing this weekend. ▶ 120A
5 We have the job of analysing the figures. ▶ 117
6 The woman is famous for impersonating the Queen. ▶ 116
7 Your not doing any work is a cause for concern. ▶ 112B
8 This crisis will necessitate me/my going into the office tomorrow. ▶ 113E
9 No boxer should resort to biting his opponent. ▶ 119

212 1 I'm looking forward to going away. ▶ 119
2 It isn't worth spending a whole day in the town. ▶ 113B
3 I was aware of not having eaten for some time. ▶ 116
4 In those days the copying of books was a laborious task. ▶ 120B
5 I was sorry to hear the bad news. ▶ 118

6 At last we succeeded in getting the car started ▶ 115A
7 I was really annoyed at having been tricked/at being tricked out of my money. ▶ 111B
8 I won't tolerate you/your telling lies about me ▶ 113E
9 I was excited by the game in spite of being a neutral. ▶ 114A
10 We haven't a hope of finishing the work in time. ▶ 117

213 1 perfect ▶ 121C
2 passive ▶ 121C
3 continuous ▶ 121C
4 passive ▶ 121A
5 past ▶ 121A

214 1 The show having been cancelled, we all went home. ▶ 122B
2 We can hear our neighbour playing the piano ▶ 122A
3 Having arrived at the flat, Karen rang the bell ▶ 122B
4 Cornered by the police, the gang tried to shoot their way out. ▶ 122A

215 1 injured ▶ 123A
2 retired ▶ 123B
3 falling ▶ 123A
4 alarming ▶ 123A
5 howling ▶ 123A
6 fallen ▶ 123B
7 unexpected ▶ 123A
8 rising ▶ 123A

216 1 a money-saving scheme ▶ 123C
2 an action-packed movie ▶ 123C
3 a glass-topped table ▶ 123D
4 hard-hitting criticism ▶ 123C
5 a strange-looking building ▶ 123C
6 a heart-breaking result ▶ 123C
7 a fair-haired, blue-eyed girl ▶ 123D

217 1 The family stood waving at the gate.
2 People ran screaming from the building.
3 The player lay injured on the grass.
4 The girls went racing down the slope.
▶ 124A

218 1 We saw a man throw a brick at the shop window. Also possible: We saw a man throwing brick at the shop window.
2 I heard someone break/breaking down the door.
3 I saw a young man being attacked by several others.
4 I observed a blue car driving very fast toward the motorway.
5 We heard people shouting and screaming.

6 I noticed a woman put two tins in her bag and leave the store without paying.
▶ 125A–C

219 1 cut/cutting ▶ 125G
2 explode ▶ 125A–B
3 kept ▶ 125D
4 spent ▶ 125E
5 ringing ▶ 125A–B
6 trying/attempting ▶ 125F
7 to ▶ 125G
8 smashed ▶ 125G
9 being ▶ 125C
10 had ▶ 125D

220 1 do some/the ironing
2 go swimming
3 do the driving
4 do the shopping Also possible: go shopping
5 do much cooking/do a lot of cooking
6 go sailing Also possible: do some sailing
▶ 124B

221 1 When you use/you are using this software
2 Once this product is opened/is open/has been opened
3 If the product is found/ has been found to be faulty
▶ 126

222 1 biting ▶ 127A
2 having achieved ▶ 127C
3 being stared Also possible: stared ▶ 127D
▶ 127D
4 looking/having looked ▶ 127E
5 having been eaten ▶ 127D
6 hidden ▶ 127D
7 Having searched ▶ 127C
8 Catching ▶ 127B/Having caught ▶ 127C

223 1 Not knowing his way around, Simon had to ask for directions. ▶ 128A
2 Having forgotten my watch, I had no idea of the time. ▶ 128A
3 (Being) recognized wherever she goes, the pop star always has a bodyguard. ▶ 128C
4 (With) the weather being so awful, we've just had to stay indoors. ▶ 128A
5 (With) the road having been closed by the police, motorists have to make a long detour.
▶ 128B, C

224 1 a comment ▶ 129E
2 result ▶ 129A
3 time ▶ 127B
4 reason ▶ 128A
5 a condition ▶ 129B

225 1 Considering/Given the effort we put in ▶ 129D
2 with piles of papers lying everywhere. ▶ 129C
3 All being well ▶ 129E
4 Judging by Tom's attitude ▶ 129D

5 spilling it all over the floor. ▶ 129A
6 Talking of holidays ▶ 129E

226 1 She lay in bed worrying all night/in bed all night worrying. ▶ 124A
2 Having been invited to the wedding, we've decided to go. ▶ 128C
3 Weather permitting, we might go out. ▶ 129B
4 Not having much money, I couldn't buy a ticket. ▶ 128A
5 It would be nice to go riding somewhere.
▶ 124B
6 The winning team will be awarded the trophy.
▶ 123A
7 Having waited hours, I was told to come back the next day. ▶ 127C
8 Considering what's happened, I think you've been proved right. ▶ 129D
9 Never use a mobile phone while driving a car.
▶ 126
10 With the stereo blasting out rock music, conversation was impossible. ▶ 128B

227 1 ticket, car, road 2 warden, engineer, friends
3 experience, attention, friendship, marriage
4 Brian, Susan
▶ 130A

228 1 minutes ▶ 131A
2 glasses ▶ 131A
3 goal ▶ 131C
4 pupils/children/students ▶ 131A
5 car ▶ 131C
6 weekends ▶ 131B
7 shops ▶ 131C
8 seat/chair/place ▶ 131C
9 questions ▶ 131C
10 runners-up ▶ 131B

229 1 the man's name 2 my friends' flat
3 someone's cat 4 the women's team
5 students' problems 6 my father's friend's son
▶ 132

230 1 the cost of a visa ▶ 133C
2 the dog's food ▶ 133B
3 the boys' football ▶ 133B
4 the names of everyone attending the meeting
▶ 133B
5 Robert's arm ▶ 133B
6 the workmen's lunch boxes ▶ 133B
7 the top of the tower ▶ 133C, 142D
8 the correct spelling of the word ▶ 133C

231 1 Your friends' behaviour was disgraceful. ▶ 134C
2 We are very grateful for our sponsor's generosity. ▶ 134E
3 The player's selection for the national team was inevitable. ▶ 134D

4 There's a women's changing room along the corridor. ▶ 134A

5 The minister's resignation surprised everyone. ▶ 134C

6 I prefer cow's milk to goat's milk. ▶ 134B

7 The star's popularity will guarantee the film's success. ▶ 134E, C

232 1 Saturday's game ▶ 135A
2 a day's fishing ▶ 135B
3 this month's code word ▶ 135A
4 last week's Time magazine ▶ 135A
5 the Wilsons' (house) ▶ 136
6 a whole week's work ▶ 135B
7 a few seconds' silence ▶ 135B

233 1 Food
2 a car
3 problems/some problems
4 violence
5 photos
6 a town
7 Health
8 an idea
▶ 137

234 1 a) much
2 b) some butter
3 c) all the
4 c) water
5 b) a job
6 b) many
▶ 137B

235 1 a box of matches ▶ 138A–B
2 a tin/can of soup ▶ 138A–B
3 two cartons of milk ▶ 138A–B
4 a/one kilo of bananas ▶ 138A–B
5 a loaf of bread ▶ 138A–B
6 a bunch/bouquet of flowers ▶ 138A, D

236 1 much work
2 litter
3 advertisements
4 little
5 baggage has
6 a shower
7 machines
8 some
9 jewels were
10 equipment
11 some
12 permission
13 some
14 research
15 pollution
▶ 139

237 1 a success ▶ 140C
2 light ▶ 140C
3 sport ▶ 140C
4 egg ▶ 140B
5 a shame ▶ 140D
6 an experience ▶ 140C
7 a conversation ▶ 140C
8 iron ▶ 140C

238 1 b) Can I have two coffees, please? ▶ 140F
2 e) I ought to wash my hair tonight. ▶ 140C
3 g) I was woken by a sudden noise. ▶ 140C
4 h) There was an interesting painting on the wall. ▶ 140C

5 j) All the men were wearing evening dress. ▶ 140C

239 1 a telephone box
2 a hospital bed
3 a fish tank
4 a door handle
5 a golf ball
6 a safety helmet
7 a church tower
▶ 141A

240 1 a glass door ▶ 142C
2 an electricity bill ▶ 141A
3 a bread knife ▶ 142A
4 a garden wall ▶ 142D
5 town centre shops ▶ 141E
6 a book exhibition ▶ 141D
7 a concrete mixer ▶ 142A
8 a beer bottle ▶ 142B
9 a shop assistant ▶ 142C
10 business news ▶ 142A
11 the sales figures ▶ 141D
12 a gas cooker ▶ 142A
13 a weather forecast ▶ 142A
14 a yogurt carton ▶ 142B
15 steel industry employees ▶ 141E

241 1 The restaurant near our office is closing down. ▶ 143A

2 The discussion yesterday was very interesting. ▶ 143A / Yesterday's discussion was very interesting. ▶ 135A

3 A piece of rock the size of a football fell down the cliff. ▶ 143A

4 Our holiday on the island of St Lucia was wonderful. ▶ 143A

5 People (who are) aware of their rights will complain. ▶ 143A

6 There's a photo of the group at a street market in France/at a French street market. ▶ 143B

7 My brother goes to a school for young children with learning difficulties/children who have learning difficulties. ▶ 143B

242 1 c) an hour's ▶ 135B
2 d) a piece of ▶ 138A, C
3 d) top of the building ▶ 132A, 133C
4 a) much money ▶ 137A, C
5 c) shelf for putting books on ▶ 142A,–B
6 b) an iron ▶ 140C
7 d) women pilots ▶ 131B
8 b) racehorse ▶ 141A, D
9 c) player's strength ▶ 132A, 134E
10 a) little progress ▶ 139A–B

243 1 Two hours is a long time to have to wait. ▶ 145C

2 Both my mother and my father are doctors.
▶ 145A

3 Either blue or green is the right colour for this room. ▶ 145B

4 Rome, my birthplace, is a wonderful city.
▶ 145A

5 The trees next to the school are going to be cut down. ▶ 145F

6 Walking up hills is quite tiring. ▶ 145G

7 The house, together with a piece of land, is now on the market. ▶ 145E

8 Fax and e-mail are modern forms of communication. ▶ 145A

9 *Antony and Cleopatra* is a play by Shakespeare.
▶ 145D

244 1 has ▶ 146C
2 were ▶ 146B
3 lives ▶ 146A
4 was ▶ 146F
5 are ▶ 146C
6 use ▶ 146D
7 have ▶ 146B
8 was ▶ 146C
9 has ▶ 146B
10 has ▶ 146E
11 goes ▶ 146B
12 thinks ▶ 146D

245 1 My clothes weren't right/The clothes I was wearing weren't right for the occasion.
2 The damage to my car is going to cost £1,000 to repair.
3 The contents of the parcel have to be listed on the form.
4 My belongings were stored in the cellar.
5 The content of the article is nothing new.
6 (All) my savings are in the bank.
7 The flat is nice, but the surroundings aren't very beautiful.
▶ 147A

246 1 Measles is a serious illness. ▶ 147B
2 The premises are locked on a Sunday. ▶ 147A
3 All means of transport have disadvantages.
▶ 147C
4 Statistics is a useful subject. ▶ 147B
5 The goods are already on their way. ▶ 147A
6 A new TV wildlife series is coming soon. ▶ 147C
7 Billiards isn't as much fun as snooker. ▶ 147B
8 The statistics are showing/The statistics show an increase in inflation. ▶ 147B
9 The odds on our winning aren't very high.
▶ 147A

247 1 pair ▶ 148C
2 pairs ▶ 148C
3 some ▶ 148B
4 are ▶ 148B
5 these/those ▶ 148B
6 them/those/these ▶ 148B
7 they ▶ 148B
8 a ▶ 148C
9 shorts ▶ 148D

248 1 The company's staff are worried about losing their jobs. ▶ 149F
2 The jury has/have decided that the man is innocent. ▶ 149A
3 The team who won are all amateur players.
▶ 149C
4 The population is ninety per cent white. ▶ 149B
5 The BBC is/are showing the programme later this year. ▶ 149E
6 The crew of the ship are taking it in turns to go on shore. ▶ 149B
7 The orchestra is the most famous ever to play in this concert hall. ▶ 149B
8 The audience are taking their seats in the theatre. ▶ 149C

249 1 knows ▶ 146D
2 want ▶ 149C–D
3 was ▶ 146C
4 are ▶ 146B
5 some binoculars
▶ 148A–B
6 doesn't ▶ 147B
7 look ▶ 148B
8 are ▶ 149F
9 are ▶ 145A
10 makes ▶ 146C
11 intends ▶ 149C–D
12 are ▶ 147A

250 1 c) One of our students has gone missing.
▶ 146A
2 d) I'm looking for some scissors. ▶ 148B
3 g) The outskirts of the town are very dreary.
▶ 147A
4 h) Everything seems to be OK. ▶ 146C
5 i) The dog and the cat get on well together.
▶ 145A
6 l) *War and Peace* is a very long book. ▶ 145D

251 1 an, a ▶ 151A
2 a, an ▶ 151B
3 a, an ▶ 151A
4 an ▶ 151A, an ▶ 151B
5 a ▶ 151B, a ▶ 151A
6 a, an ▶ 151B
7 an ▶ 151B, an ▶ 151A
8 a ▶ 151B, a ▶ 151A
9 an ▶ 151A, a ▶ 151B

252 1 It was an awful shock. ▶ 152B
2 I love books. ▶ 153B
3 the chemist's in Station Road ▶ 152C
4 But a burglar alarm doesn't always behave as it should. ▶ 153C
5 I stayed in a hotel not long ago. ▶ 152A
And it had a ghost. ▶ 152A
But the hotel was really nice. ▶ 152A
But I saw the ghost. ▶ 152A

253 1 a ▶ 152A
2 a ▶ 152G
3 The ▶ 152A
4 the ▶ 152A
5 the ▶ 152B
6 a ▶ 152B
7 a ▶ 152A
8 a ▶ 152A
9 a ▶ 152A
10 the ▶ 152B
11 The ▶ 152A
12 the ▶ 152C
13 a ▶ 152C
14 the ▶ 152A
15 a ▶ 152G
16 the ▶ 152B
17 a ▶ 152A
18 the ▶ 152A
19 the ▶ 152A
20 a ▶ 152G
21 the ▶ 152D
22 The ▶ 152A
23 the ▶ 152C
24 the ▶ 152A
25 a ▶ 152A
26 a ▶ 152A
27 The ▶ 152A
28 a ▶ 152A
29 a ▶ 152A
30 the ▶ 152A
31 The ▶ 152A
32 a ▶ 152G

254 General meaning: 6 A self-catering holiday ▶ 153C, 7 a holiday ▶ 153C, 10 the travel agent ▶ 153D, 11 travel agents ▶ 153B, 14 a holiday ▶ 153C
Specific meaning: 3 a self-catering holiday, 4 a mistake, 5 a very small flat, 8 the place, 9 the brochure, 12 the mistake, 13 the travel agent

255 1 A bad workman blames his tools. ▶ 153C
2 Galileo invented the telescope. ▶ 153D
3 Whales are huge animals. ▶ 153B
4 The mobile phone has made life easier for many people. ▶ 153D
5 A thing you cut wood with is called a saw. ▶ 153C
6 The consumer is paying too much for food. ▶ 153D

256 1 on the train ▶ 154D
2 A policeman ▶ 154E
3 the violin ▶ 154C
4 Television ▶ 154B
5 the country ▶ 154F
6 on the radio ▶ 154B
7 a television ▶ 154B
8 billiards ▶ 154C
9 the theatre ▶ 154A
10 the police ▶ 154E

257 1 the (nicest) car ▶ 152D, the (seaside) ▶ 154F, A (nice sunny day) ▶ 153C
2 The sun ▶ 152B, the sky ▶ 152B, the (countryside) ▶ 154F, the (countryside) ▶ 152A, the (radio) ▶ 154B
3 a (nice little seaside town) ▶ 152F, the (town) ▶ 152A, a car park ▶ 152A, the car park ▶ 152A, Cars ▶ 153B
4 The (road) ▶ 152C, a (steep hill) ▶ 152A, a (sign) ▶ 152A, the (edge) ▶ 152C, the (cliff) ▶ 152C
5 a (lovely view) ▶ 152A, the (English Channel) ▶ 152B, the view/the sea ▶ 152A
6 the car ▶ 152A, the (edge) ▶ 152C, the (cliff) ▶ 152A, the edge/the cliff ▶ 152A, the (rocks) ▶ 152C, a (terrible moment) ▶ 152F

7 the (top) ▶ 152C, the cliff ▶ 152A, the (wreck) ▶ 152A, the brake ▶ 152B, the (police) ▶ 154E, the (bus) ▶ 154D Also possible: a (bus)

258 1 He earns many thousands of pounds a week.
2 (When he is overtaking,) his heart beats 150 times a minute.
3 He trains five or six days a week.
4 He sleeps eight hours a night.
5 He has three good meals a day,
6 He is interviewed several times a month.
▶ 155A

259 1 one ▶ 156A
2 a ▶ 156A
3 One ▶ 156B
4 one ▶ 156C
5 one ▶ 156A
6 a ▶ 156A
7 one ▶ 156B
8 One ▶ 156B
9 one ▶ 156C
10 one ▶ 156C

260 1 (d) These are lovely photos, aren't they?
2 (e) That animal is a tiger not a lion.
3 (h) Is this salt in here, or is it pepper?
▶ 157B

261 1 Computers, The computers
2 oil, the oil
3 The furniture, The chairs, furniture
4 golf, Tennis, The golf
5 art, pictures, the pictures
6 the dogs, The noise, Dogs, cats
▶ 158A

262 1 a ▶ 152A
2 big hotels ▶ 153B
3 a ▶ 152A
4 the ▶ 152C, D
5 some ▶ 157A
6 the ▶ 152D
7 reggae music ▶ 157B
8 Noise ▶ 153B
9 the ▶ 152A
10 the ▶ 152A
11 a ▶ 152F
12 the ▶ 152B, C
13 the ▶ 152D
14 the ▶ 152B, C
15 the ▶ 152A
16 a ▶ 152A
17 the ▶ 152A
18 a ▶ 152A
19 The ▶ 152A
20 the ▶ 152A

263 1 e 3 h 5 c 7 g
2 b 4 a 6 j 8 f
▶ 159

264 1 the church ▶ 160D
2 the night ▶ 161F
3 1995 ▶ 161B
4 bed ▶ 160B
5 midnight ▶ 161F
6 Alex ▶ 162A
7 work ▶ 160D
8 the office ▶ 160D
12 the year ▶ 161B
13 the previous week ▶ 161H
14 the new school ▶ 160C
15 the Mitchells ▶ 160D
16 the bed ▶ 160B, D
17 the dark ▶ 161F
18 September ▶ 161C
19 church ▶ 160D

9 last year ▸ 161H
10 The David ▸ 162B
11 Easter ▸ 161D
20 Doctor ▸ 162A
21 lunch ▸ 161G
22 the Christmas ▸ 161D

265 1 the Brooklyn Bridge ▸ 163G, Ellis Island ▸ 163A, Rockefeller Center ▸ 163I, Macy's ▸ 163J, Chinatown ▸ 163E, Fifth Avenue ▸ 163F, the Empire State Building ▸ 163I, Central Park ▸ 163F

2 the Houses of Parliament ▸ 162A, 163H, Buckingham Palace ▸ 163H, Oxford Street ▸ 163F, Piccadilly Circus ▸ 163F, the British Museum ▸ 163I, the River Thames ▸ 163D, Kew Gardens ▸ 163F, the Tower of London ▸ 162A, 163H

266 1 a) work ▸ 160B, D
2 b) an ▸ 151B
3 b) a great game ▸ 152F
4 b) the cinema ▸ 154A
5 b) The National ▸ 163F
6 c) The boy ▸ 152A
7 a) a dog ▸ 153C
8 a) a week ▸ 155A
9 a) computer disks ▸ 157B
10 b) the ▸ 152B
11 b) breakfast ▸ 161G
12 a) Love ▸ 158A
13 a) a ▸ 156A
14 b) room ▸ 159C

267 1 a terrible nuisance ▸ 152F
2 August ▸ 161C
3 the M6 ▸ 163F
4 Birmingham ▸ 163E
5 a hurry ▸ 159E
6 work ▸ 160D
7 the same place ▸ 152D
8 the police ▸ 154E
9 a speed camera ▸ 152A
10 the camera ▸ 152A
11 a letter ▸ 152A
12 the following week ▸ 161H
13 an hour ▸ 155A
14 court ▸ 160D
15 bus ▸ 154D
16 The bus ▸ 154D
17 next year ▸ 161H
18 life ▸ 158A

268 1 his 2 their 3 its 4 my 5 your 6 our ▸ 164A–B

269 1 mine 2 his 3 ours 4 theirs 5 hers ▸ 164A–B

270 1 ours ▸ 164D
2 the ▸ 164C
3 mine ▸ 164A–B
4 of his own ▸ 164E
5 her ▸ 164C
6 your ▸ 164A–B
7 the ▸ 164C
8 his ▸ 164D
9 my own ▸ 164E

271 1 Did you take these photos?
2 This magazine is complete rubbish.
3 Who's left that motor-bike/motorcycle there?
4 Those chairs don't look very comfortable.
▸ 165A

272 1 This ▸ 165B, those ▸ 165A
2 these ▸ 165A–B, that ▸ 165E
3 this ▸ 165B, this ▸ 165B
4 that ▸ 165B, those ▸ 165B
5 this ▸ 165E, that ▸ 165B
6 Those ▸ 165B, these ▸ 165B
7 This ▸ 165B, that ▸ 165F
8 This ▸ 165D, this ▸ 165B
9 these ▸ 165A, that ▸ 165B
10 those ▸ 165F, that ▸ 165E

273 1 b) few ▸ 166D
2 c) numerous ▸ 166B
3 b) great deal ▸ 166B
4 a) bit ▸ 166D
5 d) no ▸ 166E
6 a) amount ▸ 166C
7 c) large number ▸ 166B

274 1 I drank a (little) bit of tea. ▸ 167C
2 A lot of families have only got one car. ▸ 167A
3 There aren't many/There are not many unspoilt areas left. ▸ 167D
4 There is (very) little time to relax. ▸ 167D
5 I bought a few things in town. ▸ 167C
6 There are so many things to do. ▸ 167B
7 There has been little interest in the scheme. ▸ 167D
8 We eat too much sugar. ▸ 167B

275 1 It's only a few miles. ▸ 167C
2 He has a lot of friends. ▸ 167A
3 It's one of your few faults. ▸ 167E
4 There are a great many characters. ▸ 167E
5 We've had very few problems with them. ▸ 167D
6 You could show a little bit of enthusiasm. ▸ 167C

276 1 A few. ▸ 168G
2 More than half. ▸ 168C
3 Some of it. ▸ 168E
4 A lot of stories. ▸ 168A

277 1 of ▸ 169D
2 ✓ ▸ 169C
3 of ▸ 169A
4 The ▸ 169A
5 ✓ ▸ 169B
6 the ▸ 169A
7 ✓ ▸ 169A
8 of ▸ 169D
9 of ▸ 169B

278 1 Both of them ▸ 170C
2 neither of them ▸ 170D
3 neither of them ▸ 170D
4 Both of them ▸ 170C
5 either of them ▸ 170D
6 All of them ▸ 169B
7 none of them ▸ 169C
8 most of them ▸ 169A

279 1 Neither of my/the cameras work(s)./Neither camera works. ▶ 170D
2 Either candidate/Either of the candidates would be an excellent choice. Also possible: Both candidates/Both (of) the candidates would be an excellent choice. ▶ 170D
3 Both passengers/Both (of) the passengers were injured. ▶ 170C
4 Neither of my brothers have/has sent me a birthday card. ▶ 170D
5 Both teams/Both (of) the teams were happy with the result/with a/the draw. ▶ 170C
6 Either table/Either of the tables would be OK. ▶ 170D

280 1 c) At the airport every passenger is searched. ▶ 171A
2 e) Each of the pages has a number. ▶ 171D
3 f) The Olympics are every four years. ▶ 171B
4 i) I ring my girlfriend almost every day. ▶ 171C
5 j) There was a path on each side/on both sides of the canal. ▶ 171D
6 l) None of the photos have/has come out properly. ▶ 171E

281 1 some ▶ 172A
2 no ▶ 172C
3 some ▶ 172F
4 Any ▶ 172E
5 no ▶ 172C
6 some ▶ 172D
7 any ▶ 172A
8 any ▶ 172E

282 1 any ▶ 172E
2 any ▶ 172A
3 anything ▶ 172A–B
4 any ▶ 172D
5 no ▶ 172C
6 any ▶ 172A
7 no ▶ 172C
8 some ▶ 172D
9 Anyone ▶ 172A–B
10 some ▶ 172A
11 some ▶ 172F
12 any ▶ 172A

283 1 I took too many bags on to the plane. ▶ 173B
2 We've got enough chairs. ▶ 173A
3 We bought too much food. ▶ 173B
4 I got plenty of votes/enough votes. ▶ 173B
5 There isn't/We haven't got enough time to walk to the cinema. ▶ 173A

284 1 other ▶ 173E
2 any more ▶ 173C
3 another ▶ 173E
4 others ▶ 173D
5 some more ▶ 173C
6 another ▶ 173C
7 other ▶ 173D
8 some more ▶ 173C
9 others ▶ 173D

285 1 five men. Three were later released. ▶ 174A
2 twelve new hi-fi systems. None was/were completely satisfactory. ▶ 174C
3 hundreds of job adverts. Few seem promising. ▶ 174A
4 dozens of cafés. Plenty had free tables. ▶ 174A
5 several phone boxes. Each had been vandalized. ▶ 174C
6 disappointed by the result. Many were actually crying. ▶ 174A
7 been available. Lots have been sold already. ▶ 174A
8 computer manuals. Most are incomprehensible to me. ▶ 174A

286 1 The whole story ... ▶ 169D
2 More than half of the pupils ... ▶ 169A
3 I've got quite a lot of work ... ▶ 167A
4 We each had our photo taken. ▶ 171D
5 ... and buy another one. ▶ 174A
6 We both fell ill ... ▶ 170C
7 We've had a great deal of trouble ... ▶ 166B
8 ... and he owns two other flats. ▶ 173E

287 1 We don't need any help. ▶ 172A
2 None of these sweaters are/is nice./None of them are/is nice. ▶ 168H, 169C
3 (that) little of the information/not much of the information is new/little of it/not much of it is new. ▶ 168G
4 You've got a lot of videos/lots of videos. ▶ 167B/ You've got masses/heaps/loads of videos. ▶ 166B
5 I'm not hiding anything. ▶ 172A
6 None of these (four) signatures is/are genuine./None of them is/are genuine. ▶ 171E
7 Neither of the sisters/Neither of them studied art. ▶ 170D
8 You haven't bought enough (paint). ▶ 173A–B Also possible: You've bought too little (paint).

288 1 Most of the island is forest. ▶ 169B
2 We're staying in, but the others are going clubbing. ▶ 173D
3 I had to make a small number of phone calls. ▶ 166D
4 There's hardly any food in the house. ▶ 172A
5 We watch (very) little television. ▶ 167D
6 Some garages stay open late, but a lot don't. ▶ 174A
7 Both (of) those boxes are damaged. ▶ 170C Those two boxes are both damaged. ▶ 170C
8 I write my diary every single day. ▶ 171C
9 Some people don't like heavy metal. ▶ 172D
10 Any day next week will be OK by me. ▶ 172E

289 1 it ▶ 175B, F
2 they ▶ 175B, F
3 them ▶ 175B, F
4 him ▶ 175B, F
5 he ▶ 175B, F
6 it ▶ 175B, F
7 I ▶ 175B
8 he ▶ 175B, F
9 me ▶ 175B
10 she ▶ 175B, F
11 it ▶ 175B, F
12 we ▶ 175B, H
13 us ▶ 175B
14 you ▶ 175B

290 1 Anita ▶ 175B
2 Gemma ▶ 175B
3 Karen ▶ 175B, F
4 Simon ▶ 175B, F
5 Simon ▶ 175B, F
6 Karen and Simon
▶ 175B, F
7 people in general ▶ 176A
8 Gemma ▶ 175B
9 people in general
▶ 176C
10 Gemma ▶ 175B
11 Gemma and Anita
▶ 175B, H
12 the time ▶ 175F

291 1 Me ▶ 175B, them ▶ 175B, F
2 It ▶ 175F, you ▶ 175B, I ▶ 175B, they ▶ 176C
3 they ▶ 175B, F, We ▶ 176B
4 It ▶ 175B, I ▶ 175B, they ▶ 176C, you ▶ 176A
5 it ▶ 175F, she ▶ 175B, F, they/he or she ▶ 175G

292 1 them 2 ✓ 3 ✓ 4 ✓/they 5 they 6 ✓
7 ✓/him 8 him 9 they 10 him 11 ✓/They
12 ✓ 13 ✓/them 14 ✓/they 15 ✓ 16 ✓ 17 ✓
18 ✓ 19 He 20 ✓ 21 ✓ 22 ✓ 23 ✓ 24 they
25 it
▶ 175E

293 1 herself R ▶ 177A–B
2 themselves E
▶ 177A, E
3 itself R ▶ 177A–B
4 himself E ▶ 177A, E
5 myself E ▶ 177F
6 ourselves R ▶ 177A–B
7 myself R ▶ 177A–B
8 yourselves R ▶ 177A–B
9 herself E ▶ 177A, E
10 themselves R ▶ 177A–B
11 himself R ▶ 177A–B
12 itself E ▶ 177A, E

294 1 Enjoy yourselves (, all of you). ▶ 177A, D
2 Tim and Oliver will never trust each other again. ▶ 177G
3 You've made yourself wet (all over)/all wet, Emma. ▶ 177A–B
4 Why don't you just sit down and relax? ▶ 177D
5 Sam and Joanna were getting on each other's nerves. ▶ 177G
6 I hope my brother is going to behave (himself). ▶ 177A, D
7 Families cross the border to visit one another. ▶ 177G
8 The students ought to think for themselves. ▶ 177A, C
9 I often wonder where I'll be in ten years' time. ▶ 177D
10 It's dangerous for a woman to travel by herself. ▶ 177A, D
11 All the atoms interact with each other. ▶ 177G
12 I can't afford a holiday. ▶ 177D

295 1 yourself
2 me
3 us
4 himself
5 him
6 ourselves
▶ 177C

296 1 I
2 We
3 ourselves
4 them
5 it/there
6 our
7 her
8 herself
9 it
10 it
11 her
12 He
13 himself
14 she
15 him
16 her
17 mine
18 yourselves
19 your
20 ours
▶ 178

297 1 the fair-haired one/the one who is six feet tall
2 the one on the moon/the one in a/the spacesuit
3 the small(er) ones/the ones at the front
4 the one (which is) full of helium
▶ 179A, C

298 1 I'm thinking of buying one. ▶ 179D
2 I ought to have brought some. ▶ 179D
3 ✓ ▶ 179B
4 ✓ ▶ 179B
5 I left it on the train. ▶ 179D
6 The one to Cardiff has already left. ▶ 179C
7 ✓ ▶ 179B
8 I haven't posted them yet. ▶ 179D
9 ✓ ▶ 179B
10 There are some over there. ▶ 179D
11 I think every one is in the wash at the moment. ▶ 179C
12 There are some quite interesting ones. ▶ 179A

299 1 someone/somebody ▶ 180A–B
2 anyone/anybody ▶ 180A–B, E
3 No one/Nobody ▶ 180A–B
4 anywhere ▶ 180A, D–E
5 nowhere ▶ 180A, D
6 somewhere ▶ 180A, D
7 something ▶ 180A, C
8 everything ▶ 180A, C
9 anything ▶ 180A, C, E

300 1 The doctors are doing everything possible for your friend. ▶ 180C, G
2 There's something else I wanted to tell you. ▶ 180C, G
3 Let's find somewhere quiet. ▶ 180D, G
4 During the World Cup we saw hardly anyone/anybody on the streets. ▶ 180A, E

5 Someone's/Somebody's mobile phone rang during the performance. ▶ 180B, F

6 Nothing unusual has happened during the last week. ▶ 180C, G

7 I wouldn't do a favour like this for anyone else/anybody else. ▶ 180A, E, G

8 I've looked everywhere I can think of for that computer disk. ▶ 180D, G

9 Everyone's/Everybody's luggage had to be weighed. ▶ 180B, F

301 1 a) It was ▶ 175F
2 a) each other's ▶ 177G
3 b) Something awful has ▶ 180G, H
4 b) thin ▶ 179A
5 a) her ▶ 175B, F
6 c) they say ▶ 176C
7 a) relax ▶ 177D
8 d) the one ▶ 179C
9 b) me ▶ 177C
10 d) they ▶ 175G

302 1 wonderful, coarse, sharp, careful, short, small, nocturnal, powerful, busiest, wide, old, young, blind, soft, main, natural, traditional, useless ▶ 181A
2 wonderful ▶ 181A
3 nocturnal ▶ 181A
4 their main natural enemies ▶ 181C
5 quite sharp, completely useless ▶ 181C
6 busiest ▶ 181B
7 wonderful, careful, nocturnal, powerful, natural, traditional, useless ▶ 181B

303 1 On the whole I thought Gulftown was a nice place. ▶ 182A
2 Our apartment by the water was really big. ▶ 182A
3 The weather was much better than usual. ▶ 182B
4 We were only a short distance from the beach. ▶ 182A
5 The view from our balcony was absolutely magnificent. ▶ 182A
6 If possible, I'd like to go there again some time. ▶ 182C
7 People could swim in the sea because it was so warm. ▶ 182A
8 Although expensive, the holiday was definitely worth it. ▶ 182C

304 1 central ▶ 183A
2 similar ▶ 183B
3 embarrassed ▶ 183B
4 primary ▶ 183A
5 healthy ▶ 183B
6 satisfied ▶ 183B
7 total ▶ 183A
8 a living ▶ 183B
9 complete ▶ 183A

305 1 A bus full of passengers came down the hill.
2 The men guilty of robbery were sent to prison.

3 People nervous of heights shouldn't climb the tower. 4 Some visitors tired of looking round the museum were in the café. 5 Substances harmful to our health should be banned from food.
▶ 184A

306 1 present time ▶ 184B
2 anyone famous ▶ 184C
3 involved instructions ▶ 184B
4 company concerned ▶ 184B
5 people present ▶ 184B
6 something different ▶ 184C
7 man responsible ▶ 184B
8 people involved ▶ 184B

307 1 It's an inexpensive smoke alarm. ▶ 185B–C
2 It's a stylish aluminium garden chair. ▶ 185B–
3 It's a small circular wall mirror. ▶ 185B–C
4 It's a blue polyester sleeping bag. ▶ 185C
5 It's a large wood-effect storage cupboard. ▶ 185B–D
6 It's a traditional American cowboy hat. ▶ 185B–C
7 It's a two-kilowatt oil-filled electric radiator. ▶ 185C–D
8 It's a useful folding guest bed. ▶ 185B–C
9 It's a new light grey computer workstation. ▶ 185B–D

308 1 ✓ ▶ 185F
2 X ▶ 185F
3 X ▶ 185F
4 ✓ ▶ 185E
5 ✓ ▶ 185E
6 ✓ ▶ 185F
7 X ▶ 185

309 1 very
2 absolutely
3 totally
4 a bit
▶ 186
5 very
6 completely
7 an absolutely
8 a bit

310 1 thrilled
2 amazing
3 frightened
4 terrified
5 frightening
▶ 187
6 disappointing
7 interesting
8 pleased
9 depressed
10 boring

311 1 The unemployed ▶ 188A
2 the unexpected ▶ 188B–C
3 The dead woman ▶ 188A
4 The disabled ▶ 188A
5 The good thing ▶ 188C
6 Some disabled people ▶ 188A
7 The old ▶ 188A
8 the impossible ▶ 188C

9 An old/elderly man ▸ 188A

10 the unexplained/the unexplainable/the mysterious ▸ 188B

11 the blind ▸ 188A

12 The (really) strange thing ▸ 188C

13 the homeless ▸ 188A

14 The rich, the poor ▸ 188A

312 1 b) I couldn't find anything nice in the shops. ▸ 184C

2 d) The nights are very cold. ▸ 181B

3 e) The strong have a duty to care for the weak. ▸ 188A

4 g) The view was very nice/absolutely magnificent. ▸ 186

5 i) I've got a brother (who is) good at tennis. ▸ 184A

6 j) The child leads a rather lonely existence. ▸ 183B

7 k) It was an expensive Japanese digital camera. ▸ 185C

8 m) The good thing is that we all get on well together. ▸ 188C

313 1 suddenly, adverb ▸ 189A–B

2 for six months, prepositional phrase ▸ 189 A–B

3 next week, noun phrase ▸ 189 A–B

4 carefully, adverb ▸ 189 A–B

5 on the bed, prepositional phrase ▸ 189 A–B

6 soon, adverb ▸ 189 A–B

7 all afternoon, noun phrase ▸ 189 A–B

8 Everyone put their coats on the bed. ▸ 189A, C

314 1 I never watch quiz shows. ▸ 190C

2 Someone has just been telling me the news. ▸ 190C

3 I usually have to work late. ▸ 190E

4 I don't always get up so early. ▸ 190C

5 We have recently moved house. ▸ 190C

6 You'll definitely pass the exam, but I probably won't. ▸ 190E

7 The bus is usually a few minutes late. ▸ 190C

8 But I seldom do have a day off. ▸ 190E

9 We're just getting ready to go out. ▸ 190C

10 I've been carefully checking all these figures. ▸ 190C

315 1 We're going to buy a new car soon. / We're soon going to buy a new car. / Soon we're going to buy a new car.

4 I'll have finished my course in a week. / In a week I'll have finished my course.

6 I was studying closely all the sources of information I had found. / I was closely studying all the sources of information I had found.

8 Joanna fastened the rope securely. ▸ 190F

316 1 well in yesterday's game ▸ 191A–B

2 early most days ▸ 191D

3 here soon ▸ 191B

4 to a barbecue tomorrow ▸ 191B

5 at a café(,) actually ▸ 191E

6 soundly the whole time ▸ 191A–B

7 thoughtlessly sometimes ▸ 191D

8 on time most days(,) surprisingly ▸ 191D–E

317 1 happily ▸ 192A   5 suitably ▸ 192A

2 probably ▸ 192A–B   6 high ▸ 192C

3 long ▸ 192C   7 beautifully ▸ 192B

4 dramatically ▸ 192A

318 1 daily ▸ 192F   6 lately ▸ 192E

2 highly ▸ 192E   7 well ▸ 192G

3 freely ▸ 192E   8 hardly ▸ 192E

4 good-looking ▸ 192G   9 nearly ▸ 192E

5 well-dressed ▸ 192G   10 most ▸ 192E

319 1 strange   2 quickly   3 fine   4 dizzy

5 heavily   6 quietly   7 thoughtful

8 immediately   9 slowly ▸ 193A

320 1 in an efficient ▸ 193B   4 in ▸ 193C

2 with great ▸ 193B   5 without a ▸ 193C

3 (in) a different ▸ 193B

321 1 I'll soon be on holiday.

2 I've just been looking at them.

3 I've finally made up my mind.

4 She now spends all her time on the golf course.

5 I immediately rang the fire brigade. ▸ 194A

322 1 yet, yet ▸ 194B, long ▸ 194F, already ▸ 194D

2 no longer ▸ 194E, already ▸ 194D, after ▸ 194G

3 any longer ▸ 194E, still, still ▸ 194C, afterwards ▸ 194G, far ▸ 194F

323 1 The old man doesn't often go out of the house. / The old man doesn't go out of the house (very) often./The old man seldom/rarely goes out of the house. ▸ 195A–B

Also possible: The old man hardly ever goes out of the house. ▸ 195E

2 I'm always pleased to see you. ▸ 195A–B

3 We normally/usually/generally go into town on the bus. ▶ 195A–B

4 You can sometimes/occasionally get nice things really cheap in the market. ▶ 195A–B

5 I've often/frequently stayed late at the office. ▶ 195A–B

6 The work I do is never boring. ▶ 195A–B

Also possible: The work I do isn't ever boring. ▶ 195C

7 We don't often see policemen on the streets./ We don't see policemen on the streets very often. ▶ 195A–B

8 The program sometimes/occasionally doesn't work properly. ▶ 195A–C

324 1 buys a newspaper every day. ▶ 195F

2 seldom goes to the theatre. ▶ 195B

3 has often thought about emigrating. ▶ 195B/has thought about emigrating very/quite often. ▶ 195D

4 cooks a meal most evenings. ▶ 195F

5 will never/won't ever get married. ▶ 195E

325 1 But they're fairly similar. ▶ 196A

2 It matters a lot. ▶ 196D

3 This one is easily the best. ▶ 196C

4 He behaved extremely impolitely. ▶ 196A

5 I'm half convinced by your arguments. ▶ 196A

6 Are you really running a dating agency? ▶ 196D

7 He isn't very old. ▶ 196B

8 I feel much happier now. ▶ 196C

9 We enjoyed it very much. ▶ 196D

Also possible: We very much enjoyed it.

10 I'm not at all cold./I'm not cold at all. ▶ 196A

11 She's rather nice. ▶ 196A

12 Is it any better than the old one? ▶ 196C

326 1 I've spent rather a lot of money.

2 I'll need a lot more information.

3 There's hardly any time left.

4 You've eaten almost all the sweets.

5 You've made too many mistakes.

6 I wish those people would make a little less noise. ▶ 196F

327 1 Gemma's/Her exam results aren't good enough.

2 The computer isn't powerful enough.

3 The bus drivers'/Their wages are too low.

4 The rules are too complicated.

5 Paul/He doesn't write clearly enough.

6 The car/It was going too fast/went too fast. ▶ 196G

328 1 I had quite an argument with him.

2 She's got such a nice personality.

3 He's a bit of an idiot.

4 There's too small a space.

5 We've got a fairly strong team.

6 It's rather a difficult question/a rather difficult question.

7 It's quite a big job.

8 We've walked quite a long way.

9 I haven't seen you for such a long time.

10 I couldn't do as good a drawing as that.

Also possible: I couldn't do a drawing as good as that. ▶ 196H

329 1 fairly ▶ 197A

2 rather ▶ 197C

3 fairly ▶ 197A

4 absolutely ▶ 197A

5 to some extent ▶ 197A

6 not completely ▶ 197A

7 interesting ▶ 197B

330 1 I've only just bought it. ▶ 198C

3 I'll only be away for a week. / I'll be away for only a week. ▶ 198A

4 Even young children were forced to work. ▶ 198B

6 These seats are for members only. ▶ 198A

7 And it was repaired only last week. ▶ 198C

331 1 frankly ▶ 201D

2 Presumably ▶ 200A

3 unfortunately ▶ 201A Also possible: regrettably

4 Luckily ▶ 201A

5 Culturally ▶ 199

6 Perhaps/Maybe/Possibly ▶ 200A

7 politically ▶ 199

8 Undoubtedly/Certainly ▶ 200A

9 Stupidly ▶ 201B

332 1 for example

2 consequently

3 Nevertheless ▶ 202B

4 firstly, secondly

5 After all

6 in addition

333 1 runs deep under the ground. ▶ 192E

2 I still haven't received ▶ 194C

Also possible: I haven't yet received ▶ 194B

3 For two whole days I've received ▶ 194A

4 such an awful day. ▶ 196H

Also possible: a really awful day

5 To my surprise, I found the room ▶ 201C

6 all meeting in the pub later./all meeting later in the pub. ▶ 194A

7 very tall, but Mark is even taller. ▶ 198D

8 is becoming more dangerous. ▶ 193A

9 I definitely saw that man at the scene ▶ 190C

10 stared in amazement. ▶ 192B

11 very much that you are successful. ▶ 196D

12 I have never/I've never been to Also possible: I haven't ever been to ▶ 195E

13 disabled, and in addition (to that) he's got a heart condition. ▶ 202B

14 The visit to the museum was fairly/quite/rather ▶ 196A–B

334 1 easier, harder, more difficult, more durable

2 brightest, greatest, largest, best, most exclusive, most specialized
▶ 203A–B

335 1 brighter ▶ 203C

2 most difficult ▶ 203E

3 more exclusive ▶ 203E

4 harder, hardest ▶ 203C

5 larger, largest ▶ 203B–C

6 more durable, most durable ▶ 203E

7 easy, easiest ▶ 203D

8 big, bigger ▶ 203B–C

336 1 f) ▶ 203C   3 g)▶ 203D   5 e) ▶ 203D

2 a)▶ 203C   4 c) ▶ 203B, 203D   6 b) ▶ 203E

337 1 taller than Telecom Tower. ▶ 203A–C

2 the most successful group in the world.
▶ 203A–B, 203E

3 bigger than Venus. ▶ 203A–C

4 more popular than the Tower of London.
▶ 203A–B, 203E

5 the longest river in Britain. ▶ 203A–C

6 older than Cambridge (University). ▶ 203A–C

7 the most valuable picture in the world.
▶ 203A–B, 203E

8 the wealthiest dog in the world. ▶ 203A–C

338 1 ~~boringest~~ most boring ▶ 203E

2 ~~sadest~~ saddest ▶ 203B–C

3 ~~most high~~ highest ▶ 203B–C

4 ~~wronger~~ more wrong ▶ 203C

5 ~~most~~ more ▶ 203A

6 ~~more far~~ further/farther ▶ 203G

7 ~~tidyer~~ tidier ▶ 203B–C

8 ~~attractivest~~ most attractive ▶ 203E

9 ~~badder~~ worse ▶ 203F

339 1 nearest   3 older   5 further

2 next   4 latest   6 last
▶ 203G

340 1 work more carefully ▶ 204C

2 play better ▶ 204B

3 talk more quietly ▶ 204C

4 get up earlier ▶ 204A

5 do worse ▶ 204B

6 operate more efficiently ▶ 204C

341 1 less crime in country areas   2 got the fewest/least   3 has the most   4 get more viewers
5 have/has the most   6 there are fewer/less passengers   7 has made the least   8 has less power   9 have more accidents
▶ 205

342 1 more ▶ 206B   6 most ▶ 206B

2 as/so ▶ 206C   7 as/so ▶ 206C

3 least ▶ 206B   8 less ▶ 206B

4 as/so ▶ 206C   9 most ▶ 206B

5 less ▶ 206B

343 1 Dave is as tall as Mike. ▶ 206C

2 Sunday is the least busy day. ▶ 206B

3 My new job is much more interesting. ▶ 206G

4 For this job metal is better than plastic. ▶ 206A

5 The ground was as hard as iron. ▶ 206C

6 Football is less complicated than cricket.
▶ 206B

7 This is the nicest view I've ever seen. ▶ 206F

8 The room looks bigger than it did. ▶ 206A

344 1 more and more popular   2 More and more
3 more and more profitable   4 higher and higher
5 better and better, more and more successful
▶ 207A

345 1 The later I go to bed, the better I sleep.

2 The harder I work, the less time I spend with my family.

3 The more cars come into the city, the more slowly/the slower the traffic moves.

4 The hotter you get, the more you sweat.

5 The more I think about it, the less attractive the idea becomes.

6 The bigger/larger the engine (is), the more petrol a car uses. / The greater the size of the engine, the more petrol a car uses.
▶ 207B

346 1 as/so ▶ 206C   7 better ▶ 203F

2 as ▶ 206C   8 less ▶ 206B

3 most ▶ 203B, 206F   9 than ▶ 206A

4 The ▶ 207B   10 more ▶ 203B, 203D

5 the ▶ 207B   11 further/farther ▶ 203F

6 and ▶ 207A

347 1 as old as the church ▶ 206C

2 least interesting route ▶ 206B

3 cleverer/more clever than me/than I am ▶ 203D, 206D
4 more precisely ▶ 204C
5 nicer than the old (wallpaper) ▶ 203B, 206A
6 costs, the more reliable it is. ▶ 207B
7 is the biggest city in Scotland. ▶ 203B
8 earlier than this year ▶ 204A
9 most ridiculous thing I've ever heard ▶ 203B, 206F
10 has more pages than a newspaper ▶ 205

348 1 ▶ 208A–B
  a) in Cornwall   j) during their absence
  b) on a hillside   k) at 9.15 am
  c) with a steep field l) across the field
  d) above it   m) behind the house
  e) at their house   n) of the vehicle
  f) to the building   o) on the wet grass
  g) to France   p) down the hill
  h) for a holiday   q) at high speed
  i) in the house   r) into the house
2 Luckily Mr Sloman had already jumped out of the Land Rover. ▶ 208A
3 They went to France with the idea of forgetting their problems. ▶ 208C
4 But I'm worried about how to break the news to Bill and Barbara. ▶ 208C
5 The vehicle went right through the roof. ▶ 208D
6 a) adverb b) preposition ▶ 208E

349 1 away from the dog ▶ 209A
2 past the Queen ▶ 209A
3 into a glass ▶ 209B
4 down the hill ▶ 209A
5 out of her briefcase ▶ 209A
6 outside the office ▶ 209A
7 onto the stage ▶ 209B
8 against the shed ▶ 209A
9 up a tree ▶ 209A

350 1 behind   3 among   5 into
2 against   4 beyond   6 towards
  ▶ 209C

351 1 at ▶ 210A   8 in ▶ 210D–E
2 at ▶ 210E   9 on ▶ 210E
3 on ▶ 210B   10 at ▶ 210A
4 at ▶ 210A   11 at ▶ 210D
5 in ▶ 210E   12 on ▶ 210B, E
6 in ▶ 210C
7 in ▶ 210C Also possible: at

352 1 next to the post office ▶ 211E
2 under the car ▶ 211A
3 in front of the man ▶ 211F
4 through a/the window ▶ 211C
5 on top of a/the wall ▶ 211B
6 among the/some flowers ▶ 211G
7 over the sofa ▶ 211A

353 1 among ▶ 211G   6 over ▶ 211A
2 near ▶ 211E   7 after ▶ 211F
3 bottom ▶ 211B   8 below ▶ 211A
4 around ▶ 211H   9 across ▶ 211C
5 towards ▶ 211D   10 opposite ▶ 211F

354 1 on ▶ 212B   6 at ▶ 212A
2 at ▶ 212A   7 in ▶ 212C
3 in ▶ 212C   8 at ▶ 212A
4 in ▶ 212C   9 in ▶ 212C
5 on ▶ 212C   10 on ▶ 212B

355 1 ✓ 2 on 3 ✓ 4 for 5 in 6 on 7 ✓ 8 at
  ▶ 212E

356 1 here for two years. ▶ 213A
2 seen you since Oliver's party. ▶ 213B
3 starts in half an hour. ▶ 213D
4 bought any clothes for months. ▶ 213B
5 in the sun for an hour yesterday. ▶ 213A
6 began six weeks ago. ▶ 213C
7 doing this project since March. ▶ 213B

357 1 till ▶ 214C   6 over ▶ 214B
2 from ▶ 214D   7 from ▶ 214D
3 for ▶ 214B   8 prior to ▶ 214E
4 throughout ▶ 214A 9 during ▶ 214B
5 until ▶ 214C   10 by ▶ 214C

358 1 by one of my teachers.
2 in favour of the new law.
3 via Frankfurt.
4 on careers in computers.
5 according to the newspapers.
6 on behalf of everyone here.
7 in accordance with the rules.
  Also possible: according to the rules
8 thanks to more aggressive marketing.
  ▶ 215A

359 1 by ▶ 215E   5 on ▶ 215E   9 as ▶ 215G
2 with ▶ 215C 6 of ▶ 215F   10 except ▶ 215H
3 for ▶ 215B 7 with ▶ 215D 11 without ▶ 215C
4 like ▶ 215G 8 for ▶ 215B   12 by ▶ 215D

360 1 out of work ▶ 216A   5 at the end ▶ 216C
  Also possible: on the dole   6 at last ▶ 216A
2 on time ▶ 216B   Also possible: in the end
3 for sale ▶ 216A   7 in time ▶ 216B
4 on average ▶ 216A   8 at once ▶ 216A

9 In fact ▸ 216A
10 on the way ▸ 216D
11 in advance ▸ 216A

361 1 The bell rings at the end of the lesson. ▸ 216C
2 My friends were waiting patiently in a long queue. ▸ 210E
3 We can cross the river by ferry/on the ferry. ▸ 215E
4 Debbie wanted to overtake the car in front of her. ▸ 209A, 211F
5 A woman came up to me and shook my hand. ▸ 211D
6 I go to evening classes every week. ▸ 212E
7 According to the referee, the ball did not cross the line. ▸ 215A
8 The celebrations went on for hours. ▸ 214B

362 1 d) on ▸ 212C   6 a) among ▸ 209C
2 c) on ▸ 210E   7 d) through ▸ 211C
3 b) for ▸ 213B   8 d) till ▸ 214D
4 c) in ▸ 216D   9 d) with ▸ 215C
5 b) from ▸ 215H   10 c) opposite ▸ 209A, 211F

363 1 I printed it out.
2 I took off my jacket. / I took my jacket off.
3 some people were picking up all the litter in the park.
4 they've put up the prices./they've put the prices up.
5 the birds flew away. Also possible: away flew the birds. ▸ 218B
6 you should write down a list of everything that's worrying you.
7 I must sort out my papers./I must sort my papers out.
8 I'm going to take them down.
▸ 217A, 218A

364 1 down came the rain. 4 up floated the balloon.
2 up he jumped.   5 on came another (one).
3 over they went.
▸ 218B

365 1 A hold-up   3 A hand-out
2 A breakdown   4 A stand-in
5 A takeover
▸ 218C

366 1 for him 2 with it 3 it out 4 them back 5 at them 6 from it 7 it away 8 into him
▸ 219A–B

367 1 We're hoping for fine weather. ▸ 219A–B
2 I'd switched it OFF. ▸ 219C
3 It was all eaten up. ▸ 219D

4 Can you work it out? ▸ 219A–B
5 We waited patiently for news. ▸ 219E
6 It has been disposed of. ▸ 219D
7 I've APPLIED for it. ▸ 219C
8 I got up late this morning. ▸ 219E

368 1 carry on/go on ▸ 220B   8 come down/gone down ▸ 220C
2 find out ▸ 220B   9 be over ▸ 220E
3 fix up/set up ▸ 220B   10 get by ▸ 220D
4 isn't on ▸ 220E   11 give up ▸ 220A
5 catch on ▸ 220A   12 be out ▸ 220E
6 (being) kept up ▸ 220B
7 fall out ▸ 220C

369 1 connected   6 away, disappearing
2 away   7 becoming less
3 continuing   8 clearly seen
4 to different people   9 completely
5 on paper   10 succeeding
▸ 221

370 1 cut off 2 speak out 3 cut down/chopped down 4 put out 5 turn up
6 talk over Also possible: talk through
▸ 221

371 1 for ▸ 222B   6 on ▸ 222B
2 on ▸ 222A   7 into/at ▸ 222B
3 with ▸ 222B   8 to ▸ 222A
4 for ▸ 222B   9 in ▸ 222B
5 of ▸ 222A   10 for ▸ 222B

372 1 to/with ▸ 222D   5 of/about ▸ 222C
2 about ▸ 222C   6 for ▸ 222C
3 of ▸ 222C   7 of ▸ 222C
4 with ▸ 222D

373 1 to 2 with 3 ✓ 4 ✓ 5 to 6 over
7 about 8 ✓
▸ 222E

374 1 I prefer hip-hop to reggae. ▸ 223A
2 The teacher explained the theory to the class. ▸ 223C
3 Sarah's illness has put her out of action. ▸ 223D
4 Everyone congratulated the champion on his victory. ▸ 223A
5 You should (just) take no notice of anything Mike says. / You shouldn't take any notice of anything Mike says. ▸ 223D
6 The winners were presented with a trophy./A trophy was presented to the winners. ▸ 223B
7 Witnesses blamed the van driver for the accident./Witnesses blamed the accident on the van driver. ▸ 223B

8 Two boys were asking tourists for money.
▶ 223C Also possible: Two boys were asking tourists to give them money.
9 They've turned the old hospital into luxury apartments. / The old hospital has been turned into luxury apartments. ▶ 223A
10 I want to make the most of the long weekend. ▶ 223D

375 1 go out into ▶ 224A
2 looking forward to ▶ 224A
3 looked up at ▶ 224A
4 get round to ▶ 224A
5 looks out over ▶ 224A
6 put up with ▶ 224A
7 take ... up on ▶ 224B
8 brought up against ▶ 224B

376 1 I was worried about my girlfriend.
2 The streets were crowded with festival-goers.
3 Paul was impressed with your cooking.
4 I was late for an/my appointment.
5 I'm fed up with travelling (so much).
6 The island is famous for its standing stones. ▶ 225A

377 1 at ▶ 225C   4 for ▶ 225C
2 to ▶ 225C   5 for ▶ 225B
3 with ▶ 225B   6 about ▶ 225B
                   7 for ▶ 225B

378 1 of ▶ 226B   5 from/against ▶ 226B
2 to ▶ 226B   6 for ▶ 226A
3 of ▶ 226A   7 of/about/on ▶ 226A
4 to ▶ 226B

379 1 respect for ▶ 226B
2 pride in ▶ 226B
3 relationship with Leanne ▶ 226D
4 an attack on ▶ 226B
5 no objections to ▶ 226B
6 the difference between ▶ 226D
7 a need for ▶ 226C
8 a reduction of/a fall of, in the number ▶ 226D

380 1 a) about ▶ 225B   7 d) up with ▶ 224A
2 d) through ▶ 220C   8 d) with ▶ 223B
3 b) on ▶ 222A   9 c) make out ▶ 221
4 d) them off ▶ 217A, 218A 10 c) looked into
5 a) for ▶ 226C   ▶ 219D, 222B
6 b) on you ▶ 219B, 222A 11 a) about ▶ 222B
                         12 a) resemble ▶ 222E

381 1 Next week the hospital will close (down) for good. ▶ 221
2 I've met her before, but I just can't think of her name. ▶ 222C
3 They've had to put off the game because of the weather. ▶ 220B
4 The patient suddenly cried out in pain. ▶ 219E
5 I must thank Alice for my present. ▶ 223A
6 Are you satisfied with your progress? ▶ 225A
7 We saw our friends off at the airport. ▶ 221
8 We're just going to travel around for a while. ▶ 217A
9 I had to describe the woman to the police. ▶ 223C
10 The authorities won't give any reason for their decision. ▶ 226A
11 The workers are demanding more money. ▶ 222E
12 In his speech the Prime Minister didn't refer to the recent scandal. ▶ 222A
13 Some of the UN delegates staged a walk-out. ▶ 218C
14 I'm surprised you put up with these awful conditions. ▶ 224A

382 1 a) ▶ 227B   4 a) ▶ 227A–B
2 a) ▶ 227C   5 to call the doctor ▶ 227C
3 b) ▶ 227A

383 1 No one believes that the earth is flat.
2 Well, I warned you not to touch that wire.
3 The company admitted falsifying its accounts.
4 You can teach me how to samba.
5 We arranged for our luggage to be sent on ahead.
6 I don't understand why you're so angry with me.
7 They succeeded in repairing the damage.
8 Smoke will cause the alarm to sound.
▶ 228

384 1 on copying all his files to disk/that he copies all his files to disk.
1b Also possible: that he copy all his files to disk.
▶ 231A
2 expect you to work overtime.
3 to give up his seat.
4 considering applying for the job.
5 promise you (that) everything will be OK/promise (that) everything will be OK.
6 don't mind if you bring your problems to me/don't mind you bringing your problems to me.
7 let the children sit inside the fire-engine.
8 assume (that) you have to book in advance.
9 learned (how) to use this operating system.

10 doubt if/whether the office will be open /is open now/doubt that the office will be open/is open now.

11 trying to prevent people (from) getting in free.

12 don't mind what time we meet.
▶ 228

385 1 The gallery has decided to buy more pictures painted by local artists.

2 I don't really like opera, but Mark invited me, so I went with him because I didn't want to offend him.

3 A man bought a TV, but it didn't work, so he took it back to the shop, but they wouldn't give him his money back, so he threw the TV through the shop window.
▶ 229

386 1 I don't mind helping because/as I've got plenty of time.

2 The two leaders had no common language, so/and they had an interpreter/As the two leaders had no common language, they had an interpreter (who was) present at all their meetings.

3 I'm a waitress, but/and I just work in the afternoons serving teas.

4 The president knew (that) his wife was ill and (that she) wouldn't live long.

5 Eventually we took off, and/but instead of landing at Heathrow we had to go to Manchester/but we didn't land at Heathrow, and/so we had to go to Manchester instead, which made the journey home much longer.

6 Did you know (that) there's a museum in Detroit where you can see/in which you can see the car (that/which) John F. Kennedy was riding in when he was shot/at the time he was shot.
▶ 229

387 1 c) Suppose all your dreams came true. ▶ 230A

2 d) If I were you, I'd certainly complain. ▶ 231C

3 g) I'm sure the train leaves at six tomorrow morning. ▶ 231A

4 i) It's time I went to bed. ▶ 230B

388 1 I was/were as confident as ▶ 232B

2 I'd got up/I had got up ▶ 232C–D

3 we could afford a new computer. ▶ 232B

4 I had ▶ 232B, D

5 you hadn't told everyone (the/our secret).
▶ 232C

6 you'd lock/you would lock the front door.
▶ 232A

7 only it would work/only the DVD player would work ▶ 232A, D

8 I could have been at your wedding/I'd been/I had been at your wedding ▶ 232C

389 1 well ▶ 233A
2 more ▶ 233C
3 neither ▶ 234B
4 with ▶ 233D
5 both ▶ 233E
6 otherwise ▶ 234A
7 either ▶ 233B
8 addition ▶ 233D
9 only ▶ 233E
10 alternatively ▶ 234A

390 1 I'd had a good night's sleep. All the same I felt tired. ▶ 235B

2 Alice felt optimistic despite (having) a few problems. ▶ 235D Also possible: Alice felt optimistic despite the fact that she had a few problems.

3 I couldn't speak, although I was conscious./Although I couldn't speak, I was conscious.
▶ 235C

4 Even though it was freezing cold, people were in T-shirts. ▶ 235C

5 In spite of being in a wheelchair/In spite of the fact that I'm in a wheelchair, I'm not stupid, you know. ▶ 235D

6 Yes, I do eat meat. My flat-mate, on the other hand, is a vegetarian. ▶ 235E Also possible: On the other hand, my flat-mate .../...is a vegetarian, on the other hand.

391 1 I didn't need the bike any more, so I sold it.
▶ 236A

2 I was so annoyed that I completely lost my temper. ▶ 236C

3 My health was getting worse as a result of overwork. ▶ 236B

4 Hannah is such an expert she'll know what to do. ▶ 236C

5 All the candidates were hopeless, and therefore I didn't vote. ▶ 236B

6 They've polluted the river, and consequently the fish have died. ▶ 236B

392 1 result ▶ 236B
2 alternative ▶ 234A
3 contrast ▶ 235D
4 addition ▶ 233C
5 addition ▶ 233E
6 contrast ▶ 235B

393 1 a) consequently ▶ 236B
2 b) both ▶ 233E
3 d) though ▶ 235A
4 d) while ▶ 235E
5 c) Moreover ▶ 233C
6 d) otherwise ▶ 234A
7 c) however ▶ 235B

394 1 I haven't got a car, and I haven't got a bike either. ▶ 233B

2 Although the answer was obvious, I just couldn't see it. / The answer was obvious, although I just couldn't see it. ▸ 235C

3 Neither the party nor its policies are very popular. ▸ 234B

4 I felt so emotional that I almost burst into tears. ▸ 236C

5 You'll either love this film or hate it./Either you'll love this film or (you'll) hate it. ▸ 234A

6 I was not only quoted in the newspapers, but I was also interviewed on TV. ▸ 233E

7 In addition to booking the hotel, I have to make the travel arrangements. / I have to book the hotel in addition to making the travel arrangements. ▸ 233D

8 The meal was excellent, though the surroundings were depressing. / Though the meal was excellent, the surroundings were depressing. ▸ 235C/The meal was excellent. The surroundings though were depressing./The surroundings were depressing though. ▸ 235A

9 The affair became public despite their attempts to conceal it. / despite the fact that they attempted to conceal it. ▸ 235D

10 As a result of wage cuts, people are rioting/ have been rioting/have rioted on the streets. ▸ 236B

395 1 also ▸ 233A
2 that ▸ 236C
3 but ▸ 235A
4 therefore ▸ 236B
5 despite ▸ 235D
6 or ▸ 234A
7 In spite of ▸ 235D
8 on top of ▸ 233C
9 Consequently ▸ 236B
10 alternatively ▸ 234A
11 As a result of ▸ 236B
12 Furthermore ▸ 233C

396 1 if you find this story hard to believe, before police caught up with them
2 Snatching a TV set, while being pushed along at speed
▸ 237

397 1 since it opened
2 ✓
3 when you put
4 after the start
5 ✓
6 So, having finished
▸ 238A–B

398 1 When 2 As 3 When 4 When 5 as/while
6 when 7 as; also possible: when 8 When
9 when 10 as; also possible: when
▸ 238C

399 1 Tom felt nervous before he appeared/before he made his appearance on TV. ▸ 238A

2 We had to wait till/until the performance ended/finished. / We had to wait till/until the performance was over. ▸ 238A

3 Our visitors had to leave as soon as they (had) finished/had (their) breakfast/leave as soon as breakfast was over/leave immediately they (had) finished/had (their) breakfast. ▸ 238D

4 After/When our cat (had) died, we felt very sad. ▸ 238A

5 When I was twenty, I started my first real job. ▸ 238C

6 By the time we arrive at/we've arrived at the hotel, it'll be midnight. / By the time we get to/ we've got to the hotel, it'll be midnight. ▸ 238

7 It's a month since you last visited us/you last came to see us. ▸ 238A

8 As soon as/Immediately/The moment the film (had) started, I realized I'd seen it before. / No sooner had the film started, than I realized I'd seen it before. / Hardly had the film started, when/before I realized I'd seen it before. ▸ 238D

9 Leanne's flat was burgled while/when she was on holiday. ▸ 238C

10 Just as we were leaving/Just as we left, my mobile rang. ▸ 238C

400 1 My father gave up his job on account of (his) poor health. ▸ 239C

2 Seeing (that) I'd worked all weekend, I had Monday off. Also possible: Seeing as how I'd worked all weekend, I had Monday off. ▸ 239A

3 I didn't buy the coat as it was so expensive. ▸ 239A

4 I feel much more confident now (that) I'm qualified. ▸ 239A

5 Because of its excellent condition the car is a bargain. ▸ 239C

6 I can't talk now because I'm working. ▸ 239A

7 Since there is so much street crime, you had better take a taxi. ▸ 239A

8 Joshua helped us out of kindness. ▸ 239C

9 People are staying at home because of (their fear of) terrorism. ▸ 239C

401 1 I stayed up late to watch a film. ▸ 240A

2 Put plenty of glue on the paper so that it'll stick properly. ▸ 240B

3 We talked quietly so as not to wake the baby/to avoid waking the baby. ▸ 240A–B

4 In order to meet demand the company is increasing production. ▸ 240A

5 I had to go to the newsagent's for a paper. ▸ 240C

6 I hang my keys around my neck to avoid losing them. ▶ 240B

7 A spade is a tool for digging (with). ▶ 240C

8 In order to understand the political situation, you need to know some history. ▶ 240A

402 1 purpose ▶ 240B   6 reason ▶ 239B
    2 time ▶ 238C   7 time ▶ 238A
    3 time ▶ 238B   8 purpose ▶ 240C
    4 reason ▶ 239A   9 reason ▶ 239A
    5 purpose ▶ 240A   10 reason ▶ 239A

403 1 As ▶ 241B   3 as ▶ 241C   5 as ▶ 241C
    2 like ▶ 241A   4 like ▶ 241C   6 as ▶ 241A

404 1 Wherever we looked, there were flags flying.

    2 Whoever does the cooking, it won't be me.

    3 Whenever that man comes here, I'm going to be out.

    4 Whatever's/Whatever has happened, the newspapers will invent their own story.

    5 Whichever method you use, the result is the same.

    6 You should never neglect a customer, however busy you are.
    ▶ 242A

405 1 in order to ▶ 240A   6 as if ▶ 241C
    2 since ▶ 238A   7 however ▶ 242A
    3 While ▶ 238C   8 because ▶ 239A
    4 When ▶ 238C   9 No sooner ▶ 238D
    5 because of ▶ 239C   10 than ▶ 238D

406 1 As you can imagine, I've been very worried.
    ▶ 241B

    2 Please ring me the moment you arrive. ▶ 238D

    3 However hard Justin tried, he couldn't hit the target. ▶ 242A

    4 The matter was kept secret in order not to alarm/so as not to alarm/to avoid alarming the public. ▶ 240A

    5 We look like getting approval for the plan.
    ▶ 241C

    6 As the day of the exam approached, I felt more and more nervous. ▶ 238C

    7 I must have my passport back by the time I leave/before I leave the country. ▶ 238E

    8 The journey always takes ages because of the amount of traffic/because there is so much traffic. ▶ 239A, C

407 1 When the teacher came in, everyone stopped talking. ▶ 238C

    2 I wish the team had played like they did last week. ▶ 241A

3 Since there was no evidence, the police couldn't make an arrest. ▶ 239A

4 Let's have lunch after we've played mini-golf/after we've had a/our game of mini-golf. ▶ 237A

5 Come and see me whenever you like. ▶ 242A

6 Our sales are declining due to cheap imports.
▶ 239C

7 I want everything to be ready to avoid being delayed/to avoid any delay. ▶ 240B

8 As soon as the clock struck, the doors opened.
▶ 238D

408 1 unreal – I don't live in the country.
    2 open – You may vote for me.
    3 open – Everyone may come to the party.
    4 unreal – You didn't ask politely.
    5 unreal – I can't understand computers.
    6 open – I may hear some news.
      ▶ 243A

409 1 threatening/warning   4 suggesting
    2 offering   5 criticizing
    3 requesting   6 warning/advising
      ▶ 243D

410 1 If you pour oil on water, it floats.
    2 If air gets warmer, it rises.
    3 If you heat chocolate, it melts.
    4 If you lift a heavy object, you use up energy.
    5 If water freezes, it expands.
      ▶ 244A

411 1 You'll know the right time if you wear a Minuta watch.

    2 You'll live a life of luxury if you fill your home with Superstyle furniture.

    3 If you read the Daily Dirt, you'll enjoy all the latest gossip.

    4 If you take a Kodex camera with you, you'll take better pictures.

    5 If you wear Regal jewellery, you'll be noticed.

    6 You'll save money if you buy a Maestro computer.
      ▶ 245A

412 1 If I told you the truth, you'd get angry. ▶ 246A

    2 If I wasn't afraid of flying, I might go to Disney World. ▶ 246A, D

    3 Life would be boring if there were no surprises.
      ▶ 246A

    4 If I had some money, I would pay/I'd pay all my bills. ▶ 246A

    5 If it wasn't raining, I would/I'd (want to) go to the beach. ▶ 246A, D

6 If I wasn't/weren't injured, I would be/I'd be playing tennis (right now). ▶ 246A, D

7 If Cristos and I had/If we had a common language, it would be easier to communicate. ▶ 246A

8 If I could afford a flat, I would (like to)/I'd (like to) buy one. ▶ 246A, D

413 1 If he had wanted to break up with his girlfriend, he wouldn't have booked a holiday for the two of them. Also possible: If he hadn't booked a holiday for the two of them, he would/might have broken up with his girlfriend.

2 If the cheque hadn't bounced, he wouldn't have turned to crime.

3 If the money from the first hold-up had been enough, he wouldn't have carried on.

4 If he hadn't left it so late, they would have had (some) time to spare.

5 If Alan hadn't made a silly mistake, he wouldn't have been found out.

6 If he hadn't left the envelope in the bank, the police wouldn't have discovered his identity.

7 If they hadn't returned to England, Alan wouldn't have been arrested (at once).

8 He wouldn't have committed the crimes if the holiday hadn't been so important to him.
▶ 247A

414 1 You'll make ▶ 245A

2 had crossed ▶ 247A

3 you've drunk ▶ 245B Also possible: you drank

4 worked ▶ 246A–B

5 will be ▶ 245A

6 I would have called/I'd have called ▶ 247A

7 would notice ▶ 246A–B

8 you wouldn't mind▶ 246E/you don't mind ▶ 245A

9 I could drive▶ 246D Also possible: I drove ▶ 246A

10 I could have let ▶ 247B

11 it might start▶ 246D/it would start/it'd start ▶ 246A

12 you won't get ▶ 246A

13 I didn't agree ▶ 246A

14 I might not have been listening / I wouldn't have been listening ▶ 247B

415 1 If it hadn't been for the rain, the crops would have died. ▶ 248D

2 If we were to win the contract, we might need more staff. ▶ 248B

3 If a spy should be captured, he would have little useful information. ▶ 248A

4 If anyone had spoken to me, I wouldn't have understood a word. ▶ 247A

5 If the speed limit were higher, there would be more deaths. ▶ 248B

6 Had it not been for the rain, the crops would have died. ▶ 248C

7 Were we to win the contract, we might need more staff. ▶ 248C

8 Should a spy be captured, he would have little useful information. ▶ 248C

9 Had anyone spoken to me, I wouldn't have understood a word. ▶ 248C

416 1 d) ▶ 246A   5 e) ▶ 245A
2 i) ▶ 248C   6 a) ▶ 247A
3 h) ▶ 244A   7 g) ▶ 245D
4 b) ▶ 246B   8 c) ▶ 247C

417 1 I could take a photo. ▶ 246C–D

2 If they had bought a group ticket, ▶ 247A

3 I'm going to be angry. ▶ 245B /I'll be angry ▶ 245A

4 If you could have gone to the concert, ▶ 247

5 if anyone approaches the house. ▶ 244A

6 and you'll regret it. ▶ 245E

7 If anything should go wrong,▶ 248A/If anythi goes wrong, ▶ 245B

8 it would take longer. ▶ 246B–C

9 if they know you can pay it back. ▶ 245A, 24

10 I would have refused. ▶ 247A

11 Had we delayed any longer,▶ 248C /If we ha delayed any longer ▶ 247A

12 it will burst into flames. ▶ 245A, 246C

418 1 we'll miss ▶ 245A

2 I'll watch ▶ 245B

3 I record ▶ 245B

4 we wouldn't keep ▶ 246B

5 I'd thought ▶ 247B

6 she would have watched ▶ 247C

7 will be▶ 245A/ is going to be ▶ 245B

8 did ▶ 246A

9 she won't mind▶ 245A/she wouldn't mind

10 there's (going to be) ▶ 245B

419 1 If 2 If 3 if 4 when 5 When
▶ 249A

420 1 then ▶ 249B   3 if▶ 249A   5 If wet ▶ 2
2 What ▶ 249D   4 even ▶ 249E

421 1 The hostages will be killed unless the ranso paid today.

4 The problem will get worse unless we tackl now.

5 Unless you practise regularly, you'll never le to play the piano.

7 Don't try to do electrical work unless you're sure of what you're doing.
  ▶ 250

422 1 otherwise ▶ 251B
2 on ▶ 251A
3 in case ▶ 251C
4 as long as ▶ 251A
5 Without ▶ 251B
6 In the event of ▶ 251B
7 provided ▶ 251A

423 1 condition ▶ 248C
2 time ▶ 238A
3 contrast ▶ 235C
4 condition ▶ 251B
5 wish ▶ 232D
6 condition ▶ 250A
7 condition ▶ 248C
8 time ▶ 238A
9 reason ▶ 239C
10 condition ▶ 251A

424 1 in case ▶ 251C
2 unless ▶ 250A
3 then ▶ 249B
4 without ▶ 251B
5 as long as ▶ 251A
6 otherwise ▶ 251B

425 1 If it wasn't for the view, this would be a lovely room. / If the view was better/nicer, this would be a lovely room. ▶ 246A, 251B
2 The police are already on the streets in case the protest gets violent. ▶ 251C
3 If you'd give/If you could give/If you wouldn't mind giving the book back to me some time, I'd be grateful. ▶ 245D, 246E
4 If I should lose/Should I lose my job, they'd have to pay me a month's wages. ▶ 248A, C
5 If we've received/If we receive all the replies by the weekend, we'll know who's coming. ▶ 245B
6 I'm not going to play unless you keep to the rules. ▶ 250A
7 If Simon hadn't been ill, he would have gone to the party. ▶ 247A
8 You can ring me in the middle of the night if (it's) necessary. ▶ 245A, 249C
9 (Please) leave the building immediately, or I'll call security. ▶ 245E
10 What if sea levels rise/rose dramatically?
  ▶ 249D
11 If you add six and eight, you get fourteen.
  ▶ 244A
12 If the sun was/were shining, I would be lying on the beach. ▶ 246D

426 1 He demanded that security should be increased at his concerts. ▶ 252C
2 The result of the incident was that the two guards were sacked. ▶ 252C
3 It is not clear whether he was angry at their rudeness or at their failure to recognize him.
  ▶ 252C
4 The fact that they didn't know him can't have helped. ▶ 252C

5 Americans soon realized how much more important security was becoming. ▶ 252A
6 Later he said they had done a good job. ▶ 252B

427 1 I realize (that) you didn't mean to be rude.
  ▶ 253A
2 I'd like to know when you'll/you will be back.
  ▶ 253A
3 Mark convinced me (that) he's/he is/he was telling the truth. ▶ 253A
4 I explained to the manager (that) we're doing a survey. ▶ 253C
5 I've reassured Amy (that) we won't leave her on her own. ▶ 253B
6 I suggest (that) we go to the park. ▶ 253A
7 The President announced to the media that he intends to run for re-election. ▶ 253C

428 1 It was surprising that no one claimed the prize.
2 It's/It is doubtful whether I'll be able to sell these books.
3 It's/It is a nuisance (that) we have to change trains twice.
4 It's/It is good to know (that) everyone is enjoying themselves.
5 It's/It is a mystery how this information got onto the Internet.
6 It's/It is amazing what you can find down the back of an old sofa.
  ▶ 254A–B

429 1 worried about where he's/he is going to park (the car).
2 concentrate on how they're going to pay their debts.
3 kept making comments about how awful the band were.
4 depends on what grades she'll/she will get/she gets.
5 be interested in how waste is recycled.
6 question of whether she takes/she should take a gamble (or not).
  ▶ 255A

430 1 ✓ 2 research into/on how 3 interested in how 4 ✓ 5 effect on whether
  ▶ 255B

431 1 I'm so glad you got home safely.
2 I was surprised how quickly the time passed.
3 We are very concerned that people might be injured.
4 We are hopeful the weather will improve.
5 I wasn't sure whether I was dreaming or not.
  ▶ 256A

432 1 The hope that the war would end proved false.
Also possible: The hope proved false that the war would end.
2 There is plenty of evidence that the Vikings landed in America.
3 The theory that Diana was murdered convinced many people.
4 Science has challenged the idea that God created the world.
5 I share the view that we should stop destroying the rain forests.
6 The reports that the President had resigned were untrue.
▶ 256B

433 1 We've decided that we're going on strike.
▶ 255A
2 The fact that we were lost didn't seem to matter. ▶ 256B
3 That the song will go to number one is certain.
▶ 254A / It is certain that the song will go to number one. ▶ 254B
4 I explained to your sister what was happening.
▶ 253C
5 Let's see if you're/you are right. ▶ 252B
6 I was confused about where/as to where I was supposed to go. ▶ 255B
7 Whether they're going to give us permission is in some doubt. ▶ 254A
8 The news that taxes were to go up caused an outcry. ▶ 256B

434 1 ridiculous (that) we have to fill in all these forms. ▶ 254B
2 realize (that) you're upset. ▶ 253A
3 isn't obvious how the animals have managed to escape. ▶ 254A
4 assumed (that) the figures had been checked.
▶ 256B
5 confident (that) everything will be all right
▶ 256A
6 problem is (that) my visa has run out. ▶ 254C
7 told you (that) I'm/I was going home tomorrow. ▶ 253B
8 (quite) anxious about what questions they're going to ask me. ▶ 255B

435 1 The education of children is an investment in the future. ▶ 257A, C
2 Respect for old people is no longer important in Western societies. ▶ 257A, C
3 The slight damage to my car will be paid for by the insurance company. ▶ 257A, C, D
4 The legalization of certain drugs is being discussed in Parliament. ▶ 257A, C

5 The sudden movement of troops has increased tension. ▶ 257A, C, D
6 The company's need for greater profits has led to some aggressive marketing. ▶ 257A–C
7 The emergence of the National Party is a threat to the present government. ▶ 257A–B
8 The massive over-production of coffee has pushed down prices. ▶ 257A, C, D
9 The enormous influence of advertisements on our behaviour is well known. ▶ 257A–D
10 Our request for more help was refused.
▶ 257A–C

436 1 informed Rick ▶ 259C
2 knew (that) ▶ 259B
3 explained (to the class) ▶ 259D
4 thinks ▶ 259B
5 assured Amy ▶ 259C
6 mentioned (to Elaine) ▶ 259D

437 1 've/have been told (by the boss) (that) we have to work late. ▶ 259C
2 was suggested (to us) (that) we should form a protest group. ▶ 259B
3 have been warned (by the police) that a lion has escaped. ▶ 259C
4 was pointed out (by someone) that there was a mistake in the exam paper. ▶ 259B
5 were not informed (by anyone) that there had been a nuclear accident. ▶ 259C

438 1 told ▶ 260A
2 said ▶ 260A–B
3 asked ▶ 260F
4 talked ▶ 260E
5 said ▶ 260D
6 told ▶ 260A
7 told ▶ 260A–B
8 asked ▶ 260F
9 talked ▶ 260E
10 told ▶ 260C
11 said ▶ 260A
12 asked ▶ 260F, told ▶ 260.

439 1 me ▶ 261B, before ▶ 261C
2 I'm ▶ 261B, today ▶ 261C
3 I've ▶ 261B, tomorrow ▶ 261C
4 he ▶ 261B, day before/previous day ▶ 261C
5 was ▶ 261A, that ▶ 261C
6 I ▶ 261B, immediately/at once/right away/right then ▶ 261C

440 1 studied/were studying ▶ 262B–C
2 are ▶ 262A
3 were ▶ 262B–C
4 knew ▶ 262A
5 sleeps ▶ 262A
6 were ▶ 262B–C

441 1 Max said he was going to Paris ▶ 262C
2 Polly said she'd had/she had had an e-mail from Karen. ▶ 262D

3 Mike said he didn't/doesn't like the new trainee. ▶ 262C

4 Jane said she had/she'd got/she has/she's got a new boyfriend. ▶ 262C

5 Andrew said he was being/he's being spied on. ▶ 262C

6 Mrs Lucas said she wished/wishes she was/were young again. ▶ 262D

7 Angela said she'd/she's found a place to live. ▶ 262C

8 Celia said she'd been invited to a reception. ▶ 262D

9 Alan said he knew a secret. ▶ 262C

442 spent many years in prison, but he did not feel ▶ 262C bitter, The world was changing ▶ 262C, and he wanted ▶ 262C to change with it. He loved ▶ 262C his country, and he believed it was ▶ 262C a great nation/he believed it to be a great nation. In his youth he (had) fought ▶ 262D for its freedom. He wished he could work ▶ 262E miracles, but it would be ▶ 262E foolish to think so. It would be ▶ 262E a long hard road. He urged his people to join him in the ▶ 261D task. They could do ▶ 262E it together.

443 1 They asked me if/whether I had a notebook.
2 They wanted to know where I was going.
3 They wanted to know where I had come from.
4 They inquired how long I had been in the country.
5 They wondered if/whether I had spoken to anyone on my journey.
6 They asked who (had) paid for my journey.
7 They inquired if/whether I was carrying any drugs.
8 They asked me where I planned to sleep.
▶ 263A–C

444 1 The teacher told the class to learn the new words.
2 The doctor told the patient to go on a diet.
3 The boss told the employee not to be late tomorrow morning/the next morning.
4 The traffic warden told the motorist to move his car out of the way.
5 The hotel guests asked the porter to take their luggage.
6 The security guard asked the travellers not to leave their bags unattended.
▶ 264A

445 1 Oliver said/told me (that) he'd/he would love to do a parachute jump. ▶ 262E
2 The shop assistant asked (me) what my postcode was/is. ▶ 263A–C
3 Linda asked me to look after her luggage ▶ 264A /asked (me) if/whether I would mind looking after her luggage. ▶ 264B
4 The policeman asked me if/whether anyone else lived/lives in the house. ▶ 263A–C
5 Sarah said/told me (that) she could/can drive a minibus. ▶ 262E
6 The landlord told me not to park my car in the yard. ▶ 264A
7 Tom asked (me) if/whether I'd/I had finished with the computer. ▶ 263A–C
8 The librarian asked/told me to turn the music off. ▶ 264A /asked (me) if I could turn the music off. ▶ 264B
9 Louise asked (me) where I was going. ▶ 263A–C
10 Jack said/told me (that) he'd/he had/he's/he has been dropped from the basketball team. ▶ 262C

446 1 f) ▶ 265E   5 d) ▶ 265I
2 c) ▶ 265F   6 i) ▶ 265E
3 a) ▶ 265D   7 g) ▶ 265F
4 h) ▶ 265C   8 e) ▶ 265G

447 1 Lisa has promised to fax the information. ▶ 265C
2 James warned me that the weather forecast was awful. ▶ 265I
3 We all congratulated Gemma on winning the competition. ▶ 265G
4 Someone suggested getting a group ticket. ▶ 265E
5 The office has reminded us to pay the money / that the money must be paid by tomorrow. ▶ 265D, I
6 The government is forecasting that prices will remain steady. ▶ 265H
7 The visitors were complaining about having to wait/that they had to wait in the rain. ▶ 265F
8 My tutor has advised me to sit the exam again. ▶ 265D Also possible: My tutor has advised sitting the exam again/has advised (me) that I (should) sit the exam again. ▶ 265H

448 1 I can't/couldn't get the door open. ▶ 262E
2 Are you ready to go? ▶ 263A–C
3 I like all kinds of music. ▶ 262B
4 I'm sorry (that) I got the message wrong. ▶ 265F
Also possible: I apologize for getting the message wrong.
5 I forgot my ticket. ▶ 262A

6 (Please) don't spoil the fun./You mustn't spoil the fun. ▶ 264A

7 How much money do you earn? ▶ 263A–C

8 I'll ring you next week. ▶ 261C, 262E

9 We've just seen/We just saw Madonna in the street. ▶ 262D

10 I'm not going to climb/I won't climb the ladder. ▶ 265C Also possible: I refuse to climb the ladder.

11 Would you mind waiting / Could you wait for a moment (, please)? ▶ 264A Also possible: Please wait a moment.

12 We got married last month. ▶ 261C, 262D

449 1 c) not to ▶ 264A
2 a) he'd been swimming ▶ 262C
3 a) say ▶ 260A–B
4 b) if ▶ 263A
5 b) denied ▶ 265E
6 b) could ▶ 262E
7 d) were ▶ 262B–C
8 b) informed ▶ 259C

450 1 if/whether I believed/believe in God. ▶ 263A
2 he said/he told me (that) he'd/he had come out of hospital only an hour before. ▶ 262D, 261C
Also possible but less usual: ... an hour ago.
3 asked for her key. ▶ 264D /asked if she could have her key. ▶ 264B
4 she said/she told/warned him (that) he'd/he would be sorry. ▶ 262E
5 to know when she'll/she will be getting her money. ▶ 263A–B
6 to doing all the work. ▶ 265F that he was doing all the work. ▶ 265H
7 Emily not to laugh at him. ▶ 264A
8 Jessica that it was her turn next. ▶ 259C, 262B
9 (to me) that she was waiting for Lucy. ▶ 262C
10 Paul where the secret address was/is hidden. ▶ 260B

451 1 whose house front collapsed one day
2 who lives in the English Midlands
3 it did
4 which was bad enough in itself
5 which was standing in an upstairs bedroom
6 I bought on impulse
7 who bought Elvis Presley
▶ 266A

452 1 the shop on the corner
2 a red car
3 the woman who missed her train
4 a book published last month
5 a woman waiting for someone
6 a comfortable chair
7 the people who have heard/who've heard the story before

8 a man with a gun Also possible: a gunman
9 a face recognized everywhere
▶ 266B

453 1 I'm having a visit from my favourite aunt, who lives in London.   2 ✓   3 ✓
4 The match will be played at Lord's, which is the home of English cricket.   5 ✓
6 Marian Evans, who wrote under the name of George Eliot, was a great novelist.
7 The new college, which cost £80 million to build, opens this week.   8 ✓
▶ 266D

454 1 classifying ▶ 267B
2 adding ▶ 267D
3 connective ▶ 267E
4 adding ▶ 267D
5 adding ▶ 267D
6 identifying ▶ 267A
7 identifying ▶ 267A
8 for emphasis ▶ 267C
9 connective ▶ 267E
10 adding ▶ 267D
11 adding ▶ 267D
12 identifying ▶ 267A

455 1 Tom knows the girl who/that appeared on television.
2 Louise likes the people that/who Rick has invited to the party.
3 Leanne wishes she still had the camera that James broke.
4 Adam saw them carry off the player who/that was injured.
5 Kate is going to complain about the burglar alarm that wouldn't stop ringing.
6 The company still hasn't received the letter that Paul posted on Tuesday.
7 Steve couldn't understand the woman that/who Hannah was interviewing.
8 Lisa was reading about the bridge that collapsed in a hurricane.
▶ 268A–B

456 1 The photographs show the floor on which many of the victims were trapped.
2 The Sales Manager is a young woman in whom we have great confidence.
3 We entered the territory over which so many battles have been fought.
4 Nearby are the Roman baths from which the city of Bath gets its name.
5 Washington is the man to whom Americans owe their independence.
▶ 268D

457 1 The hotel we stayed at was perfect.
2 The programme we were watching was really interesting.

3 The/These shoes I'm wearing are the latest fashion.

4 The jewellery we were looking at was rather expensive.

5 The music you were playing sounded very familiar.

6 The club I was telling you about is called the Palace (, I've remembered). ▶ 268E

458 1 People who smoke are endangering their health. ▶ 268A–B, E

2 ✓ ▶ 268D–E

3 There was a bad accident that/which closed the motorway. ▶ 268A–B, E

4 No one has said anything that/which would persuade me to change my mind. ▶ 268A, E

5 ✓ ▶ 268B, E

6 The police wouldn't tell us the source of the information on which they were acting. ▶ 268D

7 ✓ ▶ 268D–E

8 Immigrants are in jobs that/which could not be filled from the existing workforce. ▶ 268A–B, E

9 He was the leader in whom the population placed all their hopes. ▶ 268D

10 ✓ ▶ 268D–E

459 were done by black workers, many of whom had to live apart from their families ▶ 269D. Mandela was a lawyer. He joined the African National Congress, which was leading the fight against apartheid ▶ 269B. Things got even worse at Sharpeville in 1960 when police fired into a crowd of black people(,) who were protesting peacefully ▶ 269A–B. Mandela played his part in the struggle for equal rights, which led to his imprisonment ▶ 269E. He was found guilty of sabotage, for which he was sent to prison for life ▶ 269C. He stayed in prison for many long years. In fact Mandela, whose 70th birthday was celebrated with a concert in London, ▶ 269B became the most famous prisoner in the world. He was finally released in 1990, by which time he had spent 27 years in prison. ▶ 269C Soon he was President of the new South Africa. But although he had suffered for so long, he did not want to take his revenge on the white minority, whom he would have had every reason to hate. ▶ 269B

460 1 There are quite a few artists whose paintings are worth millions. ▶ 270A

2 I have a secretary whose job is to arrange my appointments. ▶ 270A

3 The camp is full of refugees who have been forced out of their homes. ▶ 268A

4 I wish to thank a number of people for whose support I am extremely grateful. ▶ 270A–B

5 We are a first-class company whose products have a reputation for quality. ▶ 270A

6 My sister married a conjuror, who soon disappeared. ▶ 269F

461 1 It's a very exclusive club, the members of which are wealthy business people.

2 The fire destroyed many treasures, the value of which is incalculable.

3 Tom told me a complicated story, the details of which I've forgotten.

4 The Romans built a huge fort, the remains of which are still visible today.

5 My flat-mates had an angry argument, the result of which is that they aren't speaking to each other. Also possible: as a result of which they aren't speaking to each other.

6 We saw a film, the plot of which was totally incomprehensible.

7 The chairman made a speech, by the end of which most of us were asleep.
▶ 270C

462 1 when ▶ 271A
2 way ▶ 271D
3 why ▶ 271A
4 Whoever ▶ 273
5 what ▶ 272
6 which ▶ 271B
7 where ▶ 271A

463 1 The dam holding back the water suddenly gave way. ▶ 274A

2 Some buildings hit by bombs are still burning. ▶ 274B

3 People wanting to smoke have to leave the building. ▶ 274A

4 A plane that/which crashed into the sea may have been a terrorist target. ▶ 274A

5 The shot fired that day signalled the start of the American Revolution. ▶ 274B

6 The letter accusing me of theft hadn't been signed. ▶ 274A

7 Tourists taking the train from London to Stratford have to change at Coventry. ▶ 274A

8 The scientist who/that discovered the neutron was James Chadwick. ▶ 274A

9 People walking across the bridge could feel it swaying. ▶ 274A

10 The man tipped to become the new President is little known outside his own country. ▶ 274B

464 1 Henry VIII of England was the only king to marry six times./Henry VIII was the only king of England to marry six times. ▶ 275A

2 John F. Kennedy was the last US President to be assassinated. ▶ 275A

3 The government has little money with which to tackle the many social problems. ▶ 275B

4 New Zealand was the first country to give women the right to vote. ▶ 275A

5 I think China will be the next country to host the Olympic Games. ▶ 275A

6 Voters are faced with a lot of parties to choose from/parties from which to choose. ▶ 275B

7 (At 24) William Pitt was the youngest person to become Prime Minister. ▶ 275A

465 1 in charge of the exercise ▶ 266C /who/that was in charge of the exercise ▶ 268A

2 time (when/that) the exercise began ▶ 271A–B

3 arrested by the military police ▶ 274B /who/that was arrested by the military police ▶ 268A

4 whose camera was confiscated ▶ 270A /who had his camera confiscated. ▶ 268A

5 (who/that) Steve was working with ▶ 268D–E / with whom Steve was working ▶ 268D /working with Steve ▶ 274A /(who/that was) working with Steve ▶ 268A

6 (who managed) to get any/some photos ▶ 275A /who/that got any/some photos ▶ 268A

7 that/which always has the best pictures ▶ 268A

8 which pleased the colonel ▶ 269E

466 1 There were people rushing about everywhere. ▶ 274C

2 Where's that magazine (that/which) I was looking at? ▶ 268D

3 I'm quite happy with what I've got, thanks. ▶ 272

4 They live in Pensford, which lies just south of Bristol. ▶ 269B

5 Peter was the only person to notice my new hairstyle ▶ 275A / who noticed my new hairstyle. ▶ 266A

6 The weather (that) we've had lately has been far too wet to go out (in). ▶ 266C

7 We've got a light that/which always comes on automatically in the evening. ▶ 268A, E

8 I can't see any reason (why/that) it shouldn't work. ▶ 271A–B Also possible: I can't see any reason for it not to work.

9 There were 35 passengers on the coach, almost all of whom were British./of whom almost all were British. ▶ 269D

10 Whoever dumped ▶ 273 /The person who dumped this rubbish here doesn't care about the environment. ▶ 266A

11 There was an accident in which four people were killed. ▶ 268D

12 They are the generation whose fathers fought in the Vietnam War. ▶ 270A–B

467 1 Do you remember the place where we all used to meet? ▶ 271A

2 There are a number of options (that/which) we are considering. ▶ 268A, E Also possible: There are a number of options, which we are considering. ▶ 269B

3 We took in a dog abandoned by its previous owner.▶ 274B / We took in a dog that/which had been abandoned by its previous owner. ▶ 268A Also possible: We took in a dog, which had been abandoned by its previous owner. ▶ 269B

4 I rang the police, who came immediately. ▶ 267E, 269F

5 In the corridor (there) was a notice board that/which several students were looking at. ▶ 268D–E Also possible: In the corridor (there) was a notice board, which several students were looking at. ▶ 269B

6 She is an artist whose work I am quite familiar with./She is an artist with whose work I am quite familiar. ▶ 270B

7 You always disapprove of whatever I do. ▶ 273

8 My favourite street is Clark Avenue, which has lots of pavement cafés. ▶ 269B

9 It isn't much evidence on which to base a whole theory. ▶ 275B